I0810102

IMAGES
of America

JARRELL

On the Cover: Shown in the early 1940s, Olga Bozon stands in the driveway of the Watkins Sinclair service station located on U.S. Highway 81 in Jarrell, Texas. (Courtesy C. B. and Mary Hodge.)

IMAGES
of America

JARRELL

Mary H. Hodge and Priscilla S. King

ARCADIA
PUBLISHING

ISBN 978-0-7385-5871-4

Published by Arcadia Publishing
Charleston SC, Chicago IL, Portsmouth NH, San Francisco CA

Printed in the United States of America

Library of Congress Control Number: 2008934527

For all general information contact Arcadia Publishing at:
Telephone 843-853-2070
Fax 843-853-0044
E-mail sales@arcadiapublishing.com
For customer service and orders:
Toll-Free 1-888-313-2665

Visit us on the Internet at www.arcadiapublishing.com

To those who lost their lives in the Jarrell tornadoes and to the Jarrell pioneers who paved the way with a "can do" attitude that is still reflected in our community today

Contents

Acknowledgments		6
Introduction		7
1.	Corn Hill	9
2.	The Railroad	21
3.	The Early Years	27
4.	Religion and Education	39
5.	Down to Business	57
6.	Historical Bits and Pieces	81
7.	Ill Winds Blow in Jarrell	89
8.	Past, Present, and Future	115

ACKNOWLEDGMENTS

Photographs came from the collections of C. B. and Mary Hodge, Fred and Eva Lee Harrison, Floyd and Claudia Goode, and Priscilla S. King. Unless otherwise noted, all images appearing in this book were from these collections. Thanks to those who went out of their way to search for special pictures. Their names are noted with their contributions.

Historical facts were taken from the manuscript, *Bicentennial Comments and History of Jarrell 1909–1976*, written by Tommy Lee Buchanan and Dorothy Jones. This manuscript contributed invaluable and irreplaceable information. Facts were also taken from *Land of Good Water* by Clara Stearns Scarbrough and the *Williamson County Sun* and the *Temple Daily Telegram* newspapers.

Additional information came from the *Story of Bell County, Texas, Vol. 1* and from the Railroad and Heritage Museum.

Thanks to Kristie Kelly for her expert guidance and her encouragement. She always had a smile along with helpful advice.

Special thanks to Tammi Cooper for her readability checks and to Milly Buford Sybert for verifying historical accuracy. Finally, the authors thank their friends and families for love and encouragement during the completion of this project.

Introduction

The small Central Texas town of Jarrell has been "on the move" since it began. The city has literally moved four different times, compliments of the Texas Department of Transportation, and has "put itself back together" several times compliments of Mother Nature. The purpose of this book is to document these unusual circumstances and to recognize the hearty and stalwart folks who participated in these events, either willingly or unwillingly. No book can be a complete history, and this is no exception. Many people and families have played an important role, and there is no way to include them all. Thus this pictorial history offers only a sampling of vintage photographs illustrating the history and tenacity of this community and its residents.

In 1852, county judge John E. King built his residence atop a hill near the stagecoach route in northern Williamson County. This home became a stop for the stage line connecting Georgetown and Fort Gates. It is reported that Judge King had dried corn hanging on the front porch of his home where the stagecoach passengers entered. It was from this dried corn that the community got its name. Passengers on the stage referred to the stop as Corn Hill, and the name stuck. This book will share with its readers photographs that depict life in Corn Hill, a town thought to be an economically sound and growing community.

As so often happens, fate has a way of changing what one thinks is predictable. In this case, it was the railroad. Corn Hill was destined to be abandoned. Readers will appreciate the enormity of the task as the town literally picked up stakes and moved—buildings and all—to be transplanted 2 miles to the north. The Bartlett-Western Railroad and its influence on Jarrell's business and residential growth are documented in photographs taken in the early 1900s. Some of the colorful stories associated with this "free and loose" time in the town's history will be retold in this volume.

Following 1909, when the first lots were sold, Jarrell was a fledgling town built on both sides of what was then U.S. Highway 81. A number of businesses and enterprises were thriving. Life may have moved at a slower pace, but it was a time of hard work as well as simple and homemade fun. There was tremendous time and energy spent on making a living. But folks had fun without the benefit of television and technology.

The 1930s brought yet another change to Jarrell. While U.S. Highway 81 had gone right through town, it was now being shifted to the east side of Jarrell. Its location is the present-day frontage road for I-35. After the highway construction, once again businesses and homes were moved, this time only a few blocks, to capitalize on the highway traffic essential to many livelihoods. Pictures show the town as it existed then with emphasis on business and social life, religion, and education.

In the 1960s, the Texas Department of Transportation again had a direct effect on the tiny town of Jarrell by building I-35, a major north/south interstate highway. The width of this major highway meant that all the businesses on the south side of Highway 81 were demolished. This was almost a deathblow to Jarrell. The population dwindled, and no new industry was present. Youngsters who were educated in Jarrell looked for jobs elsewhere. Pictures will help the reader understand the frustration the town was feeling.

All towns, no matter their size, have their share of zany and quirky stories. These are the stories that have been passed down from generation to generation. To verify their truth is impossible, but what they add to the flavor and color of a community is immeasurable. Jarrell is no exception, and some of these historical bits and pieces are included.

Mother Nature had some surprises of her own in store for this Central Texas town. Jarrell has suffered four tornadoes, each with increasing severity. The first one, in 1926, and the second one, in 1955, caused structural damage to homes and businesses. The third one, in 1989, caused severe damage, many injuries, and one fatality. The F-5 tornado of 1997 that killed 27 residents and injured many others was of such intensity it warranted national news media coverage. Each of the last two storms has been documented in photographs and stories. This chapter will leave readers with haunting images of the power that can be unleashed by nature and how quickly things can change. The few minutes during each of these events will forever leave an indelible mark on Jarrell's 100-year history.

Today Jarrell is once again on the move. It is growing and changing almost daily. The city is incorporated and has elected a mayor and city council. City services are beginning to emerge. Each month, the current residents of Jarrell welcome new neighbors in the form of families who choose to make Jarrell their home. Join the authors for a brief glimpse of current events as Jarrell once more redesigns itself to stay viable in today's modern and fast-paced world. Travel on this pictorial journey from early beginnings to present day as Jarrell, Texas, approaches its century mark in 2009.

One

Corn Hill

A decade before Abraham Lincoln was elected president and the Civil War began, John E. King, then county judge, built a residence for his family atop a hill in the rural, northernmost part of Williamson County. Transportation across America was becoming important. The Gold Rush in California was just coming to a close, railroads were being built, and stagecoach lines were transporting people as well as the U.S. mail. The stage line connecting Georgetown and Fort Gates, following the well-known Chisholm Trail, made Judge King's home one of their stage stops. Built right in the middle of rich agricultural land with head-high corn as far as one could see, this stop became known as Corn Hill. In 1869, the first store was opened, followed by a cotton gin two years later. During the next 50 years, this community developed into a thriving Central Texas town. With its economy based on farming, the town boasted a post office, a blacksmith shop, hotel, numerous businesses, and two cotton gins. Offering support were several churches, a Masonic Lodge, a newspaper, and even a college. The 1870 U.S. Census indicates a minimum of 25 dwellings in Corn Hill. By 1896, the population had increased to 350 residents, and by 1910 it is estimated that approximately 500 people resided in Corn Hill.

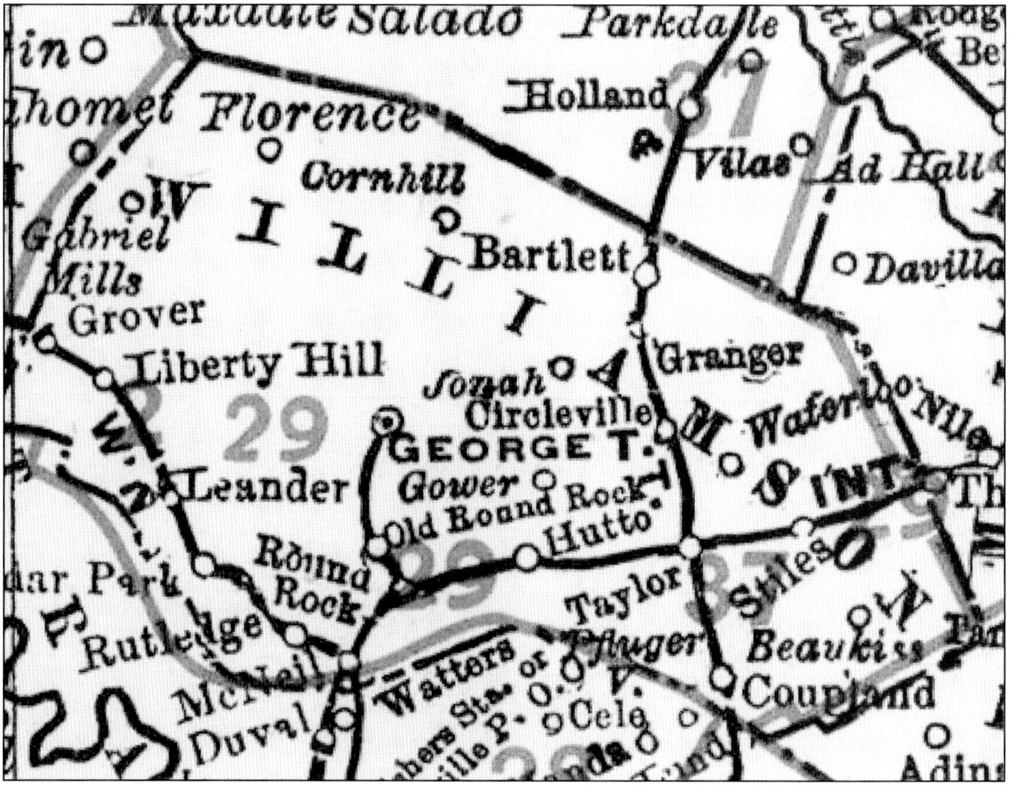

This is a map of the towns in Williamson County, Texas, in 1895. Note the town of Corn Hill is shown north of Georgetown. Jarrell at this point does not exist.

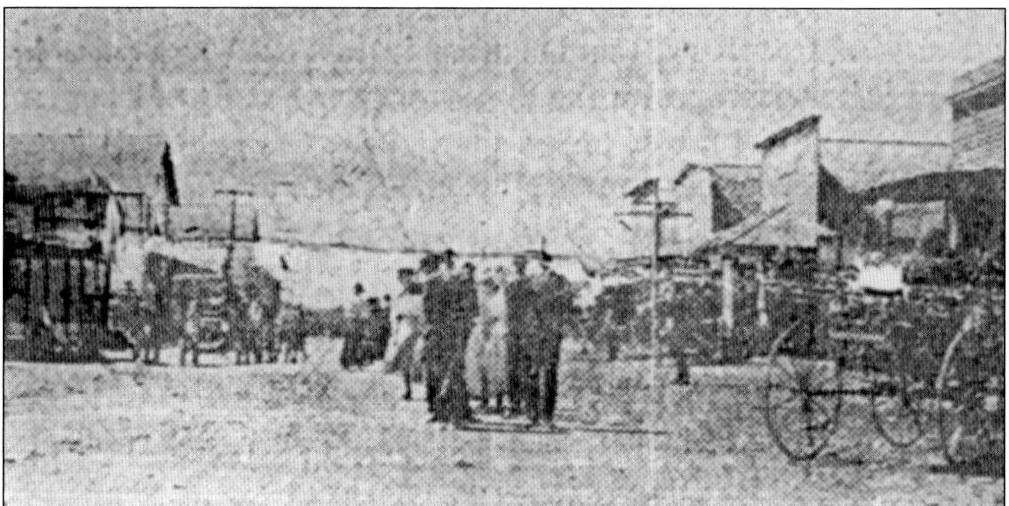

Corn Hill was a busy place in 1906. This picture was taken on Main Street. Several buggies and one car can be seen. Businesses included a mercantile store, blacksmith shop, doctor's office, druggist, livery stable, and millinery store. A member of one of Jarrell's founding families, Fred Harrison, at age 16, is standing with the young people in the middle of the street.

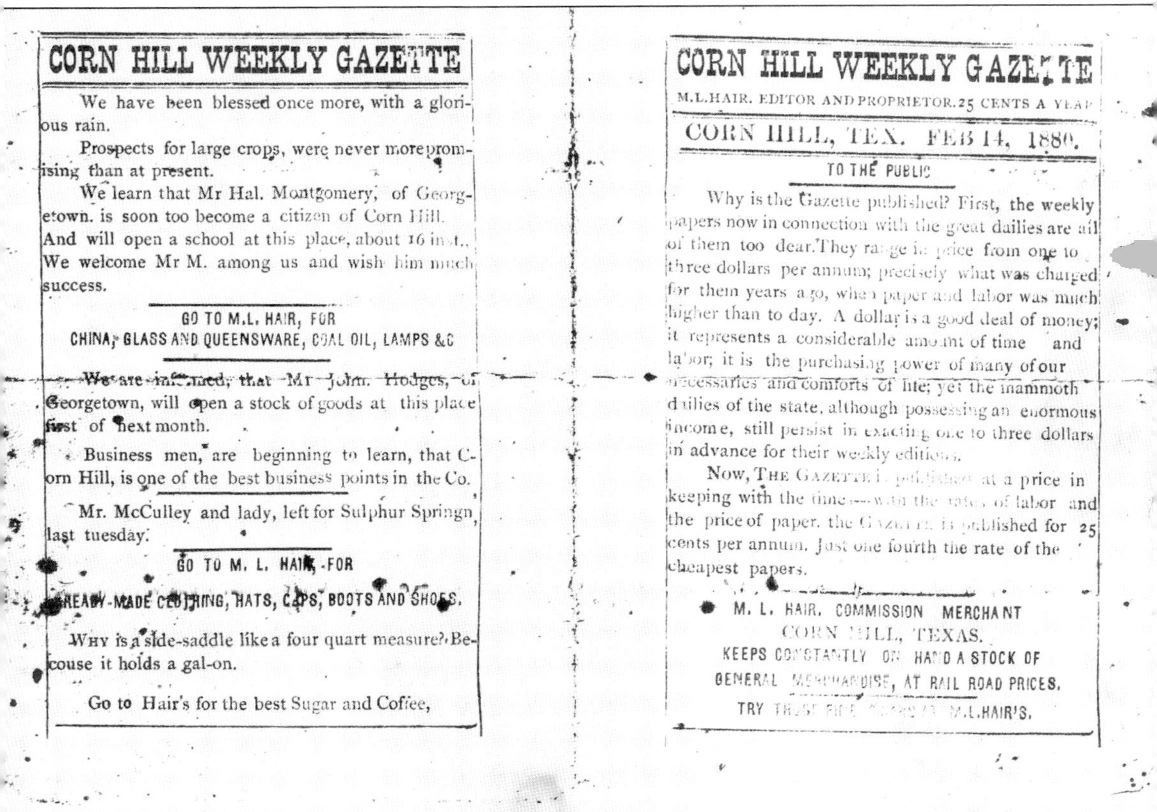

CORN HILL WEEKLY GAZETTE

We have been blessed once more, with a glorious rain.

Prospects for large crops, were never more promising than at present.

We learn that Mr Hal. Montgomery, of Georgetown. is soon too become a citizen of Corn Hill. And will open a school at this place, about 16 inst., We welcome Mr M. among us and wish him much success.

GO TO M.L. HAIR, FOR
CHINA, GLASS AND QUEENSWARE, COAL OIL, LAMPS &C

We are informed, that Mr John Hodges, of Georgetown, will open a stock of goods at this place first of next month.

Business men, are beginning to learn, that Corn Hill, is one of the best business points in the Co.

Mr. McCulley and lady, left for Sulphur Springn last tuesday.

GO TO M. L. HAIR -FOR
READY-MADE CLOTHING, HATS, CAPS, BOOTS AND SHOES.

WHY is a side-saddle like a four quart measure? Becouse it holds a gal-on.

Go to Hair's for the best Sugar and Coffee,

CORN HILL WEEKLY GAZETTE

M.L.HAIR. EDITOR AND PROPRIETOR. 25 CENTS A YEAR

CORN HILL, TEX. FEB 14, 1880.

TO THE PUBLIC

Why is the Gazette published? First, the weekly papers now in connection with the great dailies are all of them too dear. They range in price from one to three dollars per annum; precisely what was charged for them years ago, when paper and labor was much higher than to day. A dollar is a good deal of money; it represents a considerable amount of time and labor; it is the purchasing power of many of our necessaries and comforts of life; yet the mammoth dailies of the state, although possessing an enormous income, still persist in exacting one to three dollars in advance for their weekly editions.

Now, THE GAZETTE is published at a price in keeping with the times—with the rates of labor and the price of paper. the GAZETTE is published for 25 cents per annum. Just one fourth the rate of the cheapest papers.

M. L. HAIR, COMMISSION MERCHANT
CORN HILL, TEXAS.
KEEPS CONSTANTLY ON HAND A STOCK OF
GENERAL MERCHANDISE, AT RAIL ROAD PRICES.
TRY THOSE FINE CIGARS AT M.L.HAIR'S.

The copy of the Corn Hill Weekly Gazette is reproduced here through the courtesy of Mr. and Mrs. A. E. White.

Shown here is a copy of the *Corn Hill Weekly Gazette*, a newspaper published by Montgomery L. Hair, who also owned the local mercantile. This edition is from February 14, 1880. It reports that rain had been plentiful and crop prospects were good. Mentioned also is that Hal Montgomery of Georgetown was planning to open a school in Corn Hill, and John Hodges of Georgetown was planning to open a "stock of goods." The publisher pointed out, "Corn Hill is one of the best business points in the County" and then reminded his readers to shop his mercantile for the best sugar and coffee. (Courtesy Linn and Jimmy Sybert.)

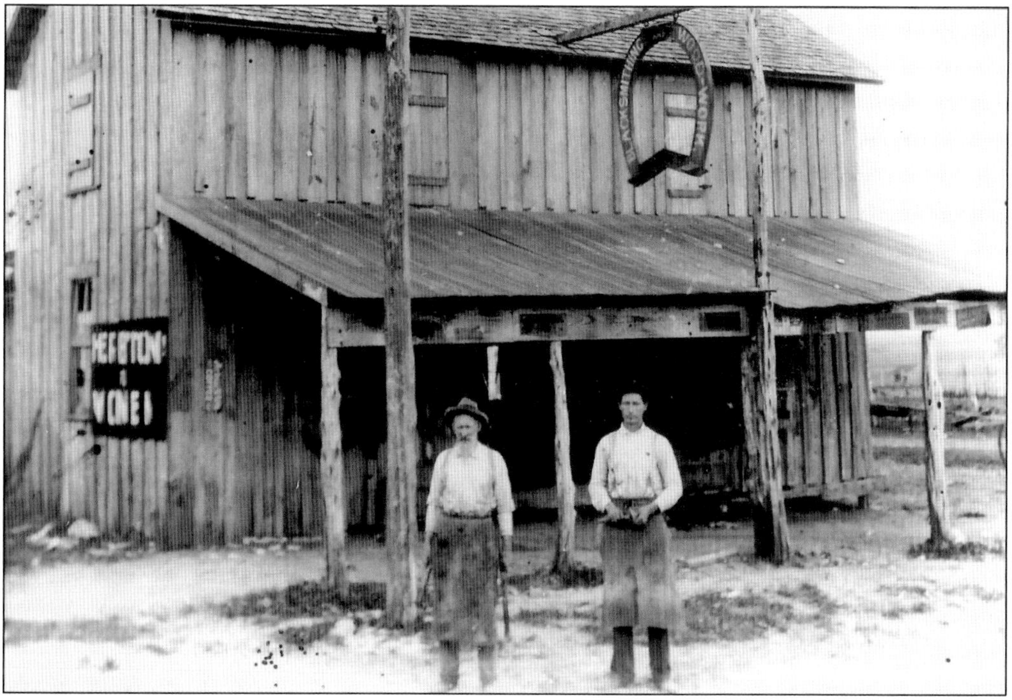

The blacksmith shop was located at the corner of Main Street and County Road 313. Taken in the 1880s, this picture shows R. W. Laws (left) and Ben Harrison, both blacksmiths. This shop was essential to the local community as the preferred mode of travel was wagons or buggies pulled by horses or mules.

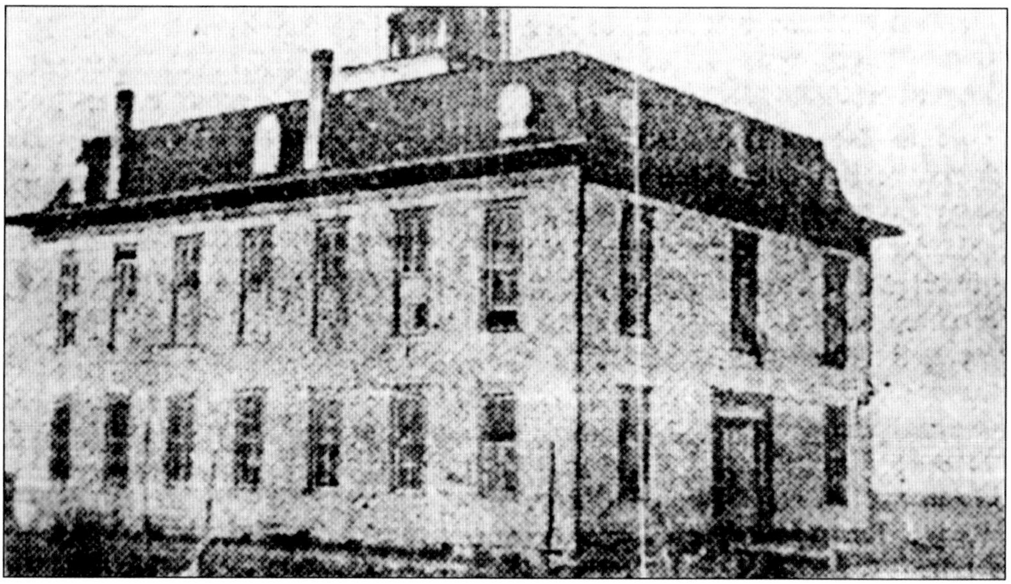

In 1886, an institution of higher learning was built on land donated by Judge John E. King. It was called Corn Hill College or Corn Hill Academy. The college building was used for church services, school programs, plays, debates, band concerts, and other similar gatherings. At some unknown date, the college burned and was replaced by a public school. The exact location of the college was at today's intersection of I-35 South and County Road 306.

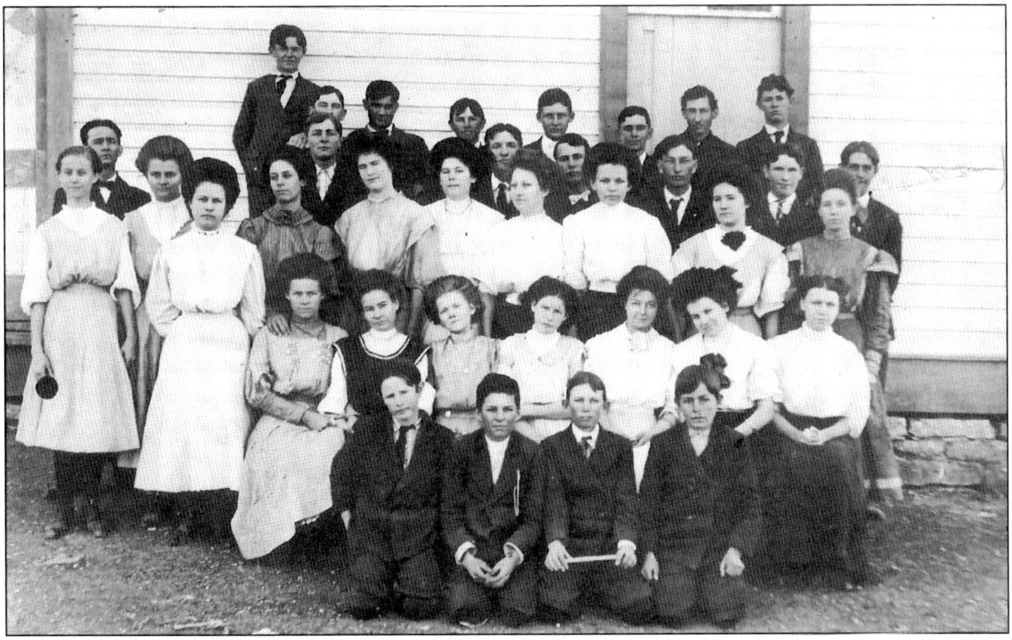

Students of all ages attended Corn Hill College. Graduates were qualified to become teachers in public schools of the state of Texas. Pictured above is the class of 1909. Among those posing are Eva White, Eunice Milam, Arlene Young, Mauytis O'Neal, May Harleson, Vera Whitley, May Shaver, Margie Coffield, Avis Frazier, Jennie Harrison, Fred Harrison, and Oran Harrison. Below is the last class of Corn Hill College in 1915. These 28 students attended school in the new Jarrell High School building completed in 1916.

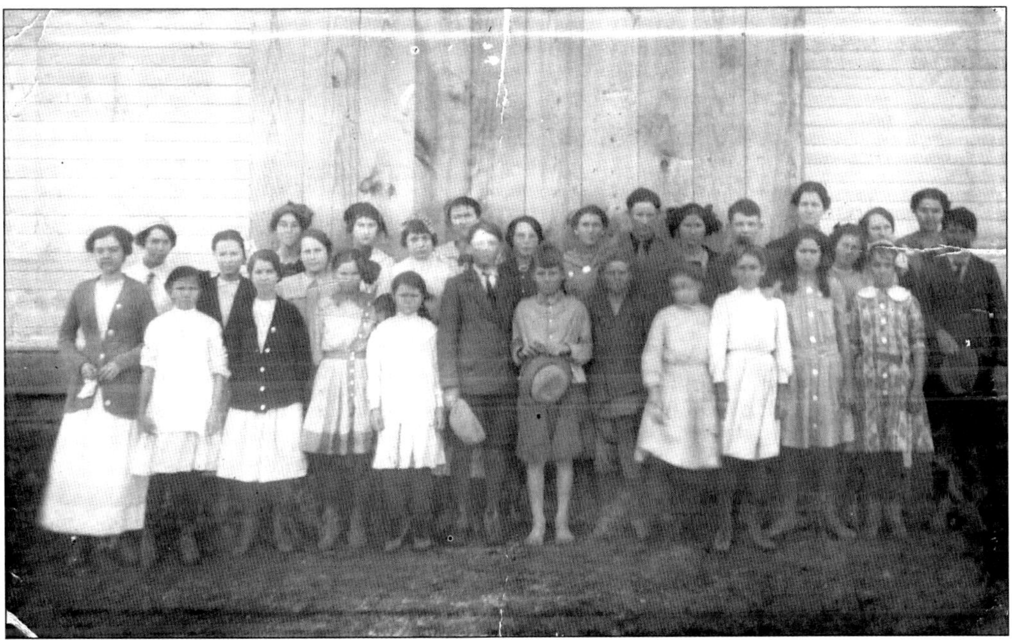

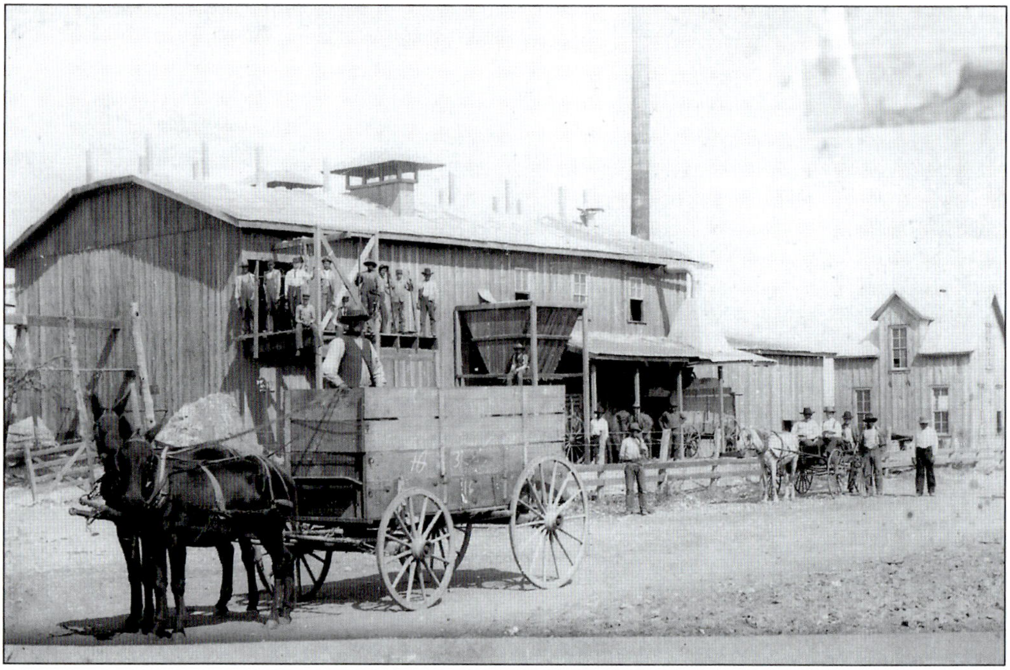

Cotton was the mainstay crop of early Corn Hill, Texas. This is one of the first wooden gins built in the area. Farmers brought their cotton to the gin in wagons pulled by teams of mules or horses. It was capable of ginning about three bales a day. The gin provided much-needed jobs for men in the area trying to provide for their families.

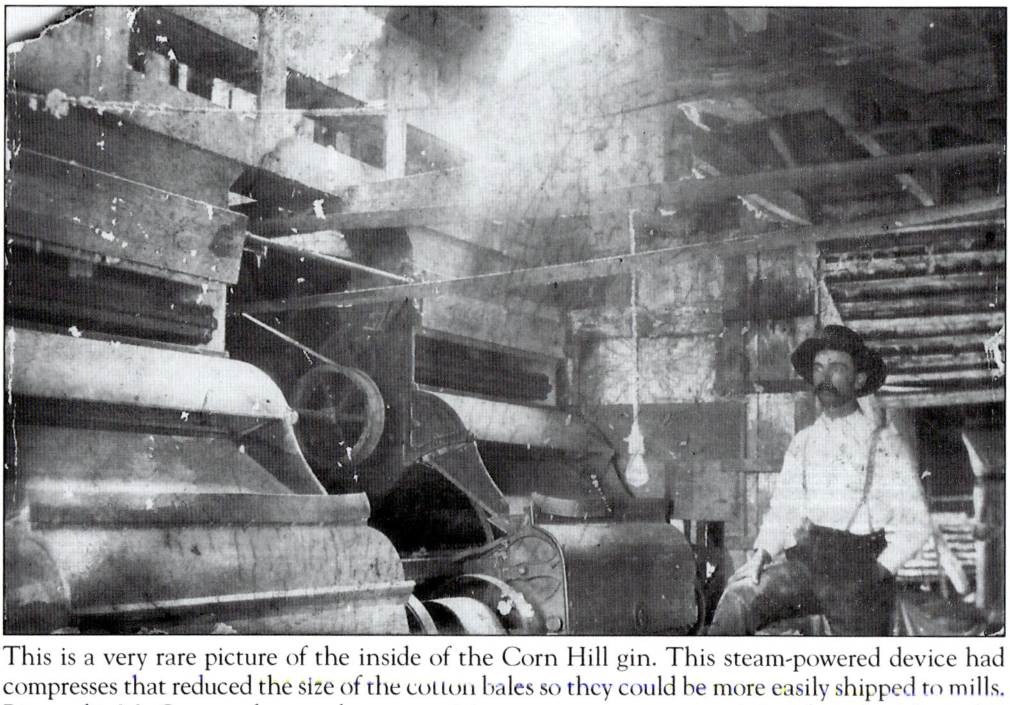

This is a very rare picture of the inside of the Corn Hill gin. This steam-powered device had compresses that reduced the size of the cotton bales so they could be more easily shipped to mills. Pictured is Mr. Storey, who ran the presses. Many press operators were injured on the job, as this was considered to be one of the most dangerous jobs at the gin.

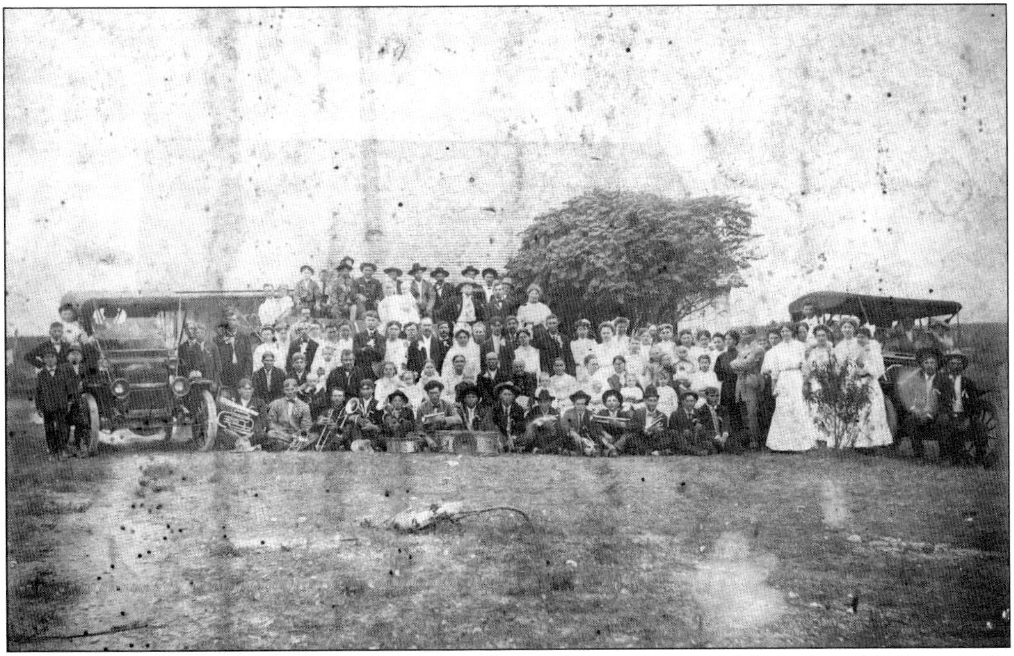

Depicted here is a c. 1910 wedding in Corn Hill. While not clearly visible in this old photograph, the whole wedding party and guests are standing outside what appears to be a church. The bride and groom are in the center of the picture, surrounded by family and friends and flanked by two early automobiles. Seated in the front is the entertainment for the day, the Corn Hill Brass Band.

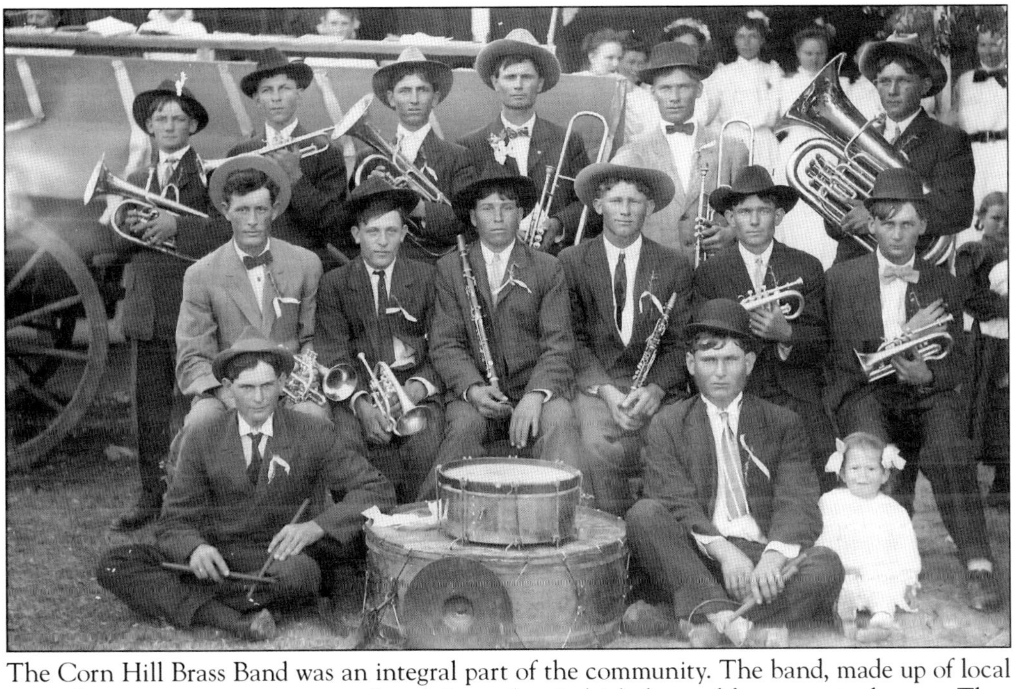

The Corn Hill Brass Band was an integral part of the community. The band, made up of local men who were amateur musicians, found themselves in high demand for events in the area. They played for church services, weddings, dances, and other special events. More about this band can be found in chapter two.

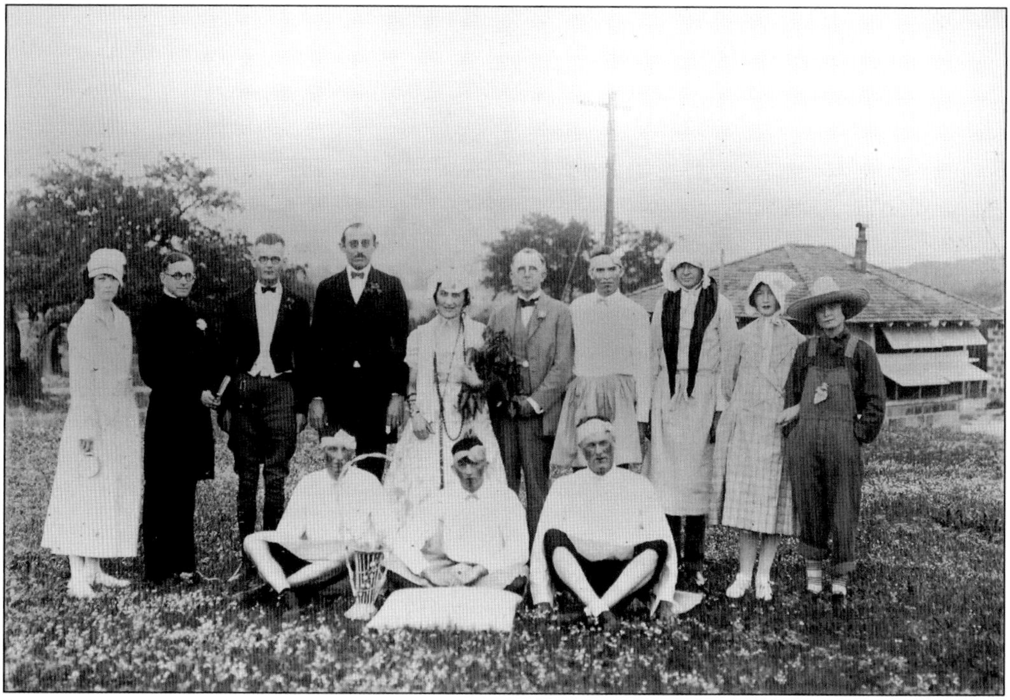

In a world without television or radio, people made their own entertainment. Pictured here is a mock wedding. Some of the men are dressed like women, and the woman on the right is in men's overalls. The mock wedding party is standing in front of the Corn Hill tabernacle. This building was used by the Baptist and Methodist congregations for services and served as a meeting place for the entire community. It was ultimately moved to Jarrell.

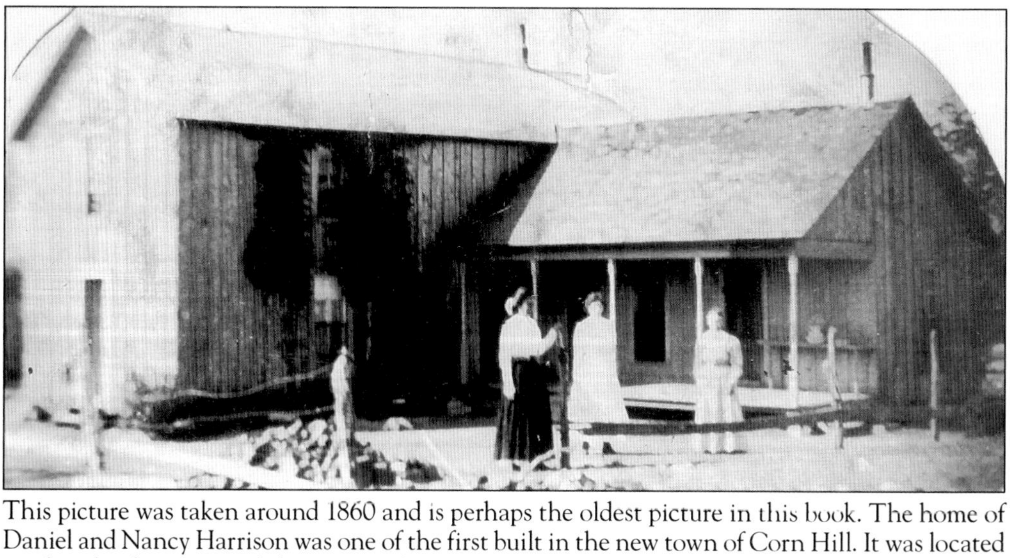

This picture was taken around 1860 and is perhaps the oldest picture in this book. The home of Daniel and Nancy Harrison was one of the first built in the new town of Corn Hill. It was located on their land just west of the present-day Corn Hill Cemetery.

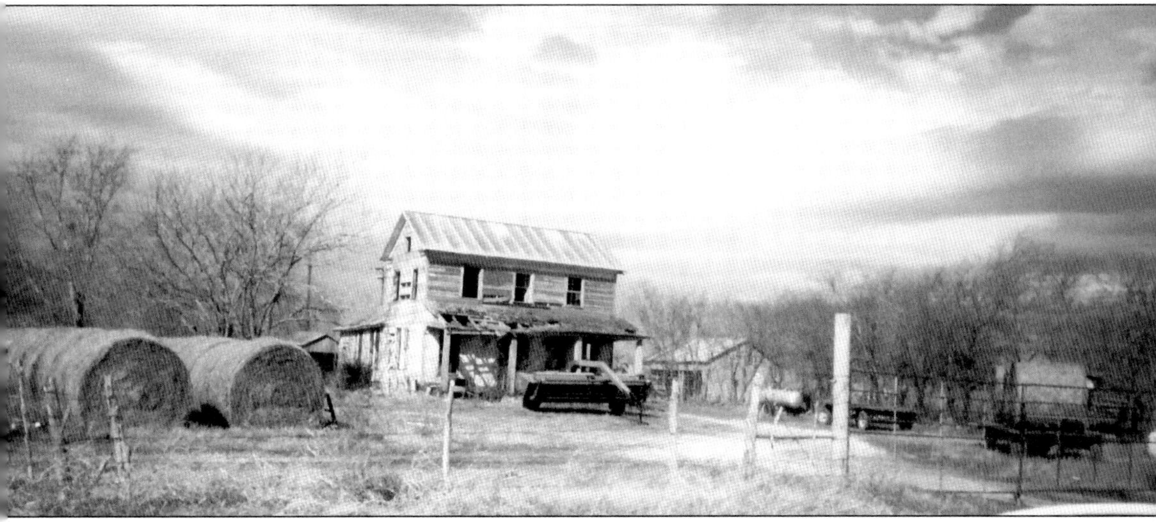

The only building in Corn Hill left standing today was built in the 1870s by the Shaver family. The lumber used in the home was hauled from South Texas. The roof consisted of post oak shingles. It took three years to build at a cost of $2,500. In later years, the J. D. Black family bought it and turned it into a hotel. It became a stage stop on the route from Waco to Georgetown. The cook at the hotel was Julia Elizabeth Ross Jones. She was the wife of a black farmer named Grant Jones. They lived in Corn Hill, and every day for many years, Julia prepared meals for the Black family. It was said there was a bell she would ring when it was time for lunch. Julia's six children were not allowed to attend the Corn Hill School because of school segregation. J. Conrad "Con" Foster, who was a teacher at the white school, took a personal interest in teaching the Jones children to read and write.

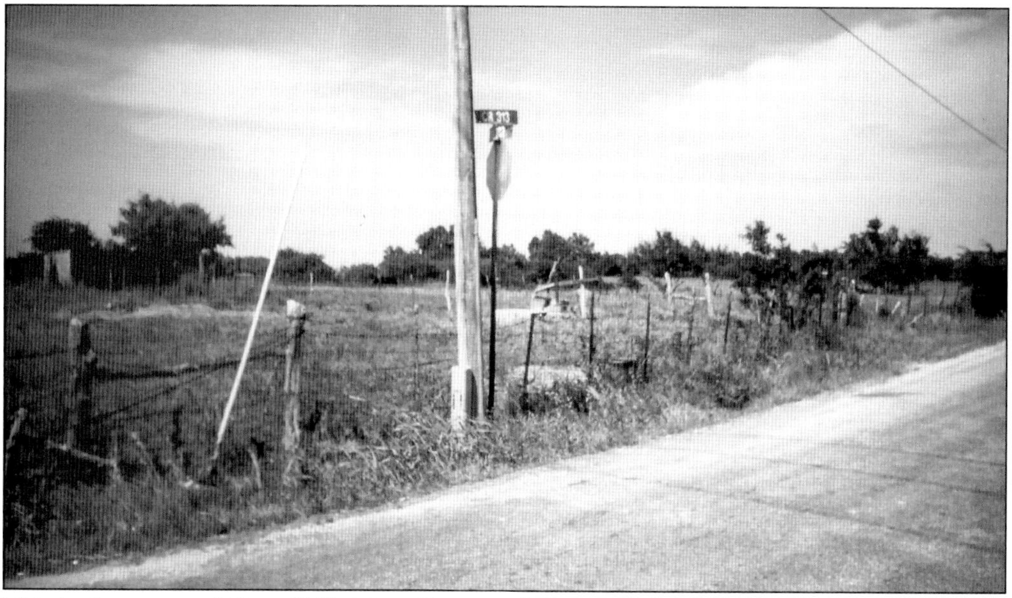

This is the corner of Corn Hill's Main Street and County Road 313 as it appears today. In the background is one of the remaining cisterns. Corn Hill built a water system after a typhoid epidemic, in which many residents died, was traced to the surface wells and cisterns. With the new system, the wells and cisterns were no longer used. The blacksmith shop shown earlier in this chapter stood on this corner.

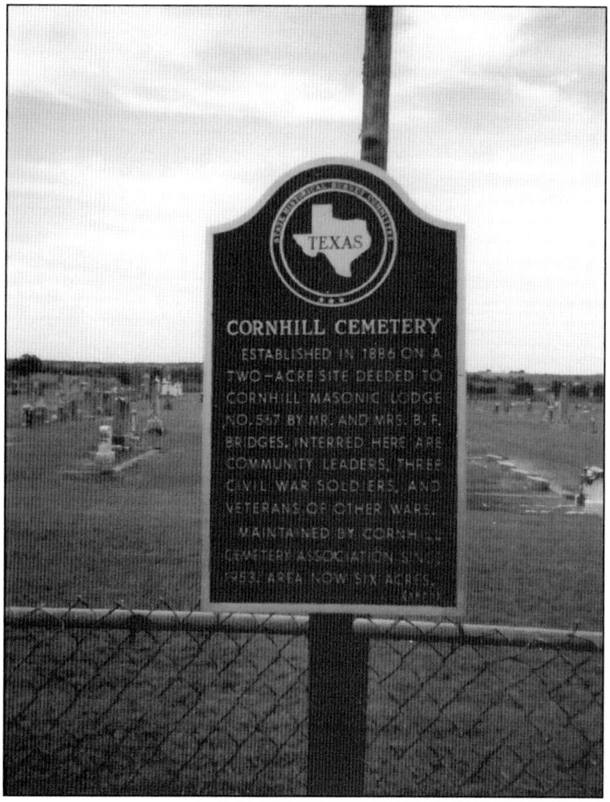

The Corn Hill Cemetery dates back to 1886 when it was maintained by Masonic Lodge No. 567. In 1953, the Corn Hill Cemetery Association was formed and is still responsible for the cemetery today. The historical marker reads, "Established in 1886 on a two-acre site deeded to Corn Hill Masonic Lodge No. 567 by Mr. and Mrs. B. F. Bridges. Interred here are community leaders, three Civil War soldiers, and veterans of other wars. Maintained by Cornhill Cemetery Association since 1953. Area now six acres."

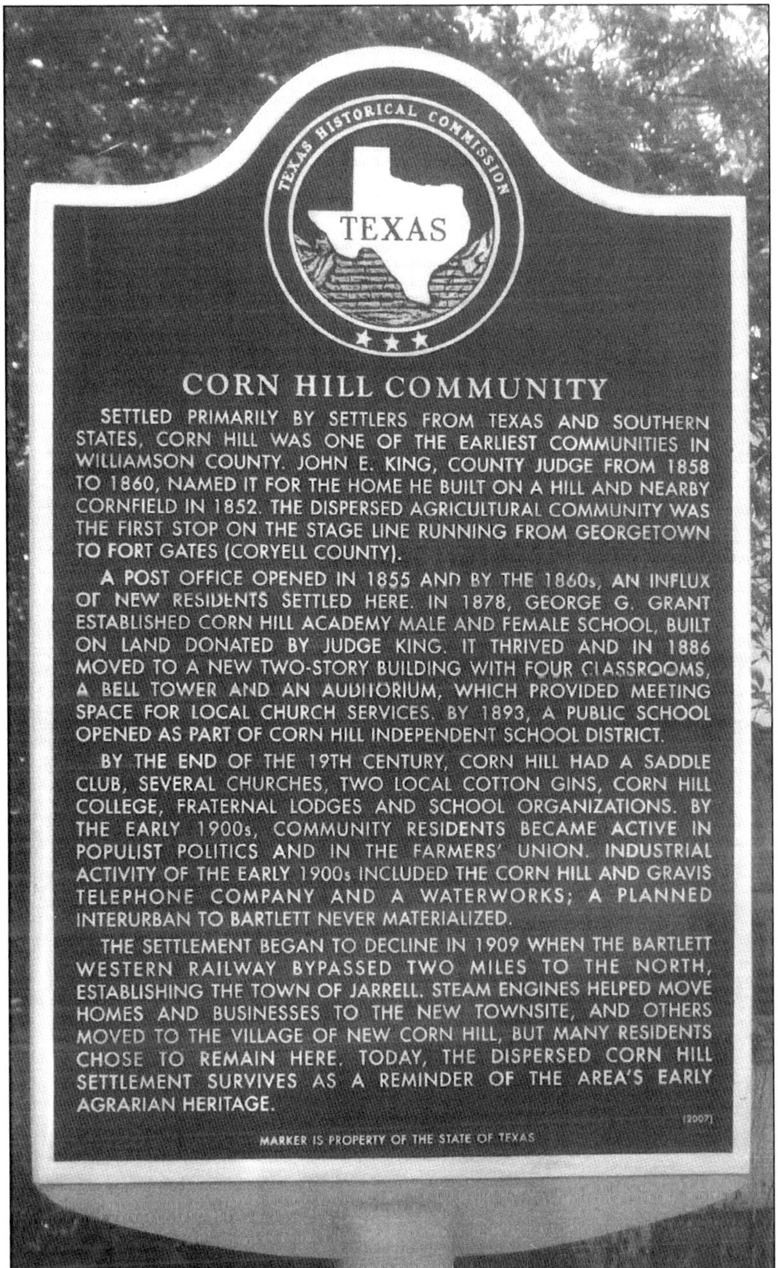

This historical marker is located on I-35 North, just south of Exit 275. It marks the spot where the town of Corn Hill once stood. The marker reviews the history of Corn Hill presented in this book and serves as a reminder of the once-thriving community. Although the town is gone, the history of Corn Hill lives on as an integral part of the fabric from which Jarrell and its people are made.

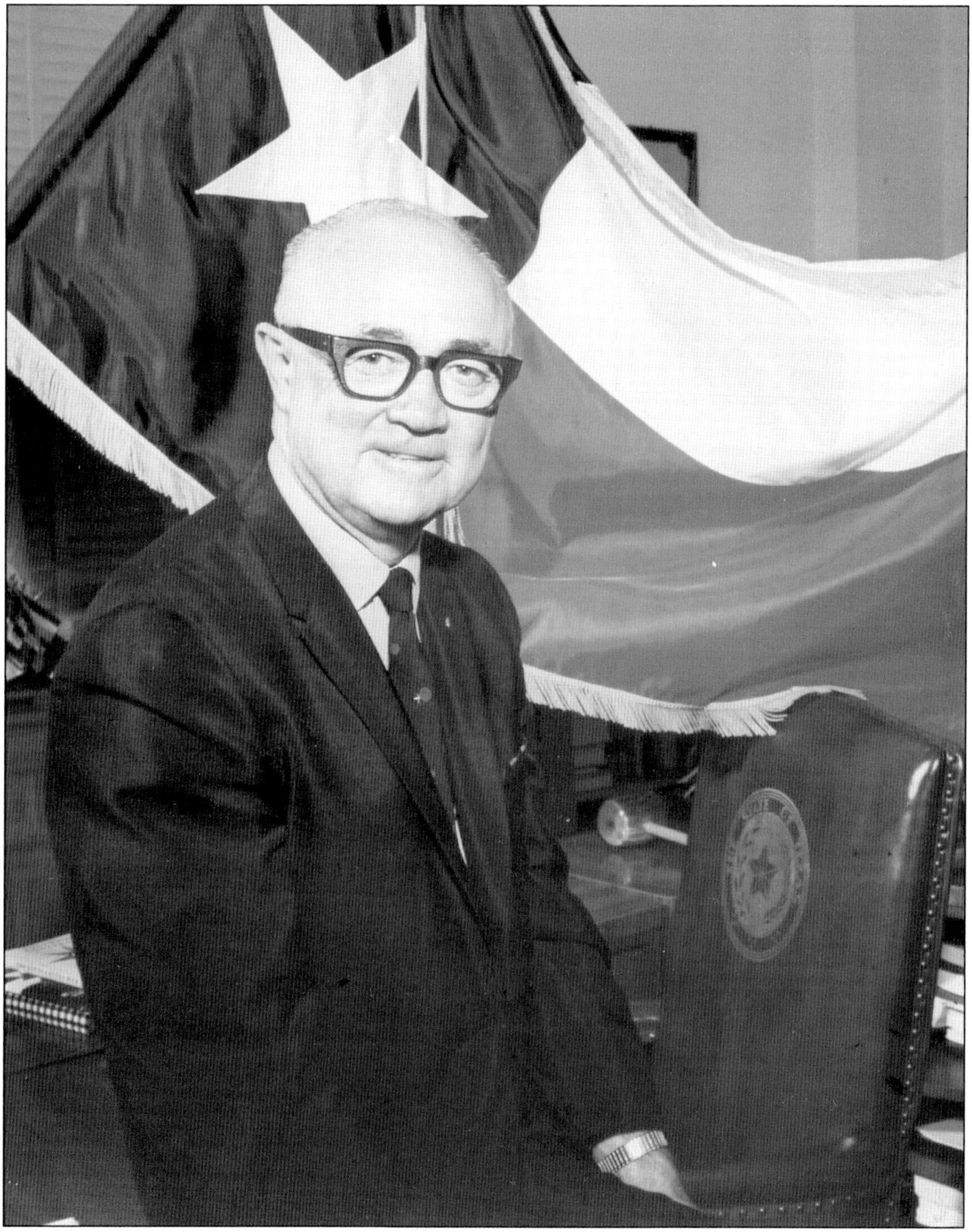

Preston Earnest Smith, the governor of Texas from January 1969 to January 1973, was born in Corn Hill, Texas, in 1912. One of 13 children, he attended school in Corn Hill when he was a young boy. Around the age of 10 or 11, his family moved to west Texas and he graduated from Lamesa High School. As a legacy to Corn Hill, Governor Smith was quoted as saying, "I was walking down a cotton row behind a span of mules and reading an old newspaper about Governor Jim Ferguson. That was the first time I'd read about a governor, and I decided right then and there I wanted to be governor of Texas. I've worked toward that goal ever since." Gov. Preston Smith died in 2003 at the age of 91 and always had a fond place in his heart for his early beginnings in Williamson County.

Two

The Railroad

In the early 1900s, the Katy (Missouri, Kansas, and Texas) Railroad ran daily through Bartlett, Texas, 13 miles east of Corn Hill. An important artery for shipping corn and cotton, the mainstay crops of the Texas Blackland Prairie, investors decided to establish a feeder line to the west to take advantage of additional productive farmland. Plans were for the new line to go from Bartlett to Florence and perhaps on to Lampasas. Of course, it was assumed that the line would be built through or near Corn Hill, a then thriving agricultural community. Imagine everyone's shock and disappointment when the proposed line instead took a more northern route. A resident of Corn Hill, Orlando D. Jarrell, being the shrewd developer he was, had been leasing a sizable piece of land near the proposed rail line, about 2 miles to the north. Seizing on this financial opportunity, he contacted E. C. Haeber from Bartlett. The two men came to an agreement and formed a partnership. Haeber was to furnish the necessary capital to purchase the land, and Jarrell was to plan the town site and promote the sale of lots. The property, previously referred to as the Jarrell Lease, became the Jarrell Townsite. This railroad was chartered in 1909, was eventually built, and for a while experienced success. With the decline of the cotton industry in the 1920s and 1930s, the Bartlett Western Railroad encountered financial difficulties and eventually closed in 1935.

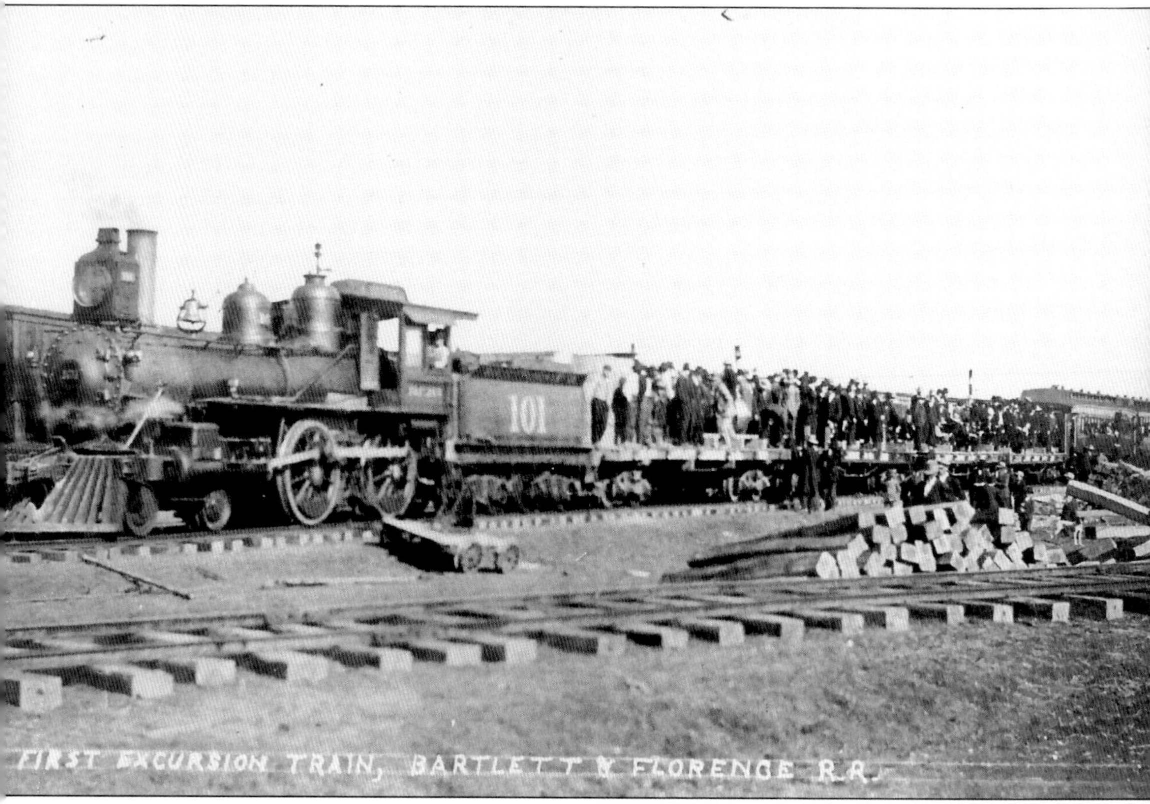

It was an exciting day in December 1911 when the first train pulled into Jarrell. People lined the track, welcoming the locomotive pulling a couple of flatbed cars and a caboose. Over 300 people had paid $1 for a round-trip ticket. The excursion originated in Bartlett, and the passengers had traveled to Bartlett early in the day in horse-drawn buggies or wagons. Folks who paid the dollar said, "It was a long day, but it was worth it just to be a part of history." In 1916, Marie Cronin, the daughter of Thomas Cronin, who was president of the Bartlett Western Railroad, nicknamed four stops on the rail line the Four Gospels. Four flag stations were named St. Matthew (Donahoe Creek west of Schwertner), St. Mark (Will Davis's country store west of Jarrell), St. Luke (Atkinson community west of Jarrell), and St. John (Armstrong community near Florence). Passengers departing at these stops were invited to read select verses from the gospel's namesake posted on the walls of each station. The rail line, for the reason above, was called the "route of the apostles."

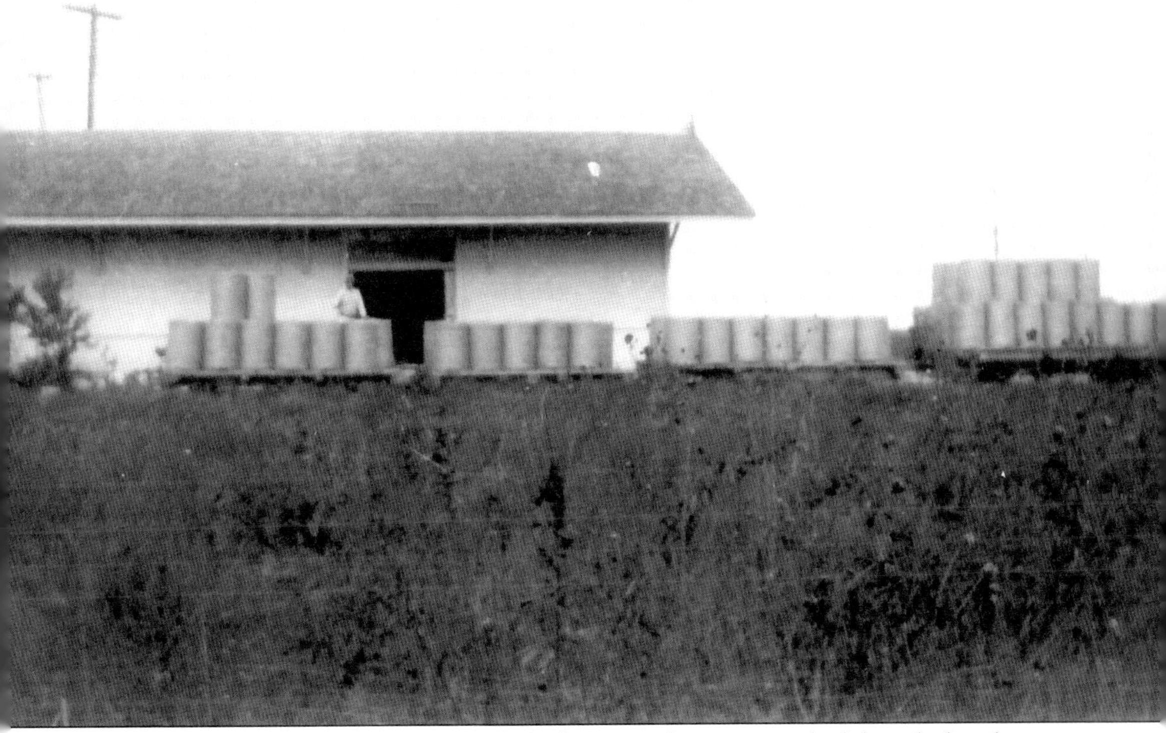

The Bartlett-Western Railroad may have lacked revenue, but it certainly did not lack in history and exaggerated folklore. Using the initials B-W (for Bartlett Western), the locals nicknamed the train "Big Windy." Passengers were often required to help push the train up the grade from Bartlett to Jarrell, so another popular nickname for the rail line was "Better Walk . . . if you don't want to push the train." Weather was a big factor in the dependability of the train. Torrential rain during the early 1920s washed out many bridges and trestles. Folks in Jarrell remember that cars of the Bartlett-Western often jumped off the track, so they dubbed the train the "Bullfrog Line." The picture above is of the Jarrell depot and flatcars loaded with cotton. Most of the cotton from this area was shipped to the ports of Houston or Galveston.

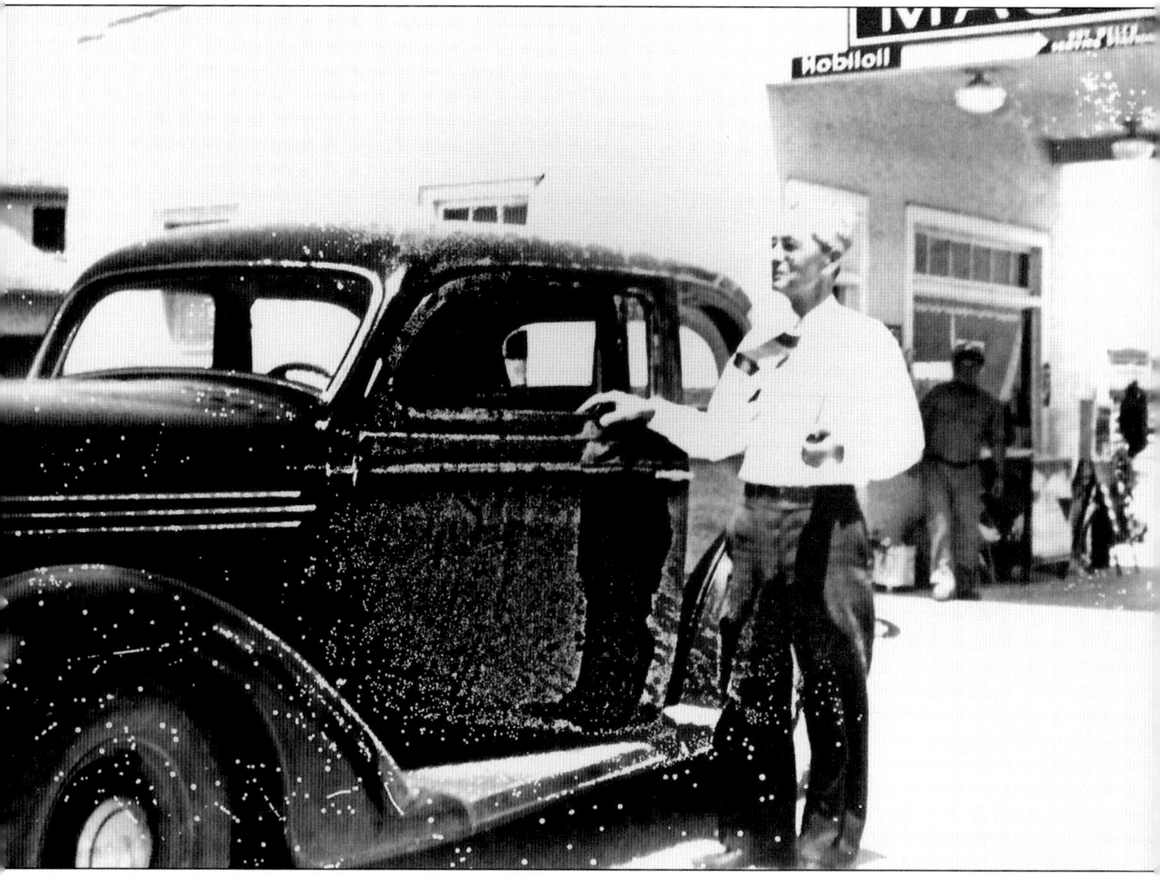

Incorporated in 1909, the Bartlett-Western Railway Company found itself in a constant struggle for revenue. In the early 1920s, the price of cotton dropped to 45¢ a bale from $1.59. In addition to cotton prices, a number of disastrous floods had weakened the railway trestles, so they were unsafe to use. For a while, the rail line used a lighter Model T truck that was outfitted with locomotive wheels in an attempt to keep the company afloat. The railroad ceased operations in December 1935. The Jarrell train depot was located between Fifth and Sixth Streets and Avenue H. It was built by T. F. Hamilton. There were two waiting rooms, a freight room, a baggage room, and an office. This picture shows Roy Welch's Magnolia station with the train depot in the background.

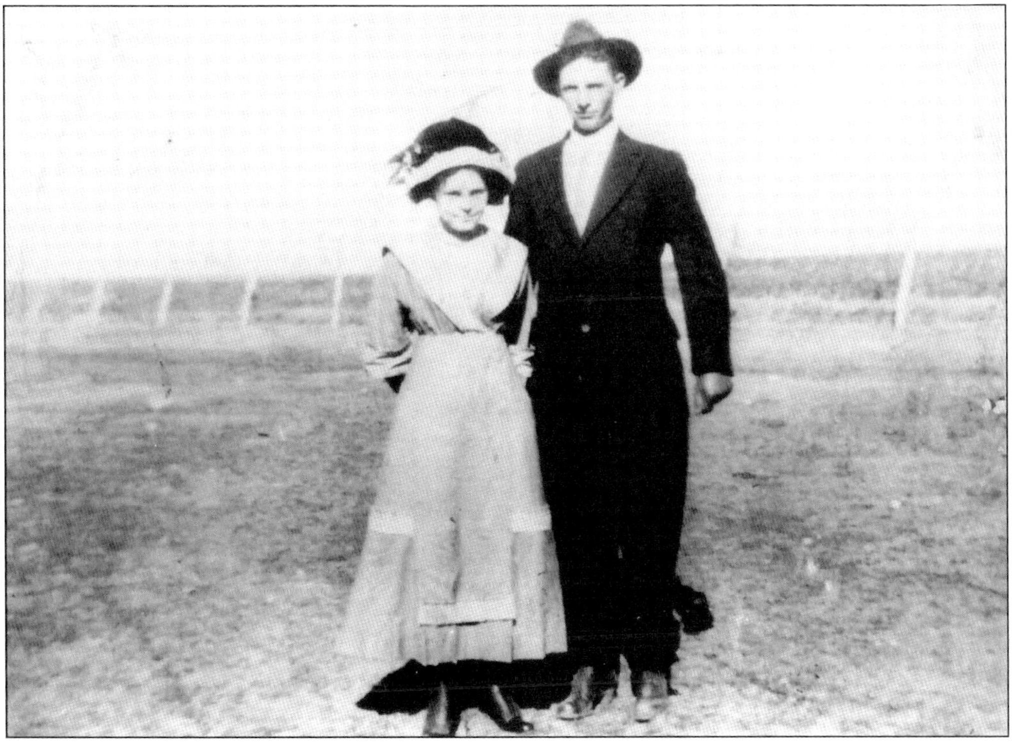

This picture was taken just around the time Jarrell became a town and the railroad was coming through. It is the wedding picture of Fred and Eva Lee Harrison on December 10, 1910. The image shows a good example of the fashion of the day.

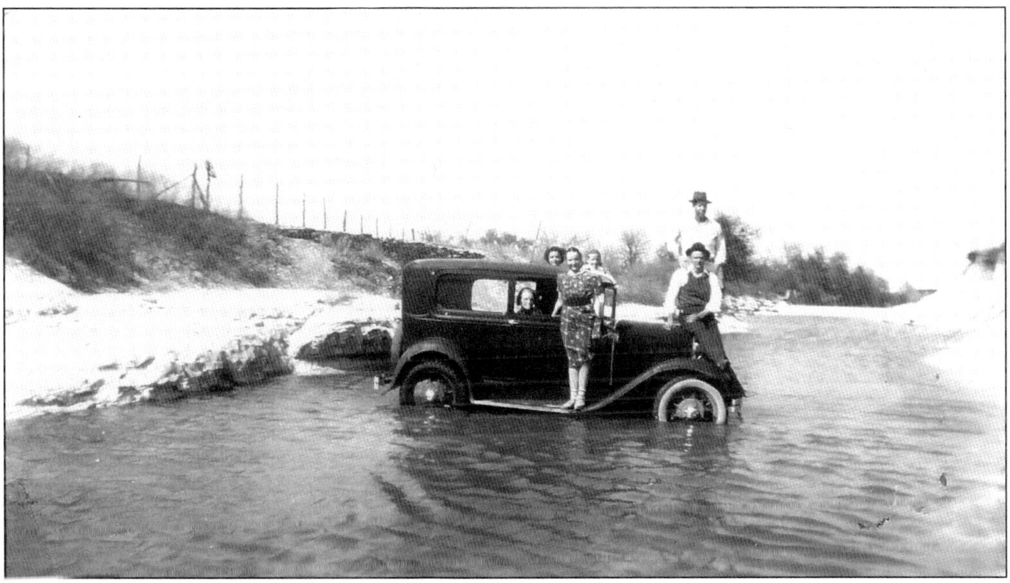

Not everything about transportation had to do with trains. Cars were becoming important as well. In this picture, a number of young Jarrell residents are taking advantage of the local car wash—in reality, Donahoe Creek, just east of Jarrell. Car owners knew just where to drive into the creek, give their car a good washing, and drive back out.

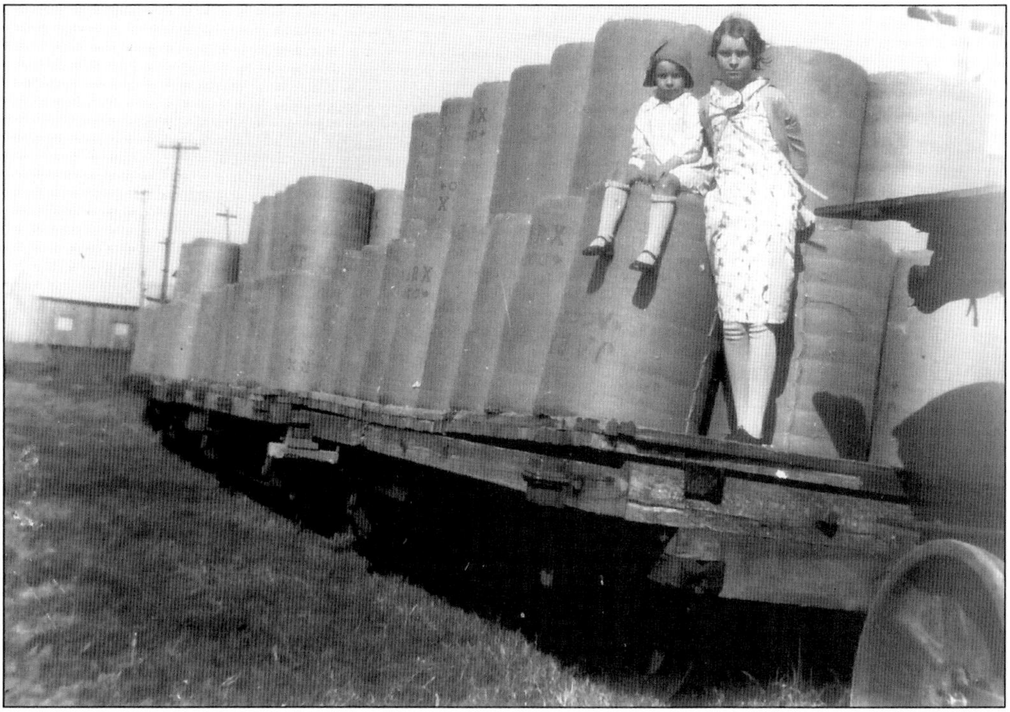

A special feeder line was built to the Harrison gin. This allowed cotton bales to be loaded on a flatcar, moved to the main rail line, and shipped to Bartlett. Pictured in 1932 are Mary Harrison (left) and her sister Claudia standing on a railcar loaded with bales from the gin. These two young girls were daughters of the owner of the gin, Fred D. Harrison.

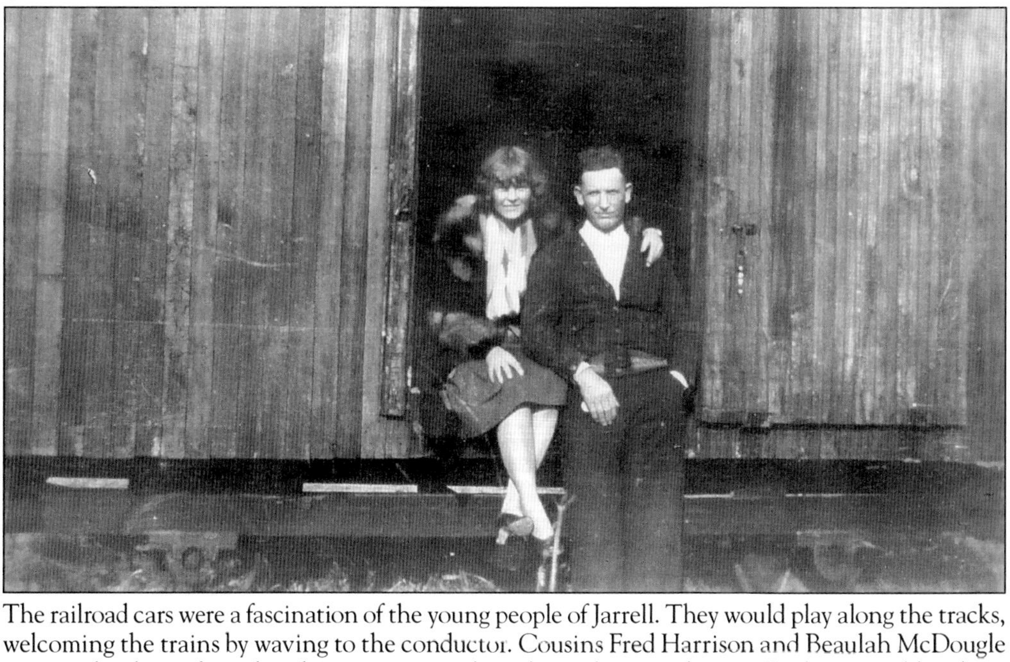

The railroad cars were a fascination of the young people of Jarrell. They would play along the tracks, welcoming the trains by waving to the conductor. Cousins Fred Harrison and Beaulah McDougle pose in the door of a railroad car sitting on the side tracks near the gin. Railcars would sit here until the cotton was ginned and baled and then hauled to the main line at the train station.

Three

The Early Years

With the plans for the railroad and the selling of lots in the Jarrell Townsite, the new town of Jarrell was on its way to becoming the northernmost city in Williamson County. The first lot was sold in 1909. The home built on that lot still stands today. The whole atmosphere around the development of the new city was carnival-like. There was much more hoopla surrounding the sale of lots than is usually associated with real estate. Weekends brought huge barbeques or fish fries with everyone invited to eat for free. The Corn Hill Brass Band provided live music, interspersed with rousing and convincing sales talks, presenting in glowing terms the bright and prosperous future of the town of Jarrell. Apparently the talks were convincing because many lots were sold. Some were auctioned off for as much as $200 or $300. All 200 lots were sold either to people who intended to reside in Jarrell or to folks from other towns who just purchased lots as an investment. The railroad became a reality in 1911, and it was with heavy hearts that the town of Corn Hill literally folded up and moved to Jarrell. J. R. Hawkins was in charge of moving the buildings to the new site. They dubbed the large homes and businesses moving down the highway "ships of the prairie" as they were put on logs and pulled with teams of mules or steam tractors to their new locations.

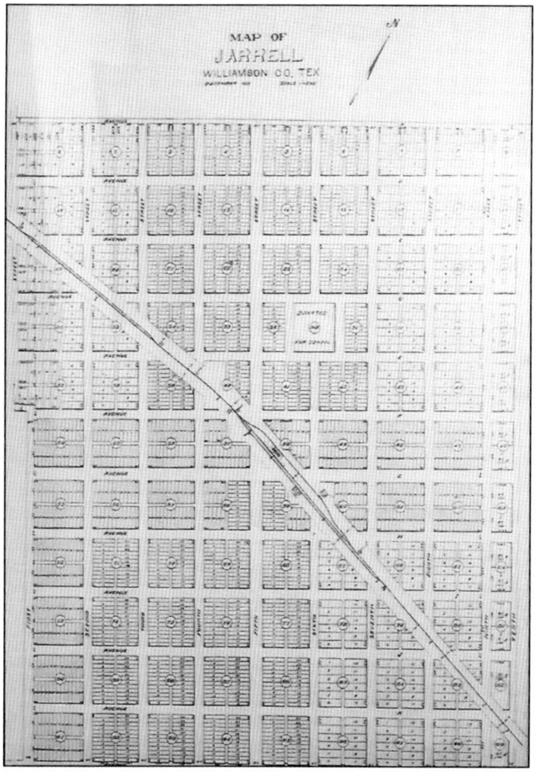

The original plat of the Jarrell Townsite still exists. It is shown here as it hangs on the wall of Jarrell's city hall. Most lots were deep but narrow. Prospective buyers were encouraged to purchase multiple lots, meaning more money for the developers. Some of the first lots were sold at auction for between $200 and $300. Many of the Jarrell lots are still owned by descendants of the original owners. All the streets shown in this plat still exist in Jarrell today. (Courtesy the City of Jarrell.)

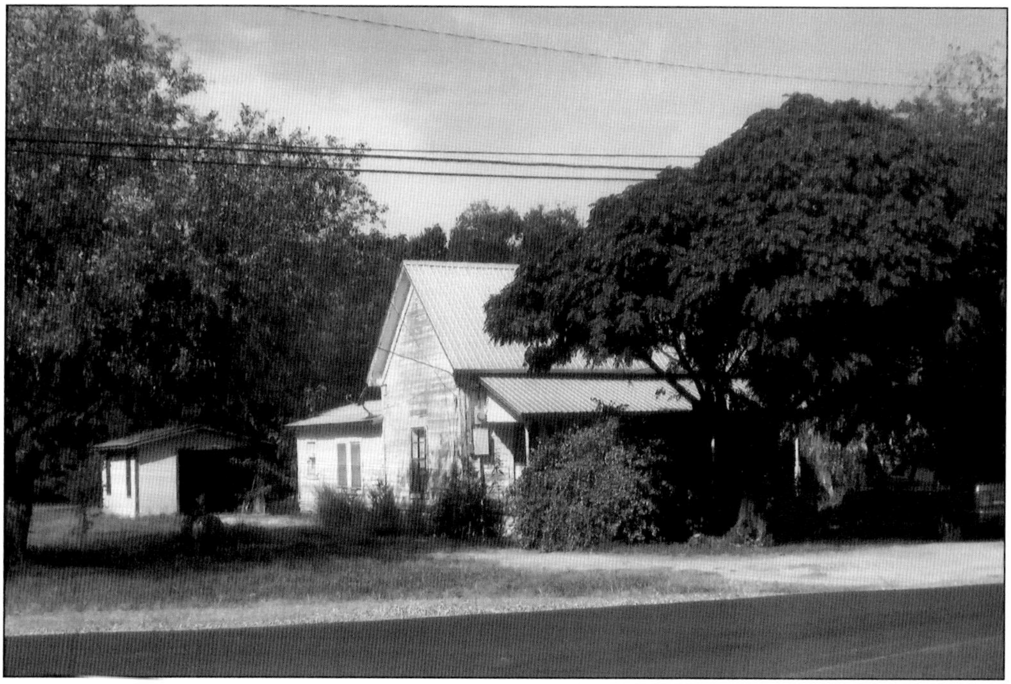

The Hickman home still stands today. It is believed the lot on which this home stands was among the first, if not the first, to be sold out of the Jarrell Townsite in 1909. This home is located at the intersection of First Street and Avenue H.

This document shows the deed to 24 lots purchased by F. R. Conlee from the Jarrell Townsite Company for a sum of $300. The date of the transaction is September 27, 1916. Notice the signatures of the original developers, O. D. Jarrell and E. C. Haeber. (Courtesy Esther Rosie Conlee Holloway.)

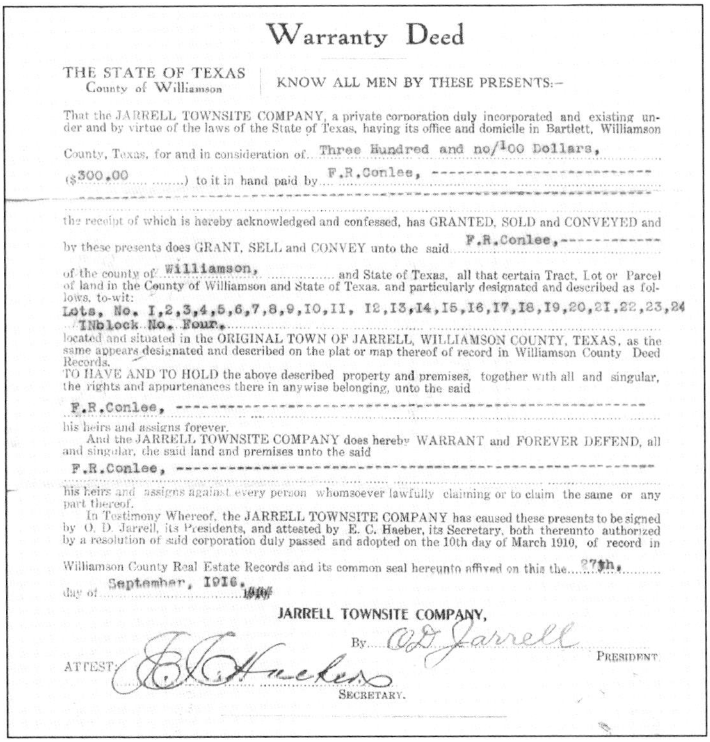

Warranty Deed

THE STATE OF TEXAS
County of Williamson

KNOW ALL MEN BY THESE PRESENTS:–

That the JARRELL TOWNSITE COMPANY, a private corporation duly incorporated and existing under and by virtue of the laws of the State of Texas, having its office and domicile in Bartlett, Williamson County, Texas, for and in consideration of Three Hundred and no/100 Dollars, ($300.00) to it in hand paid by F.R.Conlee,

the receipt of which is hereby acknowledged and confessed, has GRANTED, SOLD and CONVEYED and by these presents does GRANT, SELL and CONVEY unto the said F.R.Conlee,

of the county of Williamson, and State of Texas, all that certain Tract, Lot or Parcel of land in the County of Williamson and State of Texas, and particularly designated and described as follows, to-wit:
Lots, No. I,2,3,4,5,6,7,8,9,10,II, I2,I3,I4,I5,I6,I7,I8,I9,20,2I,22,23,24 INblock No. Four.
located and situated in the ORIGINAL TOWN OF JARRELL, WILLIAMSON COUNTY, TEXAS, as the same appears designated and described on the plat or map thereof of record in Williamson County Deed Records.
TO HAVE AND TO HOLD the above described property and premises, together with all and singular, the rights and appurtenances there in anywise belonging, unto the said

F.R.Conlee,

his heirs and assigns forever.

And the JARRELL TOWNSITE COMPANY does hereby WARRANT and FOREVER DEFEND, all and singular, the said land and premises unto the said

F.R.Conlee,

his heirs and assigns against every person whomsoever lawfully claiming or to claim the same or any part thereof.

In Testimony Whereof, the JARRELL TOWNSITE COMPANY has caused these presents to be signed by O. D. Jarrell, its Presidents, and attested by E. C. Haeber, its Secretary, both thereunto authorized by a resolution of said corporation duly passed and adopted on the 10th day of March 1910, of record in Williamson County Real Estate Records and its common seal hereunto affixed on this the 27th. day of September, 1916. 1910

JARRELL TOWNSITE COMPANY,

By O.D. Jarrell
PRESIDENT.

ATTEST: E. C. Haeber
SECRETARY.

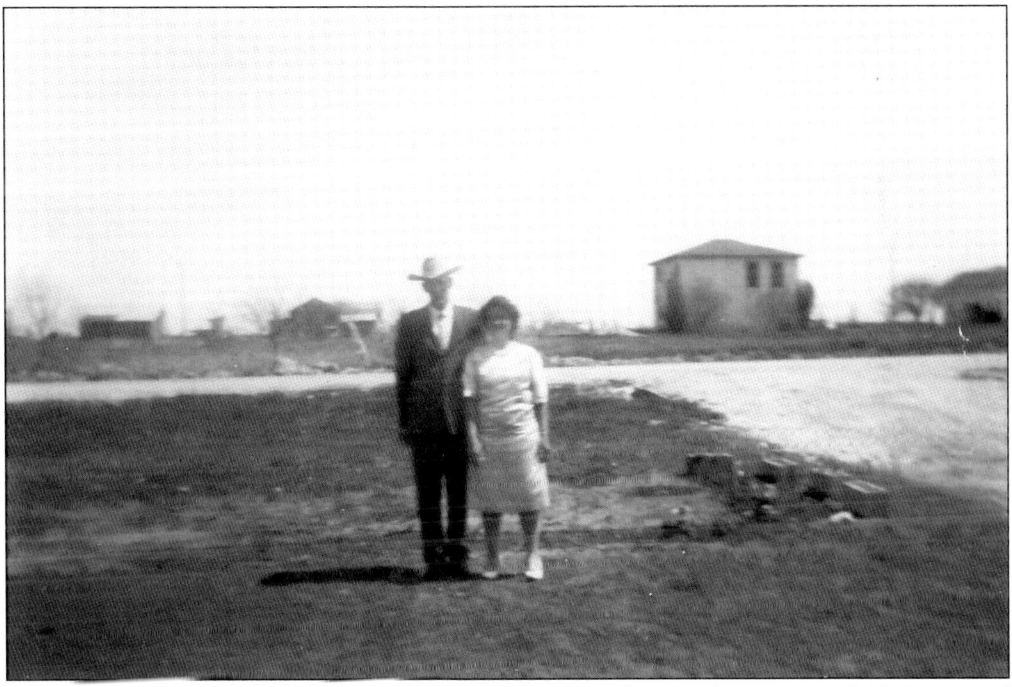

Shirley Frank Conlee and his wife, Myrtle, are shown standing on the corner of Fifth Street and Avenue A near their residence in the early 1960s. The deed previously shown is for this property purchased by Shirley Frank Conlee's father, F. R. Conlee. The two-story home in the background belonged to the Ramsey family. (Courtesy Esther Rosie Conlee Holloway.)

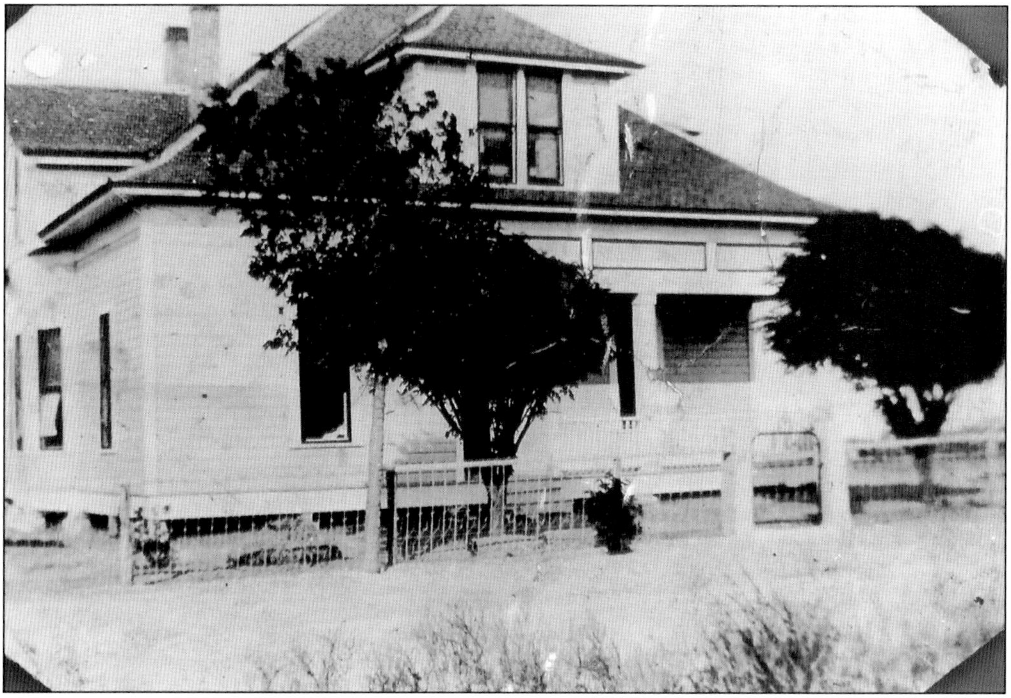

This beautiful old home owned by the G. T. Harrison family was located on the corner of the Bartlett Highway and Farm to Market Road 487 (FM 487). Most of the homes of this era were built with wide, deep porches, and all were on pier-and-beam foundations. The piers were usually large blocks of limestone found naturally in this part of Texas.

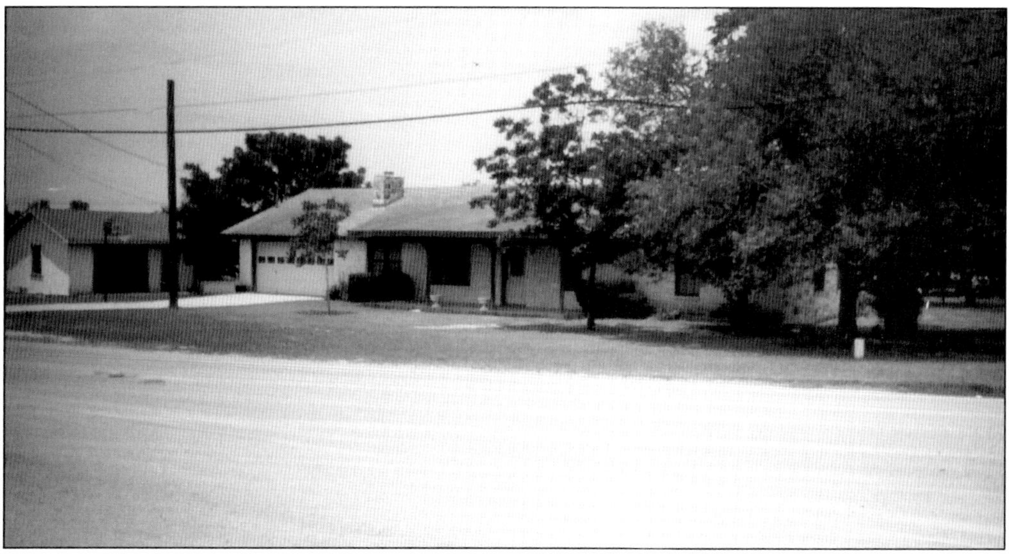

The Harrison home was torn down in the 1960s. The house that was subsequently built there was destroyed in the 1989 tornado. The home pictured here is built on the same site. Note the detached garage to the left. It is part of the original Harrison home and was built to accommodate their Model A Ford.

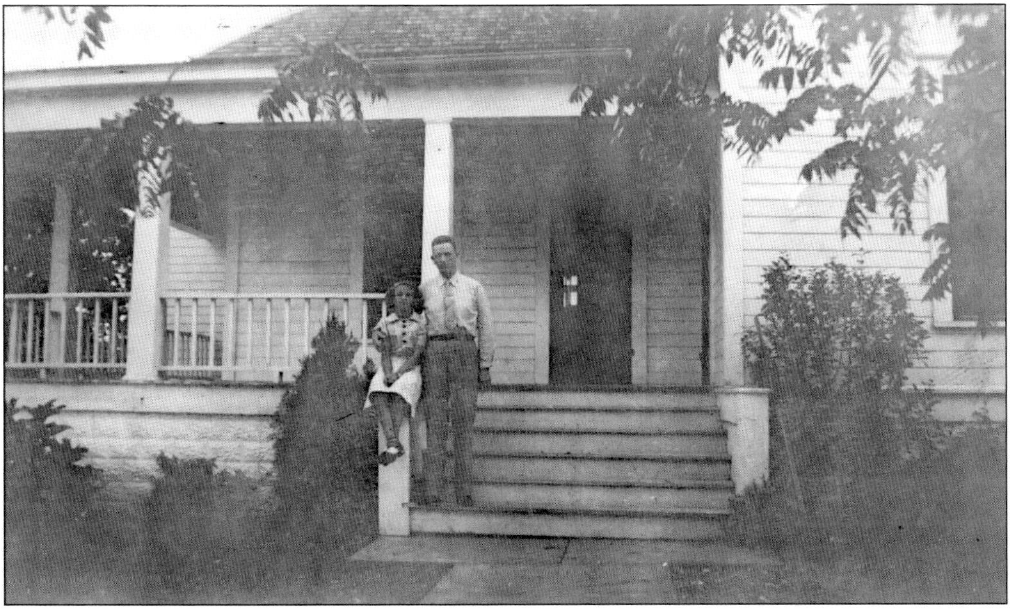

This lovely home was located on the southwest corner of Second Street and Avenue G. It was one of the homes moved from Corn Hill in or about 1912. It was originally owned by the Foster family. In 1939, when this photograph was taken, it belonged to Fred and Eva Lee Harrison. Mary Harrison and Fred Harrison are shown in the picture.

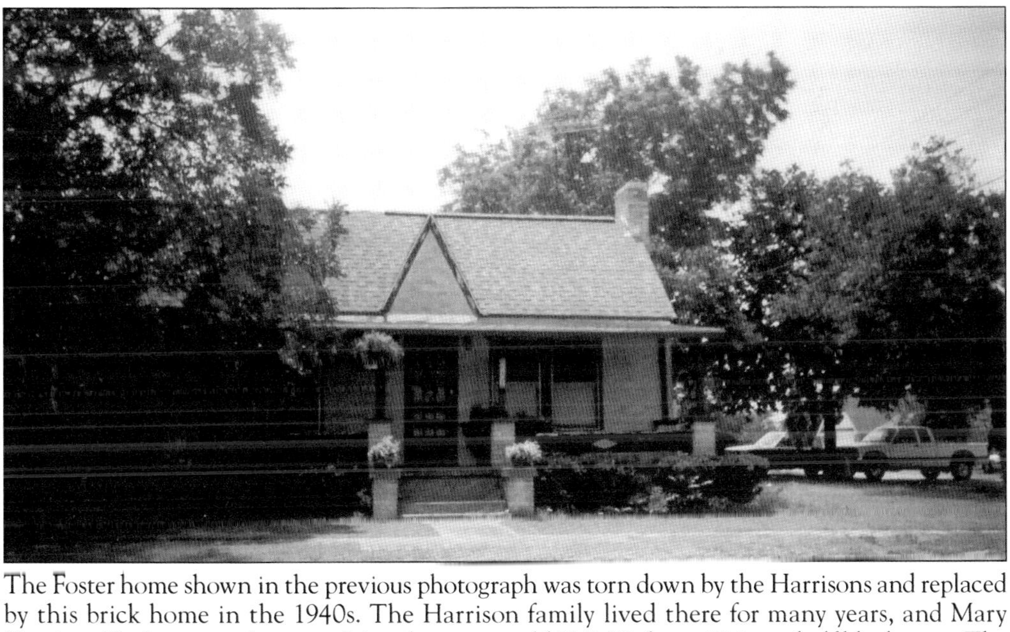

The Foster home shown in the previous photograph was torn down by the Harrisons and replaced by this brick home in the 1940s. The Harrison family lived there for many years, and Mary Harrison Hodge remembers watching the cars on old U.S. Highway 81 just a half block away. The home is currently owned by Kevin and Vinette Makal, who have both been teachers in Jarrell schools for many years.

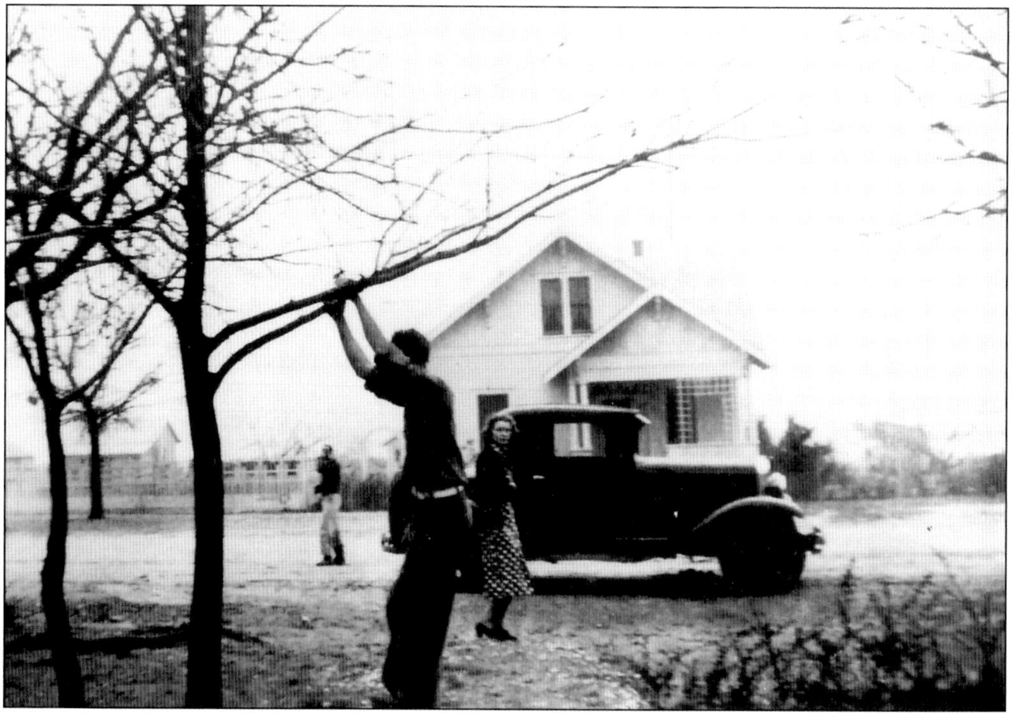

Across from the Harrison home on Avenue G was a home owned by the Valenta family. John Valenta owned the local lumberyard and built this beautiful craftsman-style home around 1920. Avenue G was just a gravel road at that time. The outbuildings to the left of the house were for the Valentas' cow and chickens. In this 1939 picture are, from left to right, Floyd Goode, Jesse Sybert, and Claudia Goode.

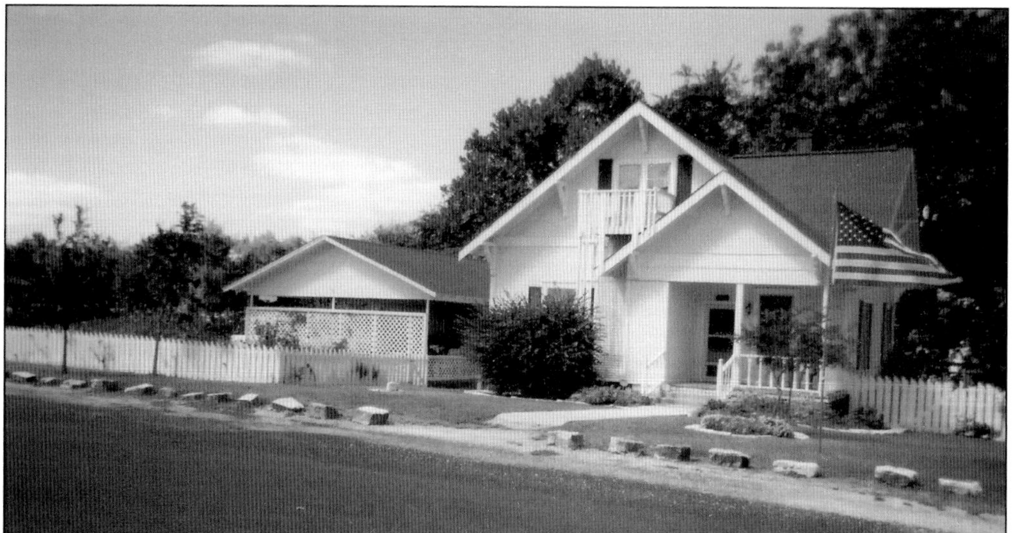

In 2001, the Valenta home was purchased by the late James King and his wife, Priscilla. Prior to that, it was owned by Floyd and Claudia Goode and was also owned at one time by Boyd and Lucille Goad. It is truly one of the treasures of Jarrell's Old Town. The original woodwork, steep staircase, and interior French doors, along with old double-hung windows, are still visible inside.

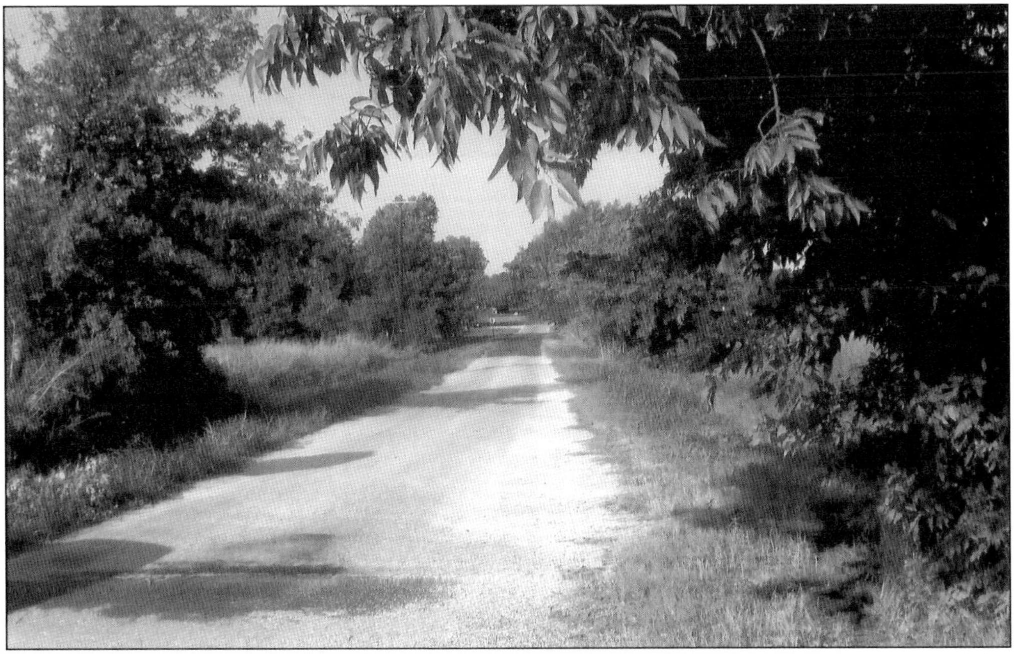

Avenue G is home to many of the older residences in Jarrell, as mentioned in some of the photograph captions. It is a picturesque street shaded by large trees. When the houses were built, it was a wide gravel road. Mary Hodge remembers neighbors telling her to "slow down" when she drove down the road and to quit "kicking up the dust."

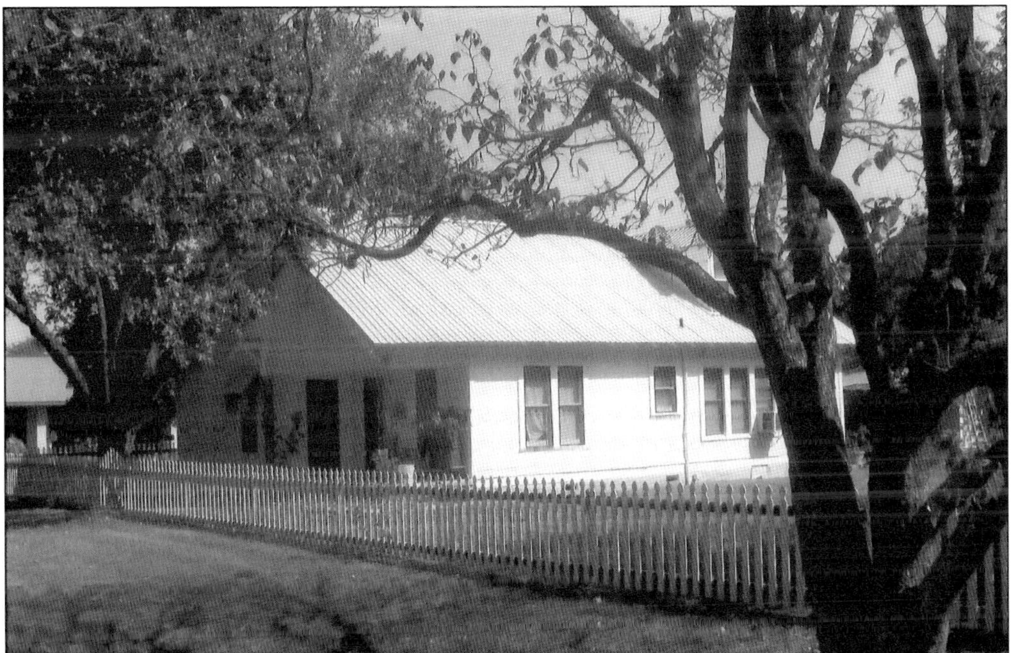

Graced by beautiful old trees, another of the well-preserved homes in Jarrell originally belonged to the Shaver family. Later it became home to the Frymires. Located on the corner of Second Street and Avenue J, it is currently owned by Johnny and Alison Martone Jr.

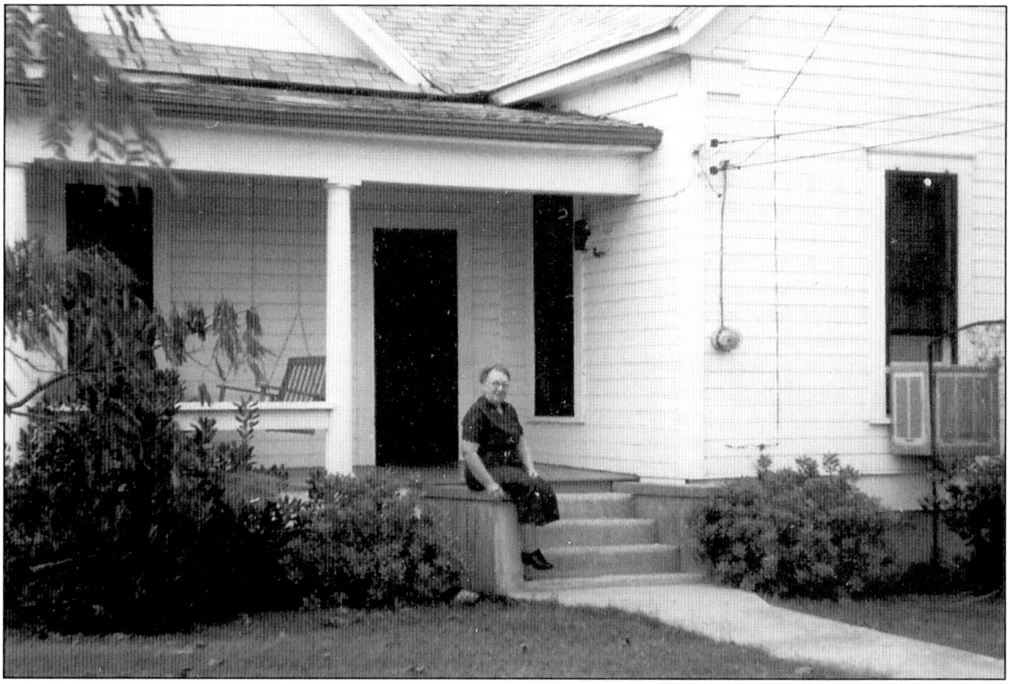

The home belonging to Mr. and Mrs. Robert Kalmbach was built on the corner of Second Street and Avenue J. Taken in the 1940s, the above photograph shows Ida Ella Kalmbach on the front porch. The Kalmbach name is still visible in the concrete sidewalk at the front of the house. A number of Jarrell families have lived in this home over the years. Today it is owned by Eugene "Tookie" and Sena Mullen. As can be seen from the picture below, the home is well maintained and the trees indicate many years of memories and growth. Even though the swing has been replaced by rocking chairs, the front porch and sidewalk are still exactly as in the older picture. (Both courtesy Mr. and Mrs. Curtis Andrews.)

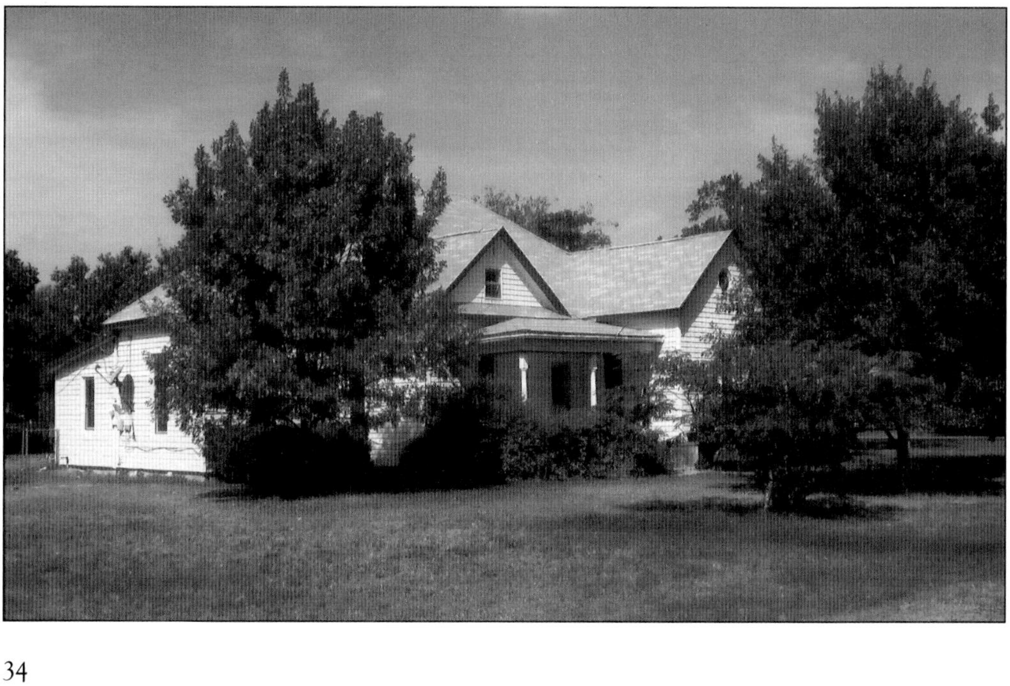

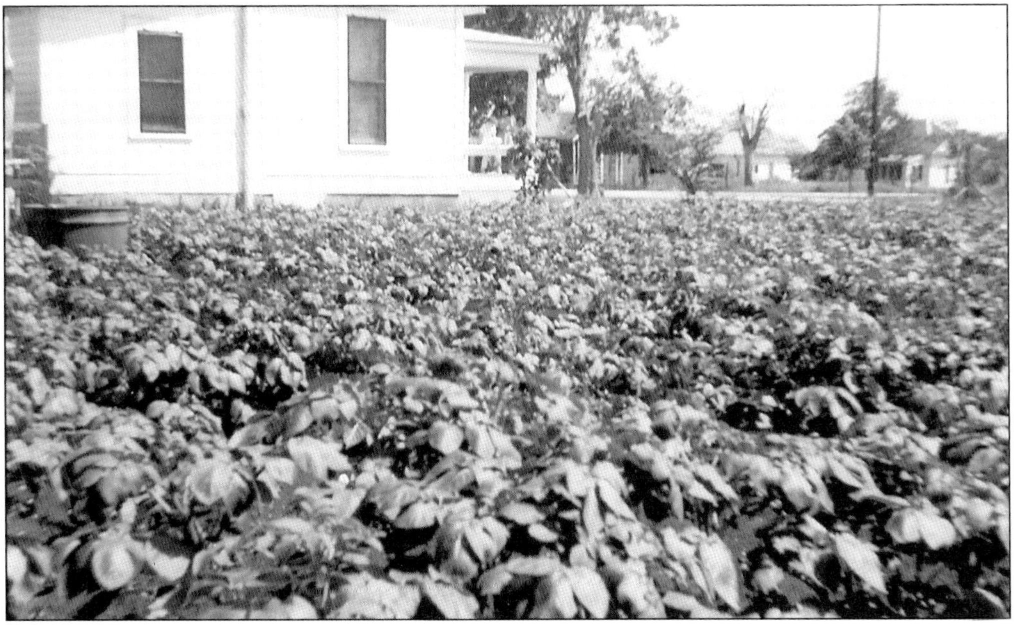

Here is an unusual picture and side view of the Kalmbach house. This is a large 2-acre patch of German potatoes. As the story is told, seed potatoes were brought over from Germany, planted, and cultivated to provide a special treat for the Kalmbach family and friends. (Courtesy Mr. and Mrs. Curtis Andrews.)

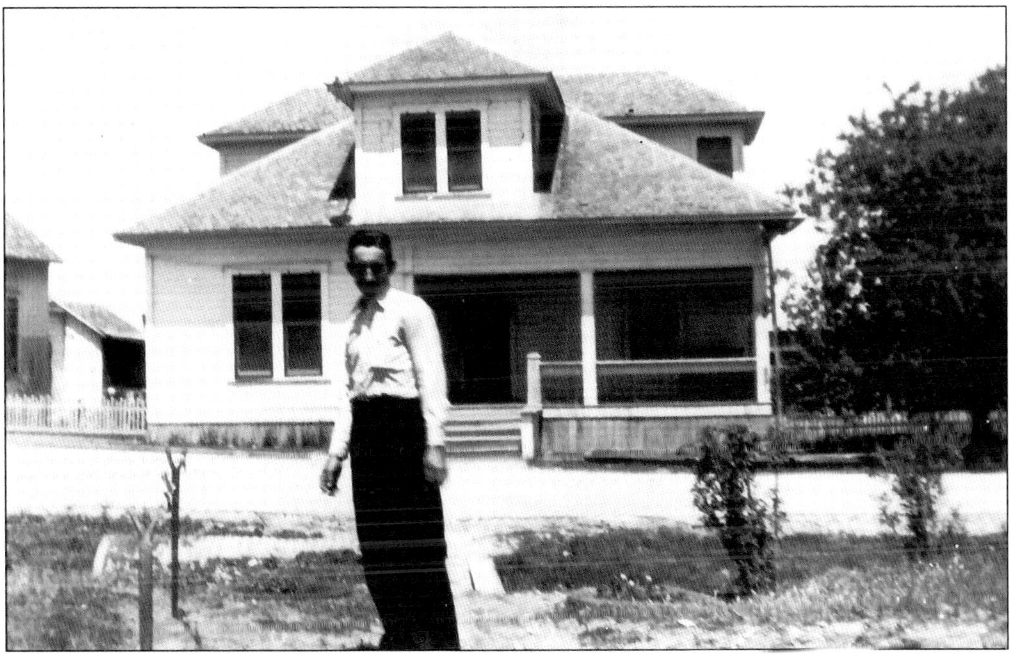

Shown here is Jesse Gistinger standing in front of the family home. Bertha and Carl Gistinger's home was located on the north side of Avenue H at the east end. To the left of their home was the family meat market. They were known for their homemade bologna sausage made from a family recipe brought over from Czechoslovakia. The shop was frequented by shoppers from both Jarrell and the surrounding areas.

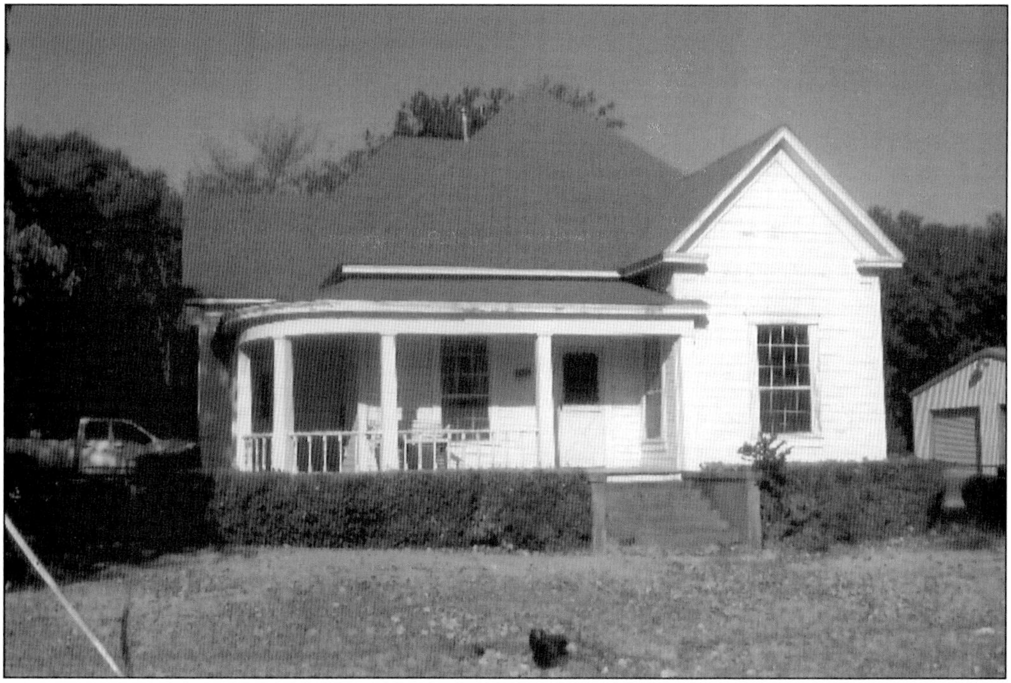

A beautiful old home built by J. A. Buchanan stands on the corner of Avenue G and Third Street. It was built at the same time as the Valenta home down the street, using lumber from the local lumberyard. Both houses were built around 1920. They each have the same woodwork and coal-burning fireplaces. It is currently owned by John and Stephanie Alto.

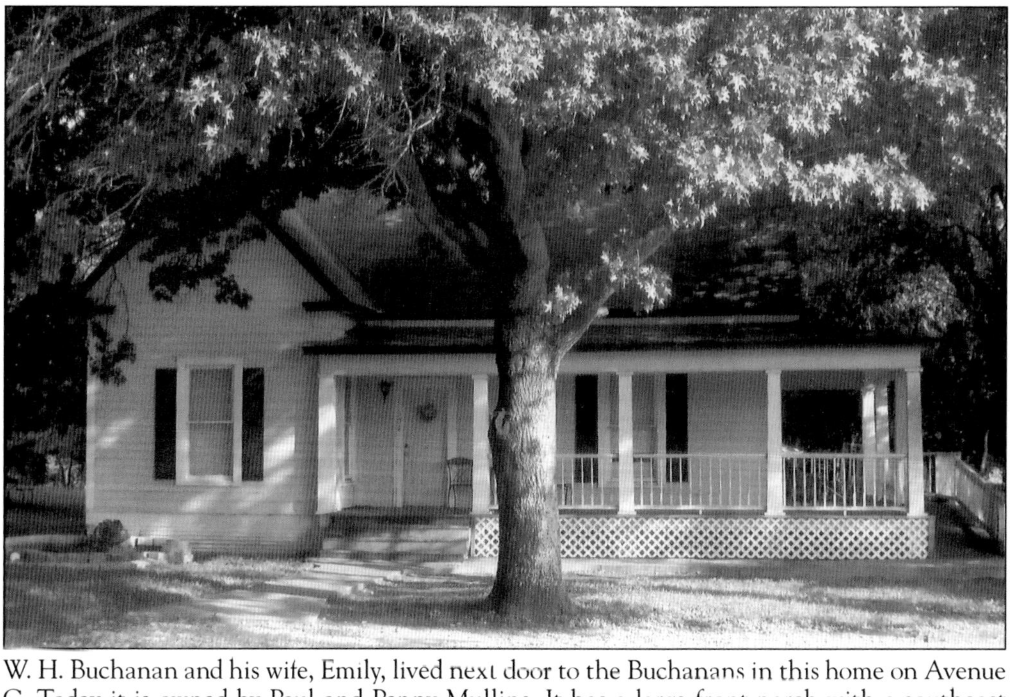

W. H. Buchanan and his wife, Emily, lived next door to the Buchanans in this home on Avenue G. Today it is owned by Paul and Penny Mullins. It has a large front porch with a southeast exposure to take advantage of Texas summer breezes.

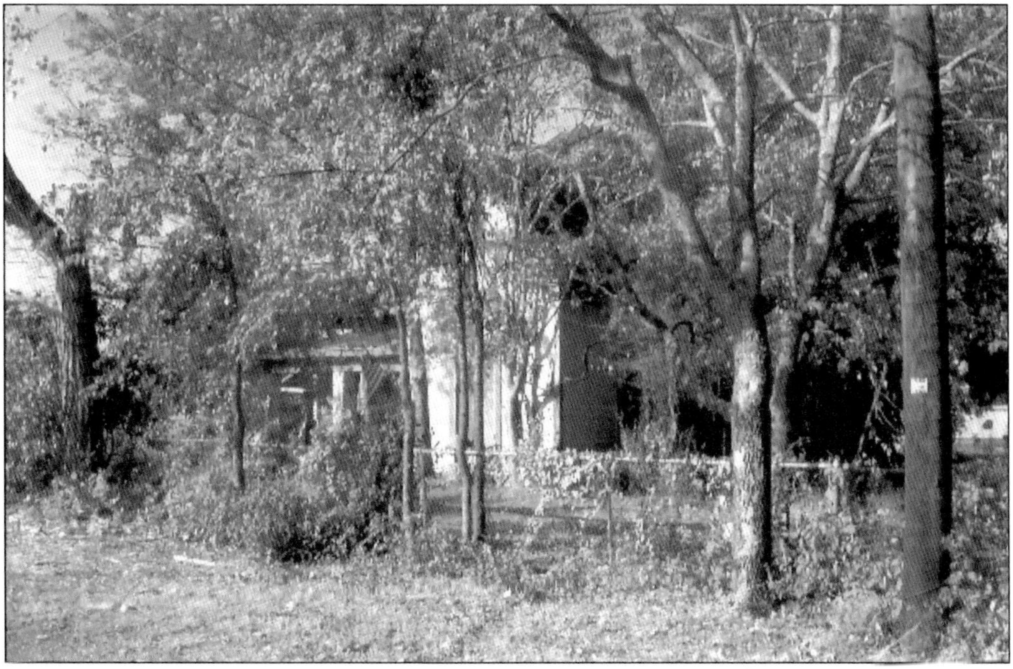

One of the first homes to be moved from Corn Hill to Jarrell was the Myron Ponder home. The date of its construction is unknown, but it is well over 100 years old. Arthur Carlisle, who was a conductor on the Bartlett-Western Railroad, and his family also lived in this home for some time.

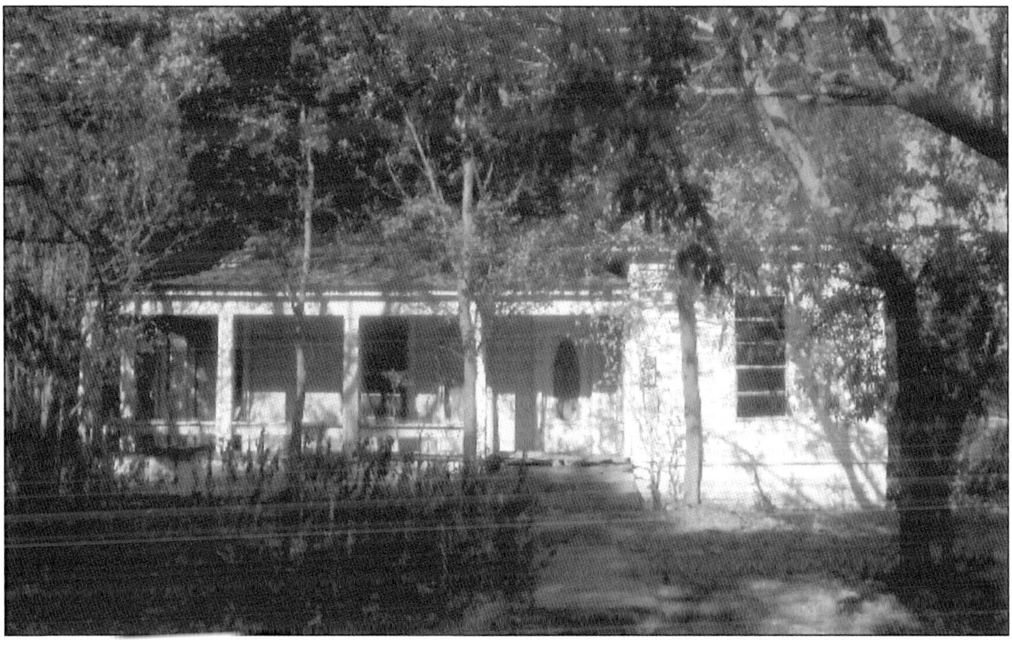

The J. D. Black home was the first home actually built in Jarrell. It was constructed by Dave Walthall. Along with others, it was home to the Stach family. Unfortunately, it is in a sad state of disrepair. It was one of most prestigious homes in town with a beveled glass front door and beautiful wraparound porch. It stands at the corner of Avenue H and Third Street.

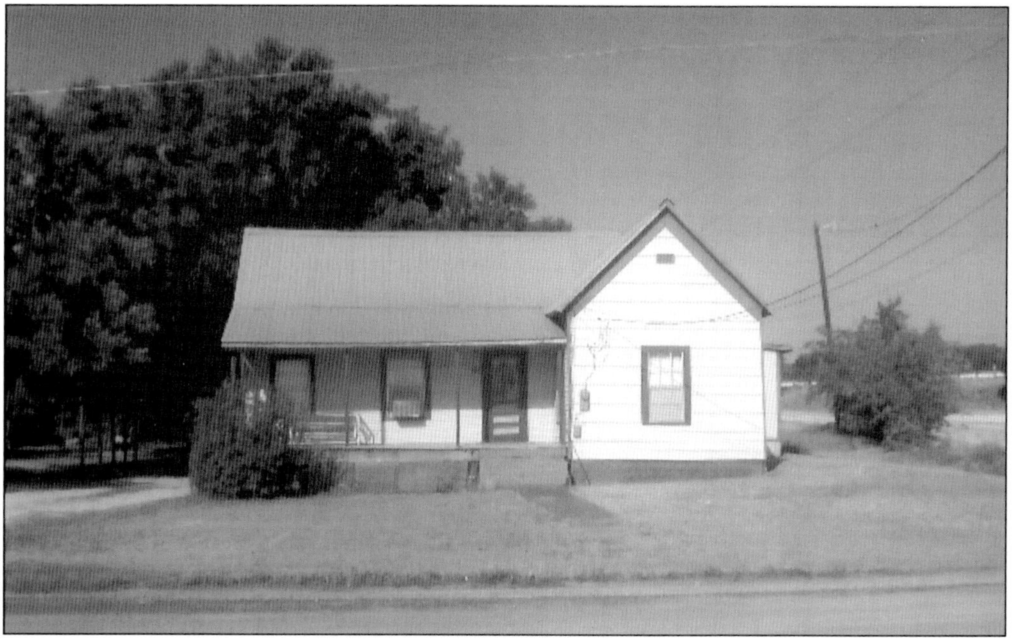

The J. A. Stinnett home sat on the south side of U.S. Highway 81. It was built between 1913 and 1915. The simple style of this home was very popular during the early years. Myrtle Stinnett was a sales clerk at the Jarrell Mercantile. This is one of the few remaining homes on the south side of the highway that was unaffected by the 1989 tornado.

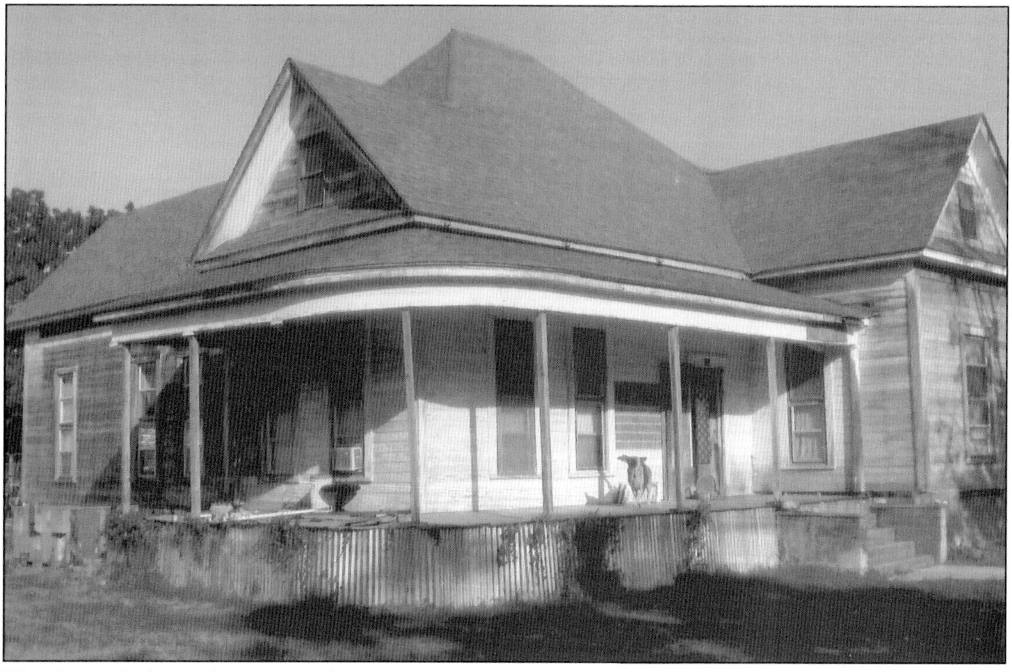

This home belonged to Mr. and Mrs. H. L. Jones. They moved to Jarrell from Arkansas, and in 1940 H. L. Jones purchased the Jarrell Mercantile. He operated the business until 1973. Rev. Max Johnson, pastor of First Baptist Church, and his wife, Charlotte, have resided in this home for many years. It is located at the corner of Third Street and Avenue H.

Four

Religion and Education

Once homes and businesses had been moved from Corn Hill to Jarrell, the churches were also moved. In 1912, the First Baptist Church was placed just north of the Bartlett-Western Railroad tracks. The Jarrell Methodist Church was moved in July of the same year to a position just south of its current location on First Street. It stood until a windstorm destroyed it in 1926. The current building was constructed from the salvaged lumber. The Corn Hill tabernacle was owned by both the Baptist and Methodist churches. It was moved from Corn Hill and placed on six lots, three owned by the Baptist church and three by the Methodist church. Combined revival services were held under the tabernacle each year with large crowds attending. Parents brought quilts and pallets so young children could play and sleep during evening services. This tabernacle was also used for a variety of civic and cultural activities and gatherings, including Chautauqua programs. Chautauqua was an adult education movement in the United States during the 19th and early 20th centuries that brought cultural events to rural America. The first school building erected in Jarrell was a wooden structure, but voters elected to pass a bond to construct a modern, two-story school building, which was completed in 1916 and has been used continuously since. This building has been the center of Jarrell, both actually and figuratively, for generations. Additions and renovations were made, but it continued to house all grades from kindergarten through 12th until 2007, when a new high school was built on West FM 487.

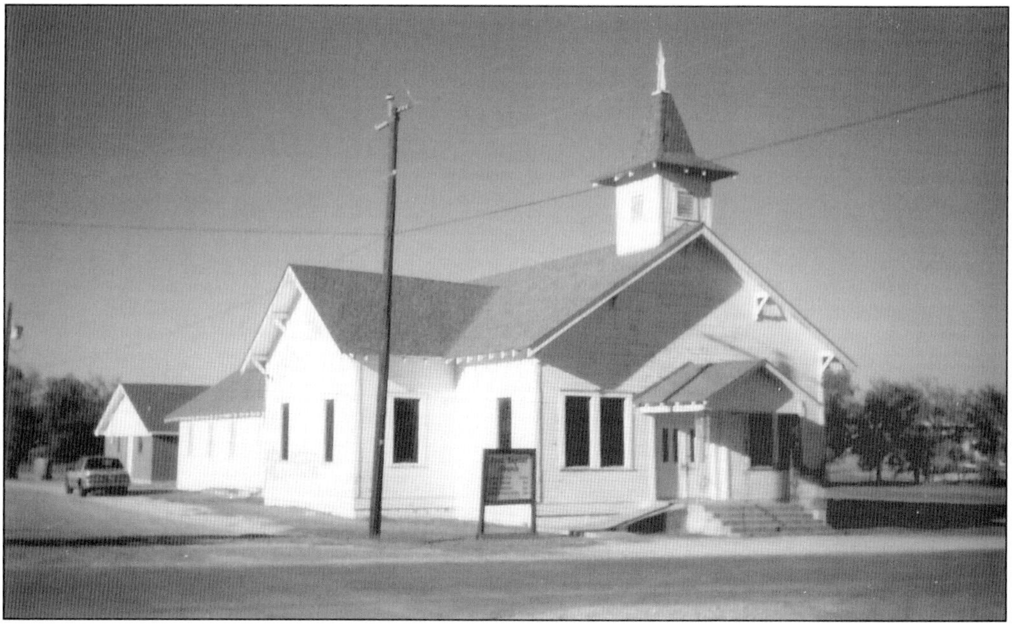

The original building that housed the Baptist church was moved to Jarrell from Corn Hill. Men from the congregation took the building off its piers and lowered it onto a set of logs used as rollers. Six teams of mules moved the church forward slowly inch by inch as it rolled down the hill to Jarrell. A thunderstorm dumped several inches of rain on the procession, causing the building, teams, and all the men in the congregation to become totally bogged down in the gumbo clay. The church was stuck in the mud somewhere between Corn Hill and Jarrell. Consequently, planks were laid down so members could attend services out in the field. Finally, after six weeks, conditions improved and the church was moved to Jarrell and placed on a lot north of the Bartlett-Western Railroad tracks. The church as shown above was built in 1924 at its current location closer to the business district. The same building is shown below with the addition of trees planted in memory of the 1997 tornado victims. Rev. Max Johnson is the pastor. (Above, courtesy Charlotte Vancil; below, C. B. and Mary Hodge.)

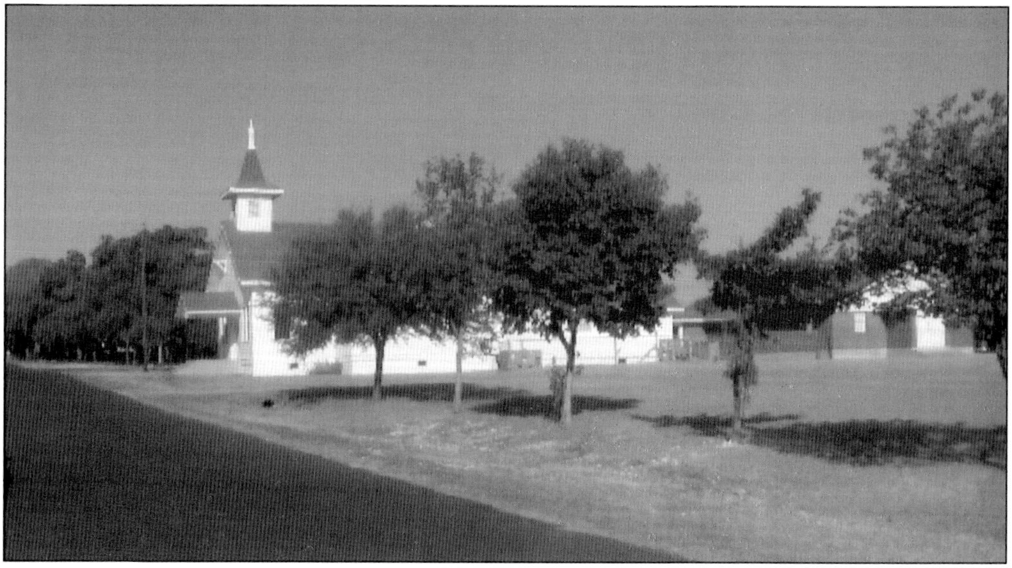

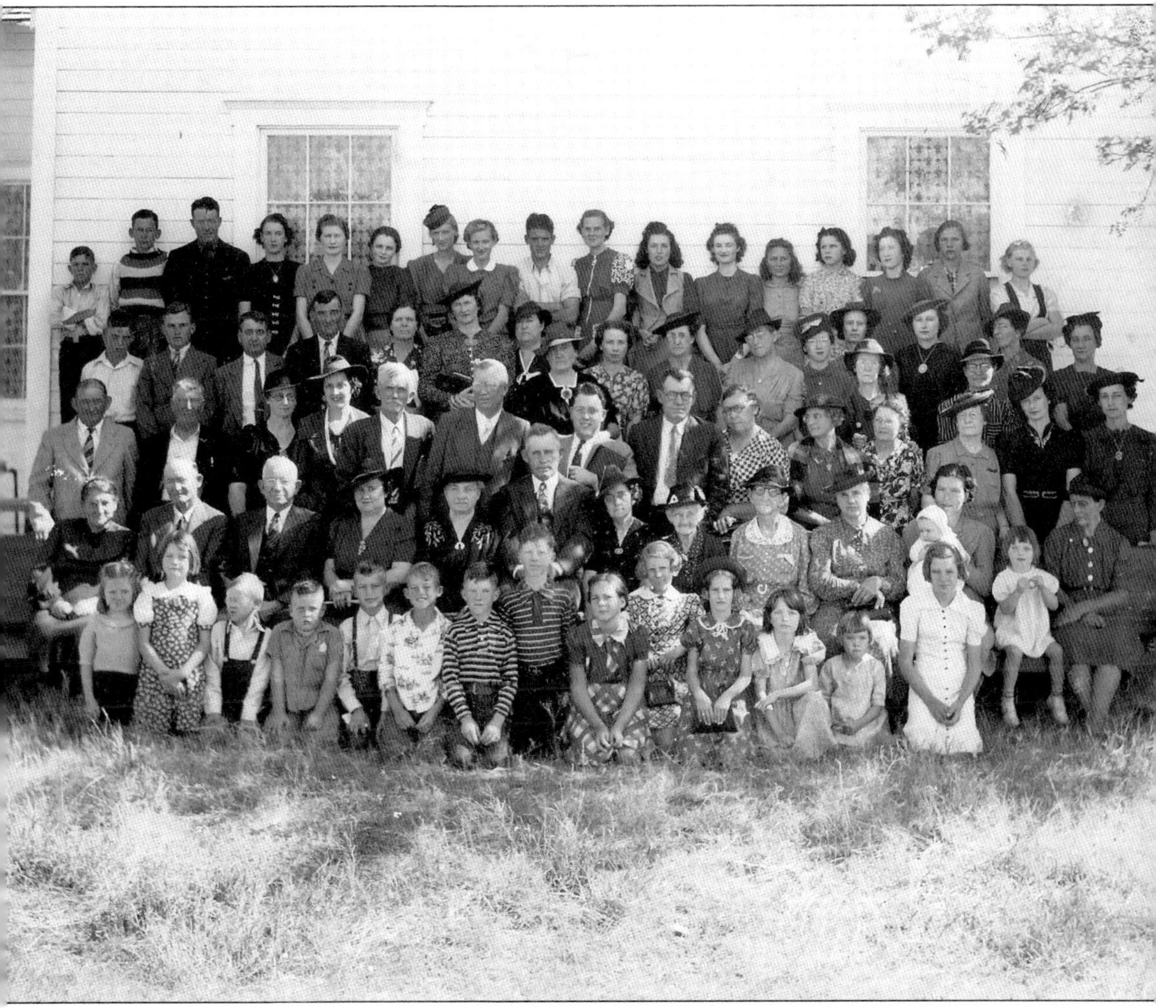

Always the center of religious and social events, the early churches in Jarrell were quite active and well attended. Services were held each Sunday, along with Sunday school for children and Bible class for adults. Potluck dinners or suppers were popular, along with musical programs, holiday celebrations, and regularly scheduled prayer meetings. The Baptist and Methodist churches would combine for Christmas and special services. This picture was identified by Buck Jones and Lillian Smith as being taken outside the Baptist church. The exact event is unknown, but it is thought to be after a combined service of the two congregations in the late 1920s or early 1930s. The church pews shown here are still used by the Baptist church today. (Courtesy W. E. and Albena Proctor.)

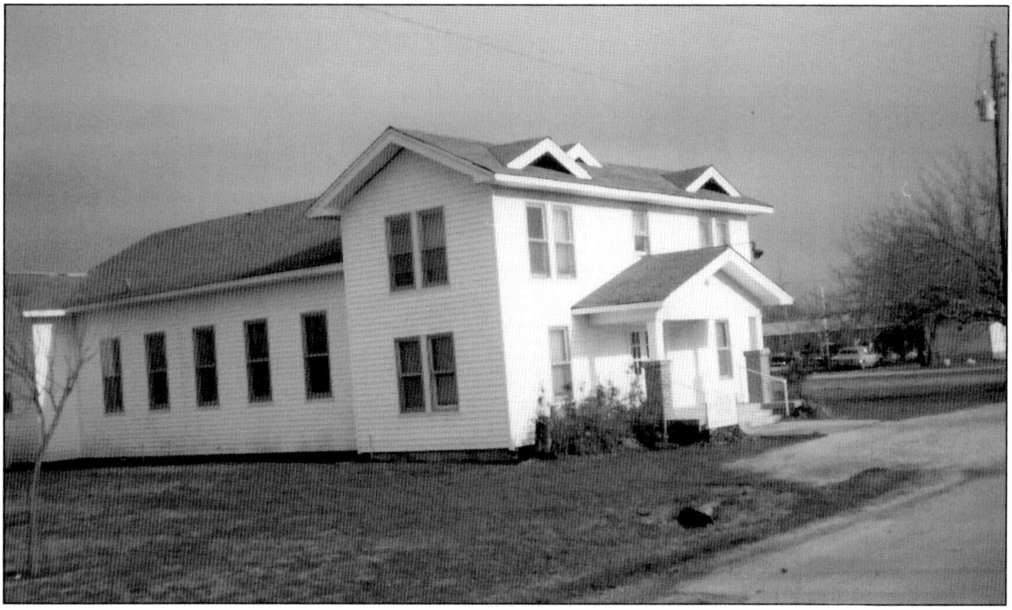

A Methodist church was built north of Corn Hill in 1872, and in 1890 one was built in town. In July 1913, the building was moved from Corn Hill to Jarrell. This church building served the community until 1926, when it is believed that a high windstorm, or possibly a tornado, destroyed it. Lumber from the building was saved to rebuild the current sanctuary shown here. The parsonage was built in 1924 is shown below. The current pastor of the Jarrell United Methodist Church is G. Dean Coultas.

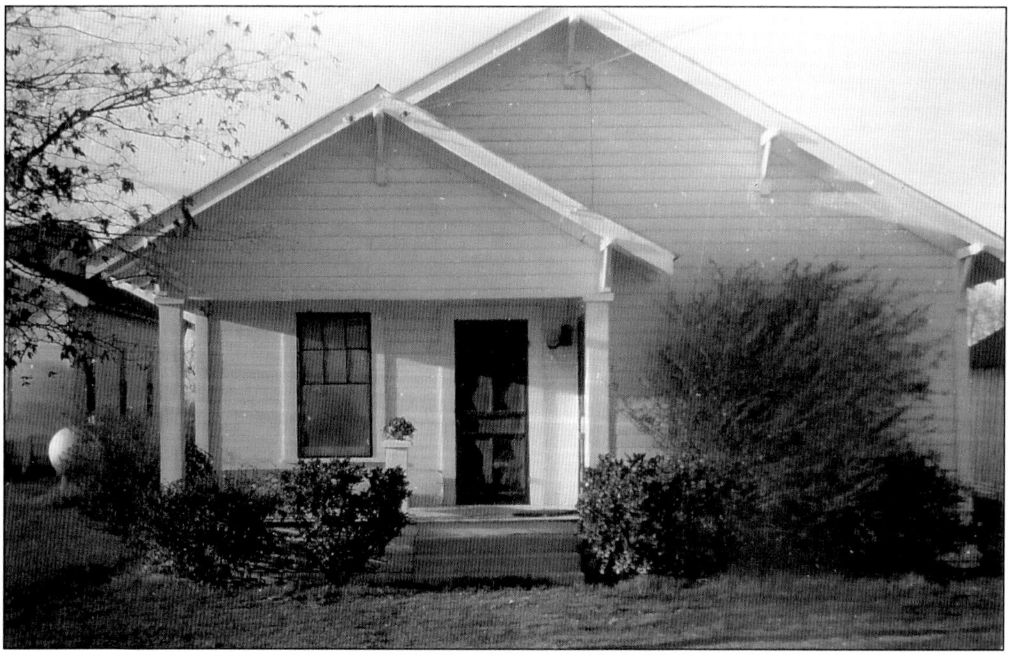

Here is a copy of the Jarrell Methodist Church's 1952 budget. Note that the pastor's salary was $1,800 per year, and electricity was budgeted at $30. The pastor was Rev. William F. Osborn. His phone number was 384, and he was available day and night for pastoral services. With approximately 100 members, it was necessary to hold two services each Sunday. Four children were listed on the "Cradle Roll": Leo Edgar Johnson, Eddie Ray Wallace, Gladys Liane Mihlberger, and Larry Lee McLaurin. (Courtesy Linn and Jimmy Sybert.)

CHURCH SUPPORT

Pastor's Salary	$1800.00
World Service	60.00
Advance Fund	40.00
General Administration	2.00
Jurisdiction Administration	4.00
District Administration	20.00
Missouri Corp	18.00
District Superintendent	225.00
Episcopal Fund	31.50
Conference Claimants	225.00
Minimum Salary	30.00
Sunday School Literature	150.00
Stationary and Stamps	30.00
Music	25.00
Insurance	72.50
Fuel	50.00
Lights	30.00
Church Cleaning	52.00
Flowers and Miscellaneous	75.00
Repair Fund	300.00
Total	$3240.00

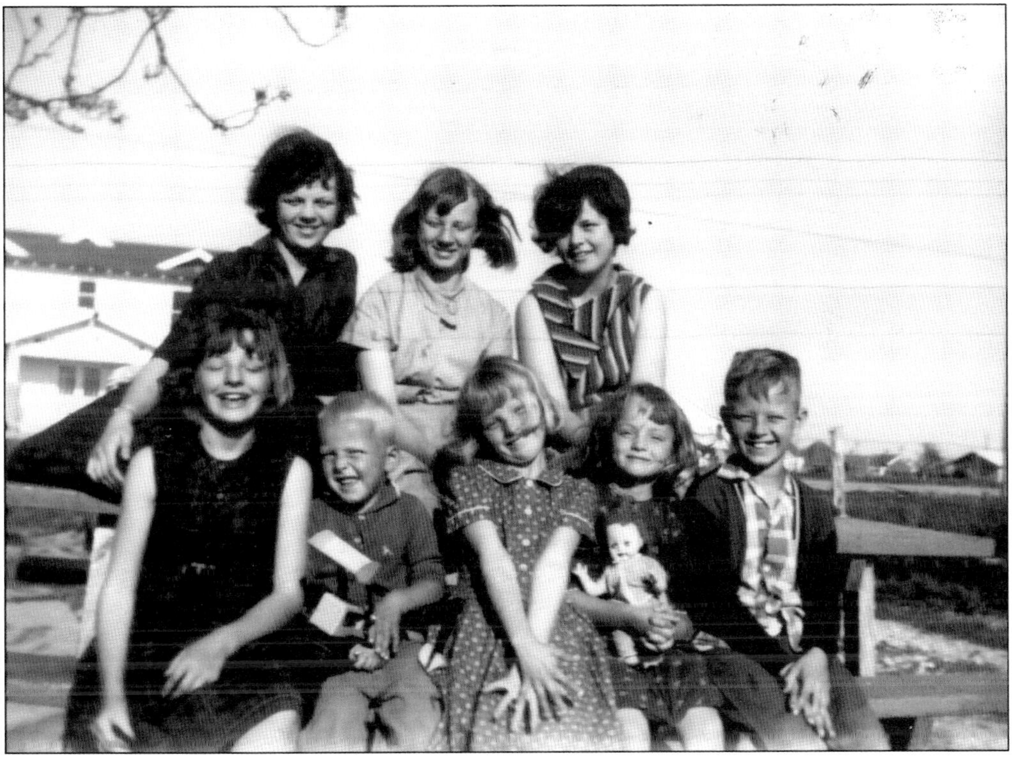

If anyone asked the Clarence Mertink family their address, it was "across the street from the Methodist Church." This photograph of the Mertink children, all eight of them, was taken in April 1966. Pictured are (first row) Ruth Mertink Wildenstein, Howard Mertink, Dorine Mertink Otteson, Doris Mertink (with the Tiny Tears doll she received at Christmas) and David Mertink; (second row) Mary Mertink Kubala, Joyce Mertink Manning, and Clarice Mertink Proctor. (Courtesy Doris Mertink.)

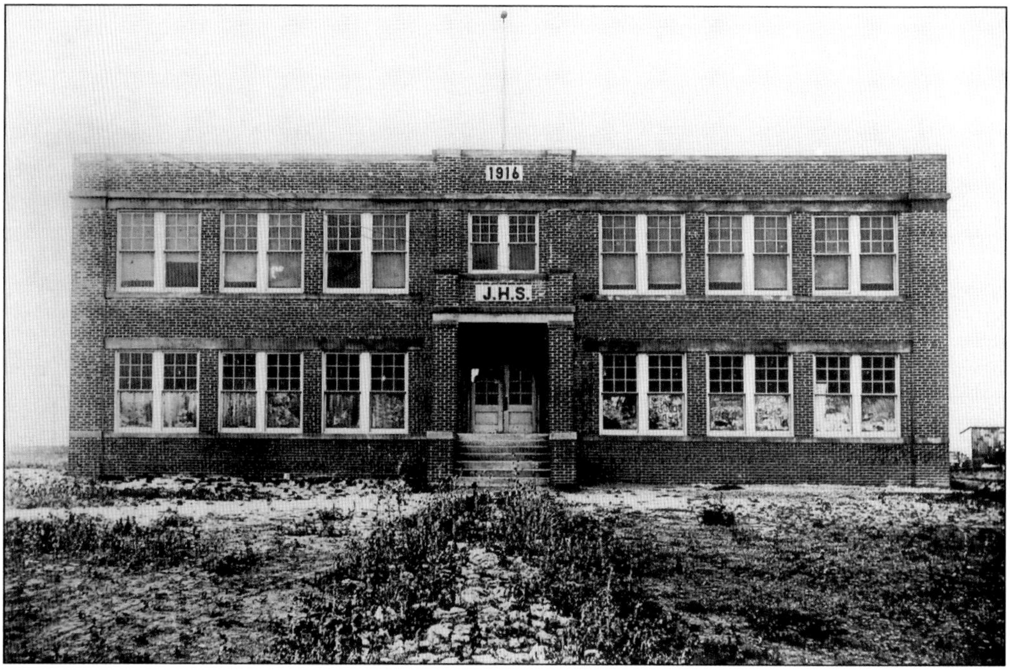

The year 1916 was an important one in Jarrell's history. It was marked by the construction of a brand-new, brick, two-story school building. Pictured above is how it appeared when construction was complete. It was pronounced a well-built and beautiful building, and indeed it was. The building has been remodeled several times but has been in continuous use since 1916. Today it houses administrative offices for the Jarrell Independent School District. Even though many other things have changed in Jarrell, this dominant fixture of the Jarrell landscape has been a constant, providing a backdrop for education of generations of residents.

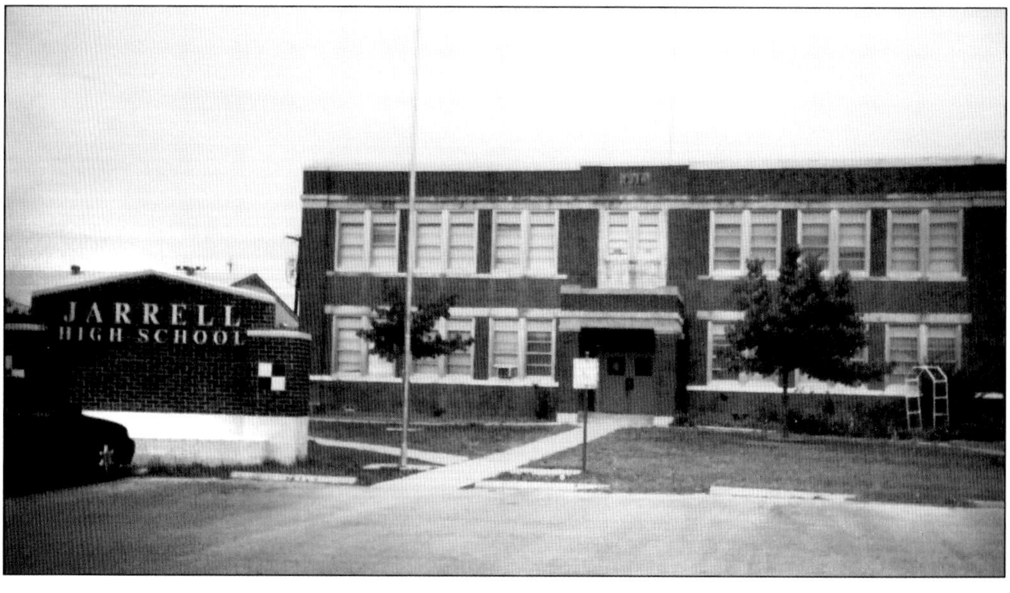

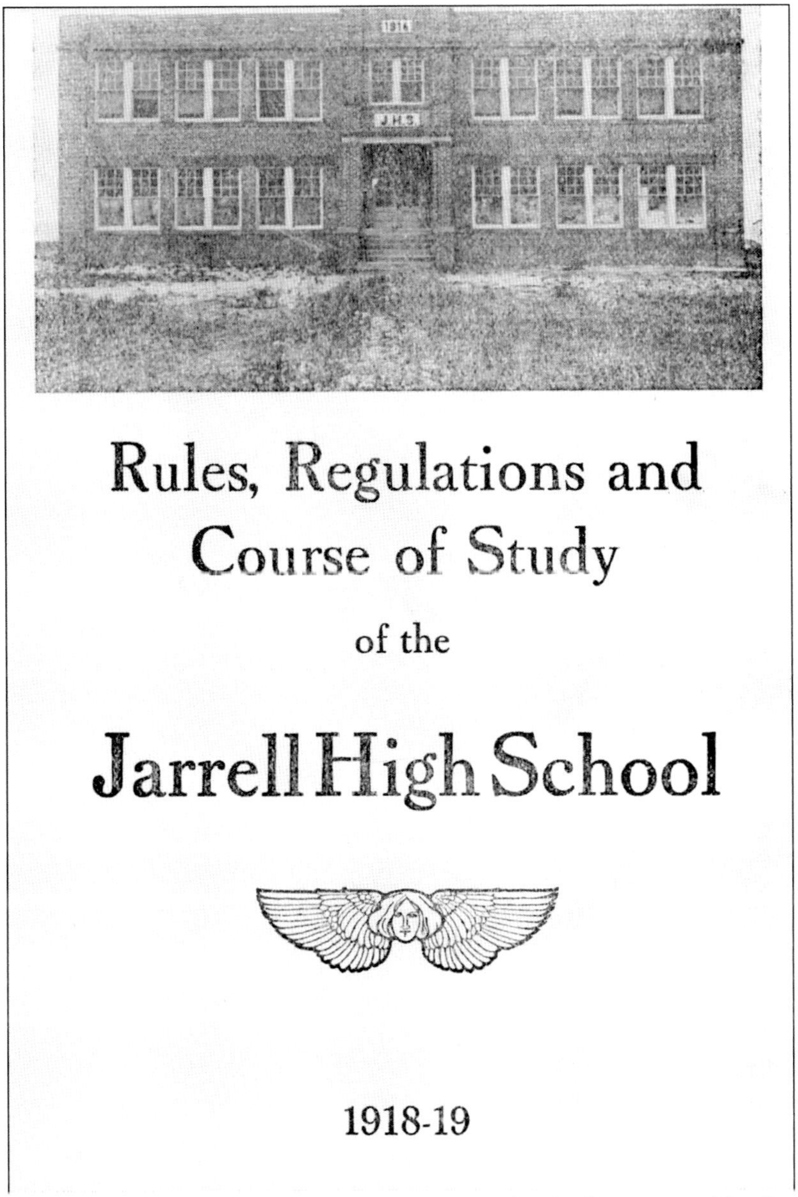
Rules, Regulations and
Course of Study
of the
Jarrell High School

1918-19

The *Rules, Regulations and Course of Study of the Jarrell High School* was printed for the 1918–1919 school year. The following are excerpts from the book: "Tuition per year: first through third grade, $1.50, fourth through seventh grade, $2.00 and eighth through tenth grade, $2.50. . . . To parents: juvenile crime is increasing rapidly since the war began. This, to the sane mind, demands a careful watch on the part of parents. . . . To students: Students are not expected to loiter about town. . . . To students: Students of the High School will be awarded diplomas by the School Board upon the completion of twelve High School credits. . . . To the teachers: When the number of minutes lost by a teacher, due to tardiness, amounts to more than thirty minutes during the week, a deduction of one per cent of the week's salary will be made for each ten minutes. . . . The Principal: The Principal, especially, has the best interest of the school at heart, and he will be glad to discuss school matters with anyone who is interested. . . . Patriotism will be taught throughout the High School."

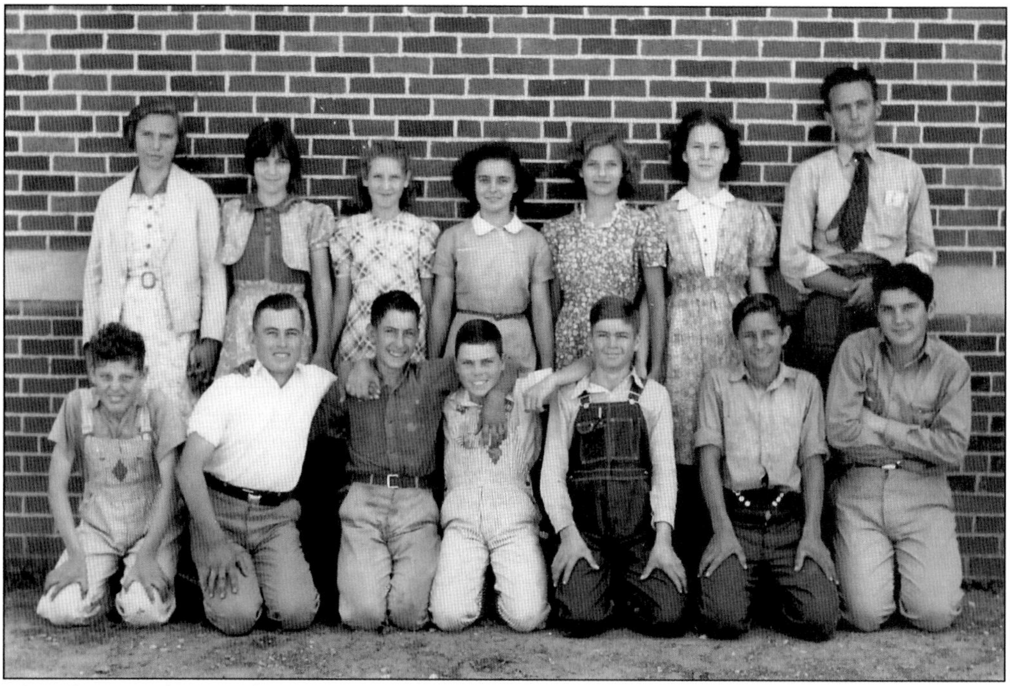

This photograph was taken in 1948. Standing in front of the 1916 school building from left to right are (first row) Hulen Stanford, J. W. Stone, Maurice Teddlie, Jack Smith, unidentified, Robert Lang, and unidentified; (second row) Lillie Ora Watson, Mary Clyde Woodward, Mary Harrison, Lora Jackson, Neba Jean Grumbles, Milly Buford, and Isham Coward, the teacher.

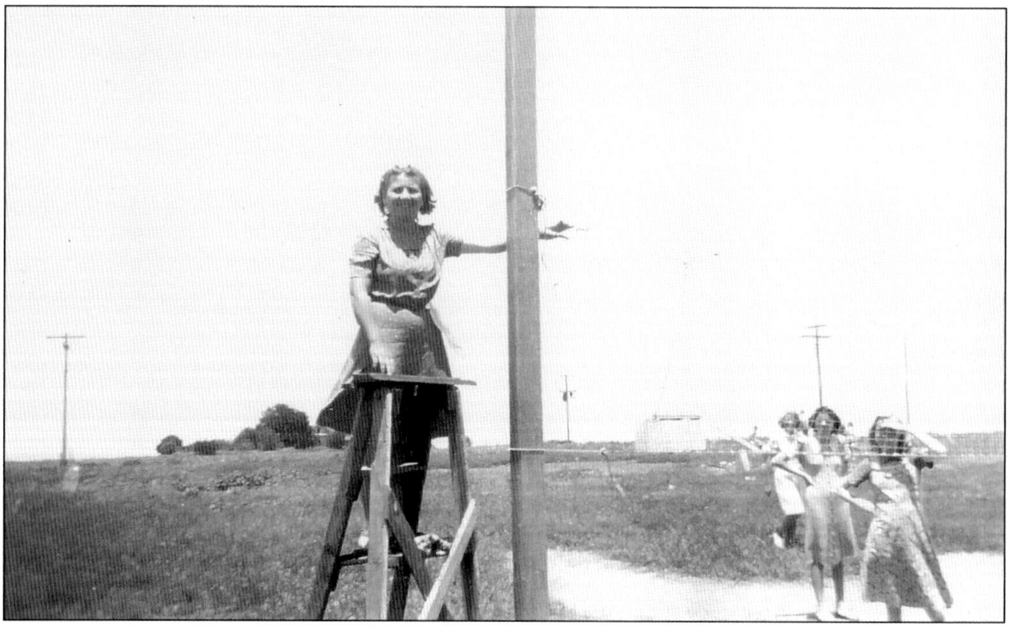

Since there was no gymnasium, all school sports were played outdoors. The volleyball court was located just west of the 1916 school building. This photograph shows Alice Kalmbach (left) adjusting the net with Miriam Grumbles (second from the right) and Margaret Sybert (far right). Notice the "ladies restroom," better known as the outhouse, in the far background.

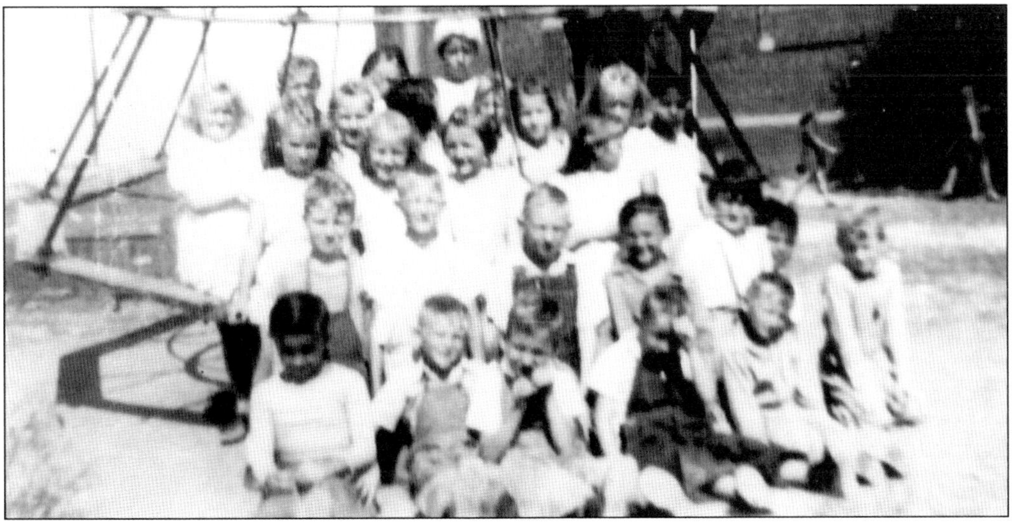

This photograph was taken during the 1946–1947 school year. Children are posed on the old merry-go-round. Local children loved to play on this apparatus, and boys would compete to see how fast they could push it, which occasionally resulted in injury. Pictured from left to right are (first row) Edward Martinka, A. B. Warrick, Roy Castleberry, Byron Goode, ? Williams, and Jesse Ray Moore; (second row) Daniel Mersiovsky, Norman Noack, Walter Ischy, and J. W. Breeden. The rest of the children are unidentified.

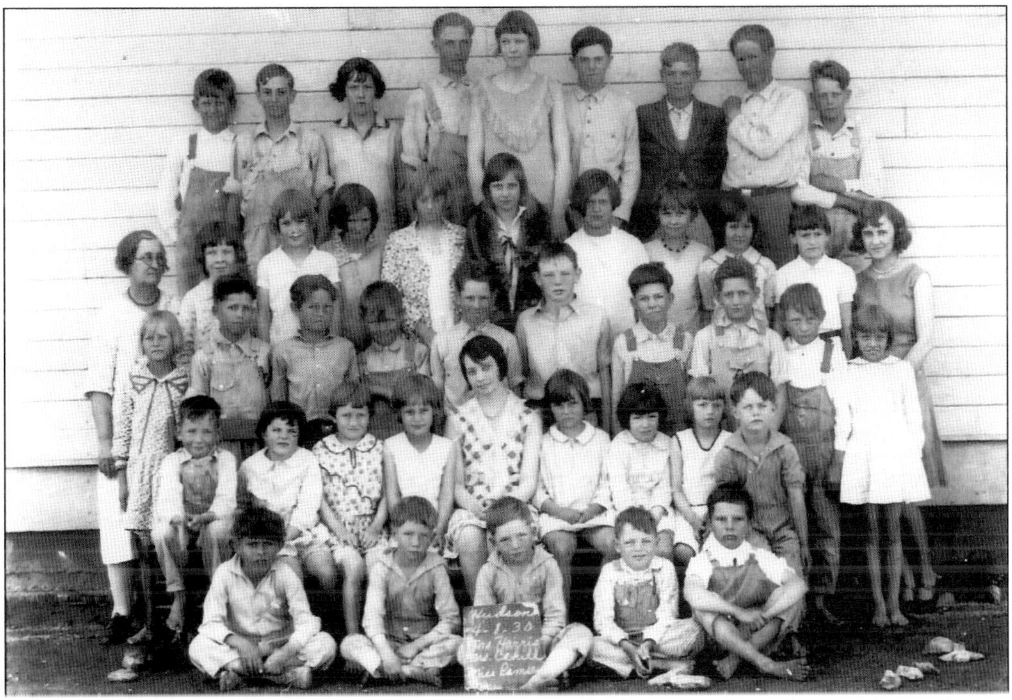

Taken in 1930 at the Hudson School, this photograph shows teachers Annie Harris (fourth row, far left), Ella Ramsey (second row, center), and Iris Cahill (fourth row, far right) along with children of all ages. The only children identified are in the first row, second and third from the left—twins Doyle and Tom Sybert, who attended Hudson School until it closed. Both men and their families made their homes in the Jarrell community.

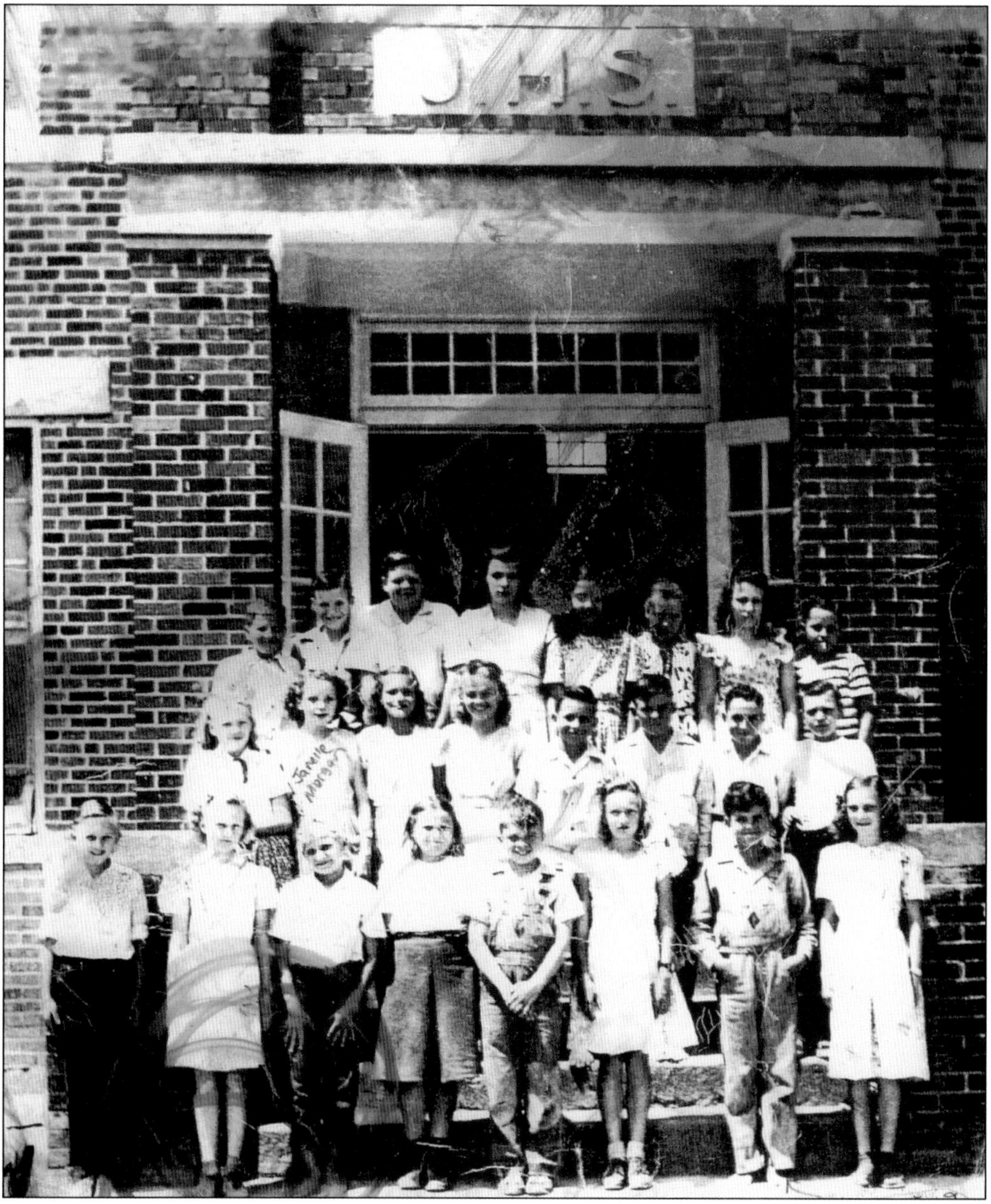

Pictured here are students in 1947–1948 standing in front of the 1916 school building. From left to right are (first row) Charles Tonn, Bobbie Jean Conlee, Johnny Bridges, Zona Gail Thompson, Jimmy Langston, Linda Langston, Anson Kelly, and unidentified; (second row) unidentified, Janelle Morgan, Georgia Dutchmann, unidentified, Ray Cowart, ? Castleberry, Richard Black, and Roger Sedbery; (third row) Elvin "Snuffy" Ischy, John Wiley, Dick Burson, two unidentified children, Pauline Castleberry, unidentified, and Earl Hawthorne. Many of these students went on to become prominent leaders in the Jarrell community. Zona Gail Thompson served as a teacher and librarian for the Jarrell schools for many years. (Courtesy Byron and Patsy Goode.)

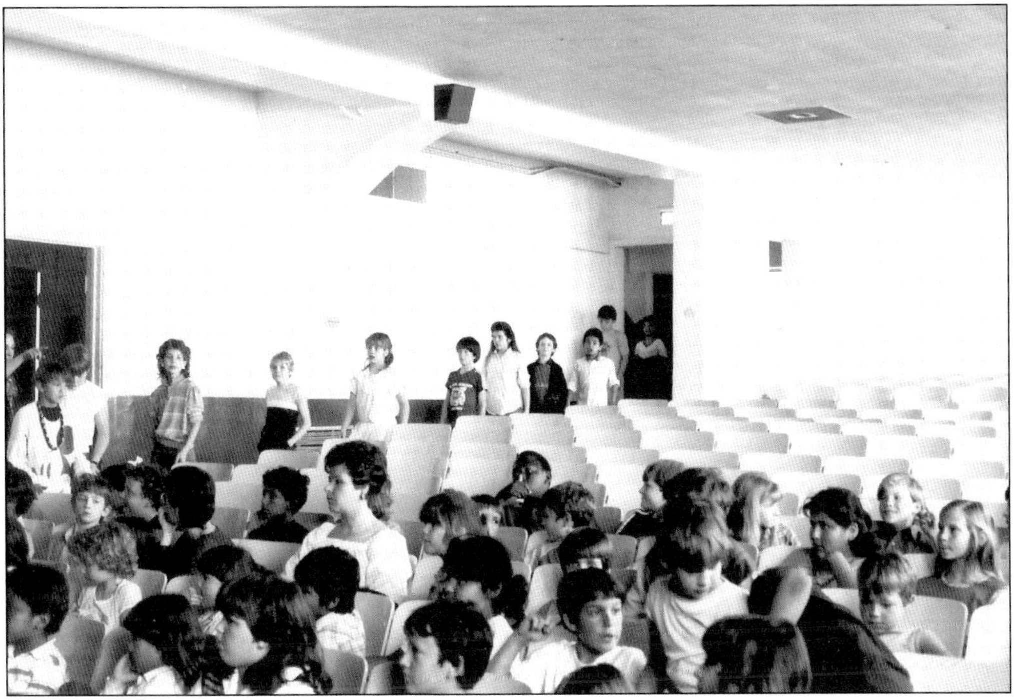

A full auditorium with sloped floor and wooden theater seats was built into the lower story of the 1916 building. Over the years, many events benefited from this grand old auditorium, including school plays and assemblies, community presentations, lectures, and civic gatherings. When the building was remodeled, the auditorium was turned into classrooms and a school library. Shown below is a Girl Scout event held on the old auditorium stage. (Both courtesy Charlotte Vancil.)

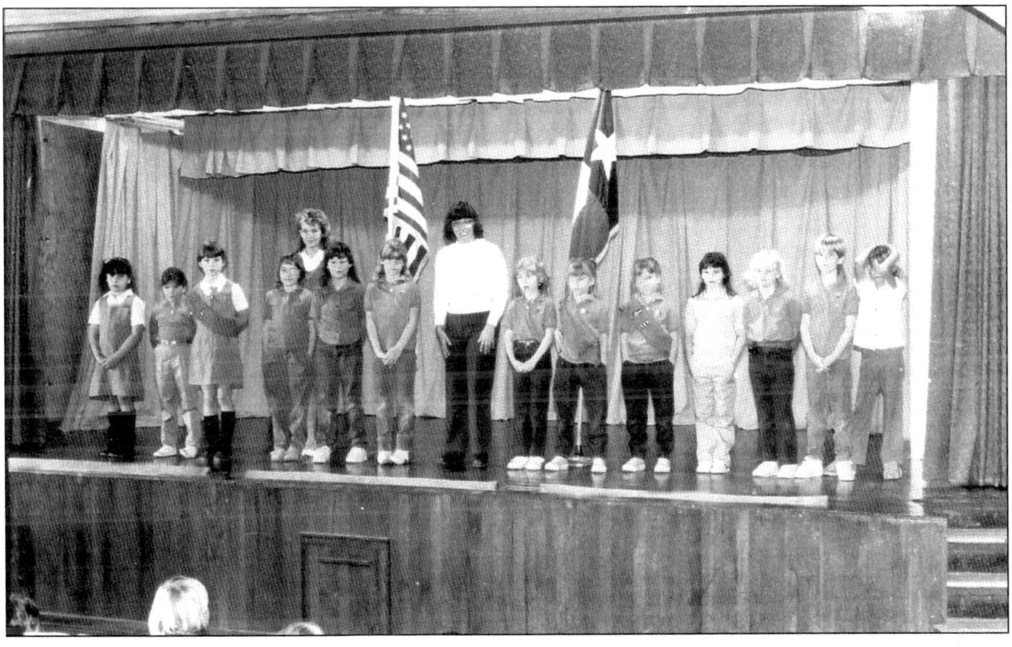

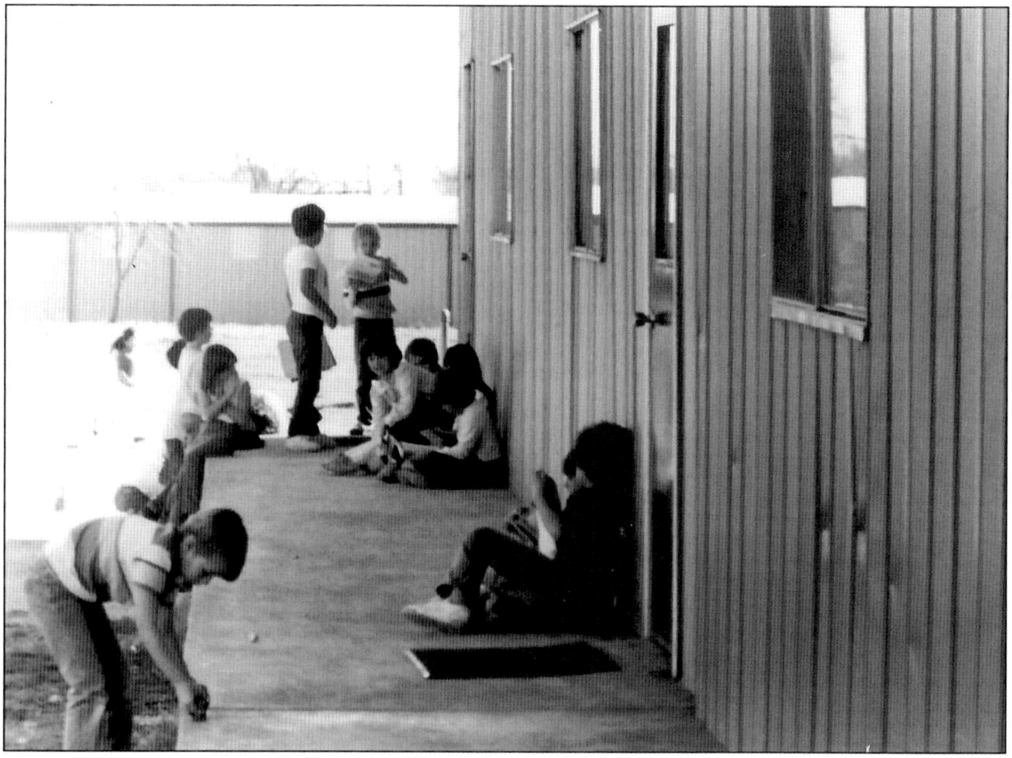

Slowly but surely over the years, the school campus expanded to accommodate the increase in students. Children shown here will remember going to school in the "blue building." Referred to as the west wing, this was the first building addition since the original one in 1916. (Courtesy Charlotte Vancil.)

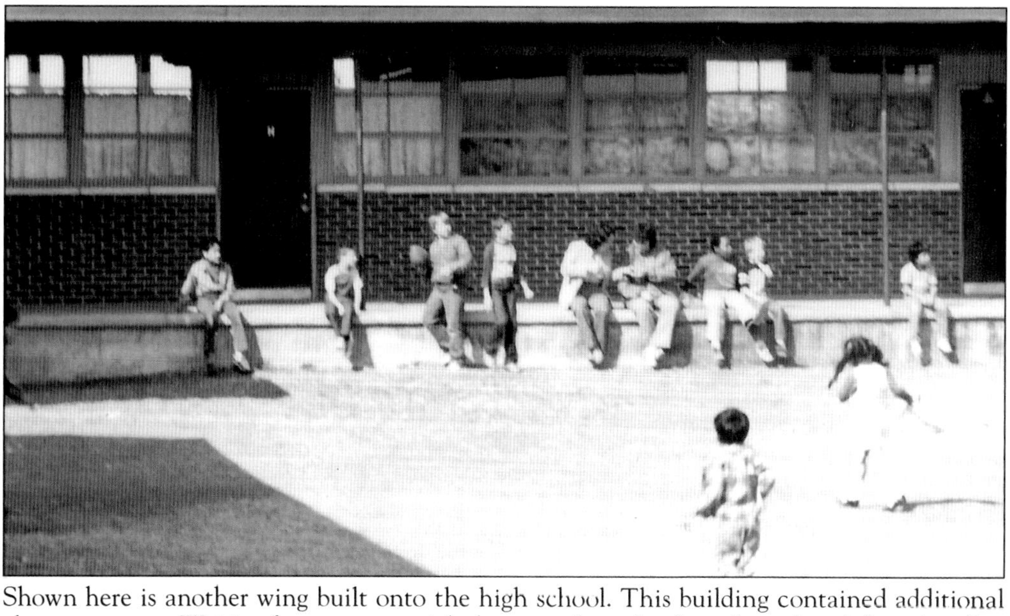

Shown here is another wing built onto the high school. This building contained additional classroom space. Waiting for parents to pick them up after school, students found the sidewalk a popular place to sit. (Courtesy Charlotte Vancil.)

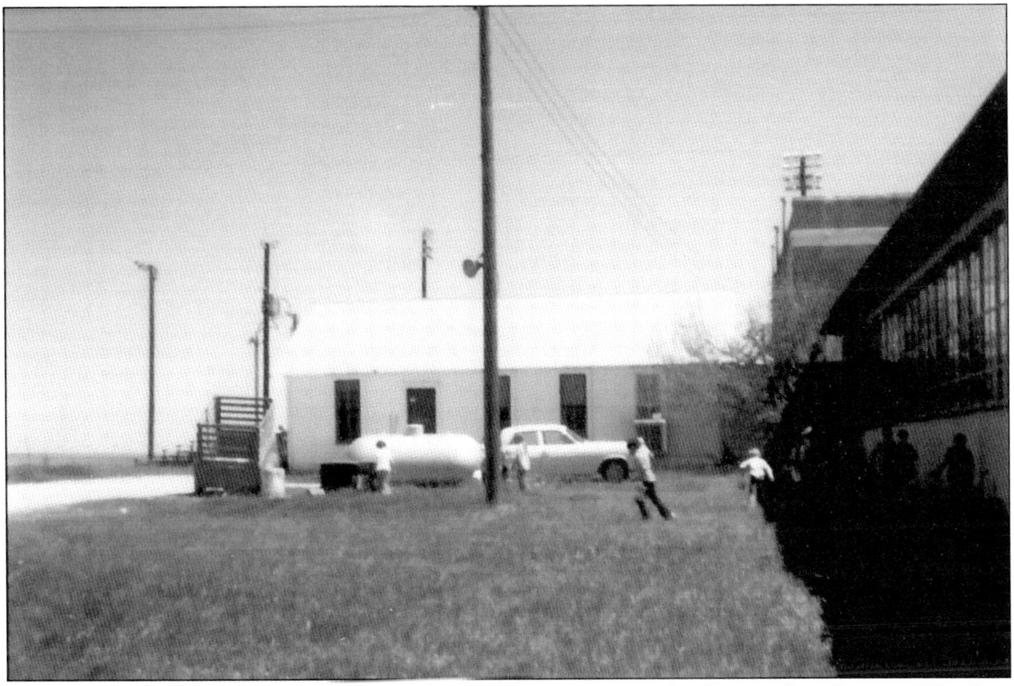

Students brought their lunch to school or ran to town to gulp down a hamburger. The first cafeteria was upstairs in the 1916 building. Food was prepared in a small room, and the students would pick up a tray and eat at their desks. Pictured here is the old cafeteria, built onto the back of the school. This building has served many purposes over the years, from concession stand to book room to storage. (Courtesy Charlotte Vancil.)

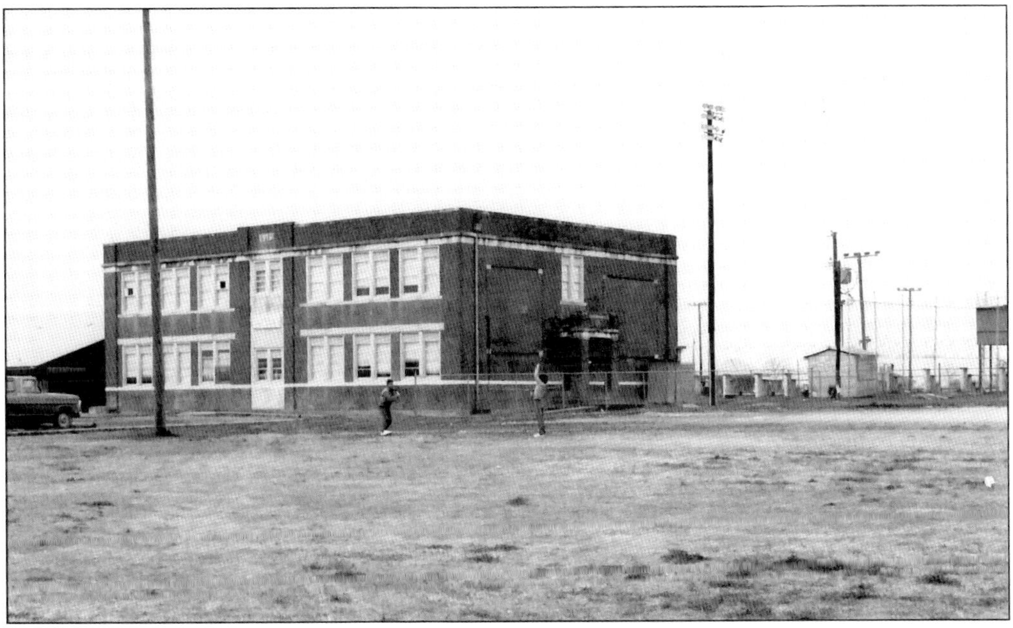

This photograph shows evidence of the old football stadium. Notice the bleachers to the back and right of the school. Many football games were played here on Friday evenings throughout the school's long history.

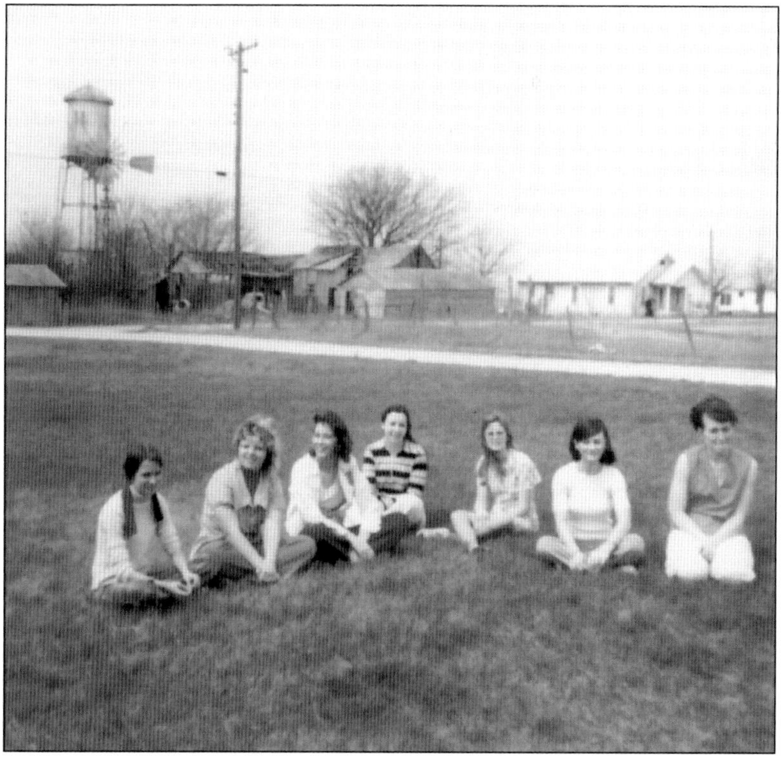

Girls taking a break at school are seated on the lawn on the west side of the campus. The water tower and some of the original buildings in Jarrell are shown in the background across Fifth Street.

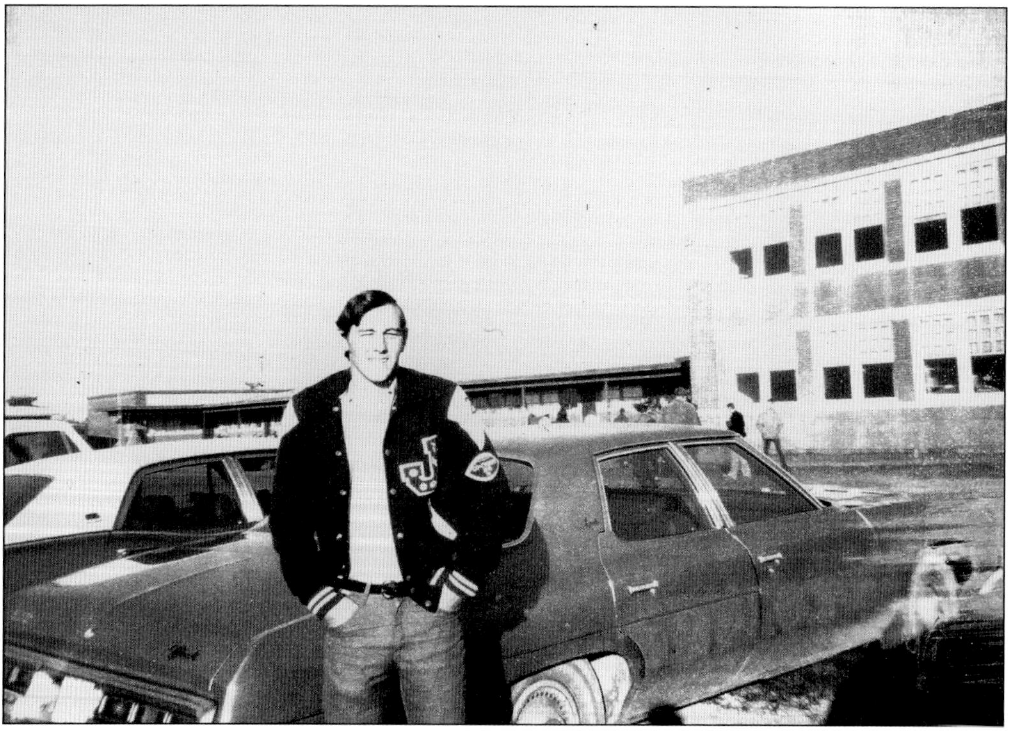

Roy Arldt, in his athletic letter jacket, stands in the parking lot of Jarrell High School in the 1970s. During these years, Jarrell was still playing six-man football. (Courtesy Roy and Donna Arldt.)

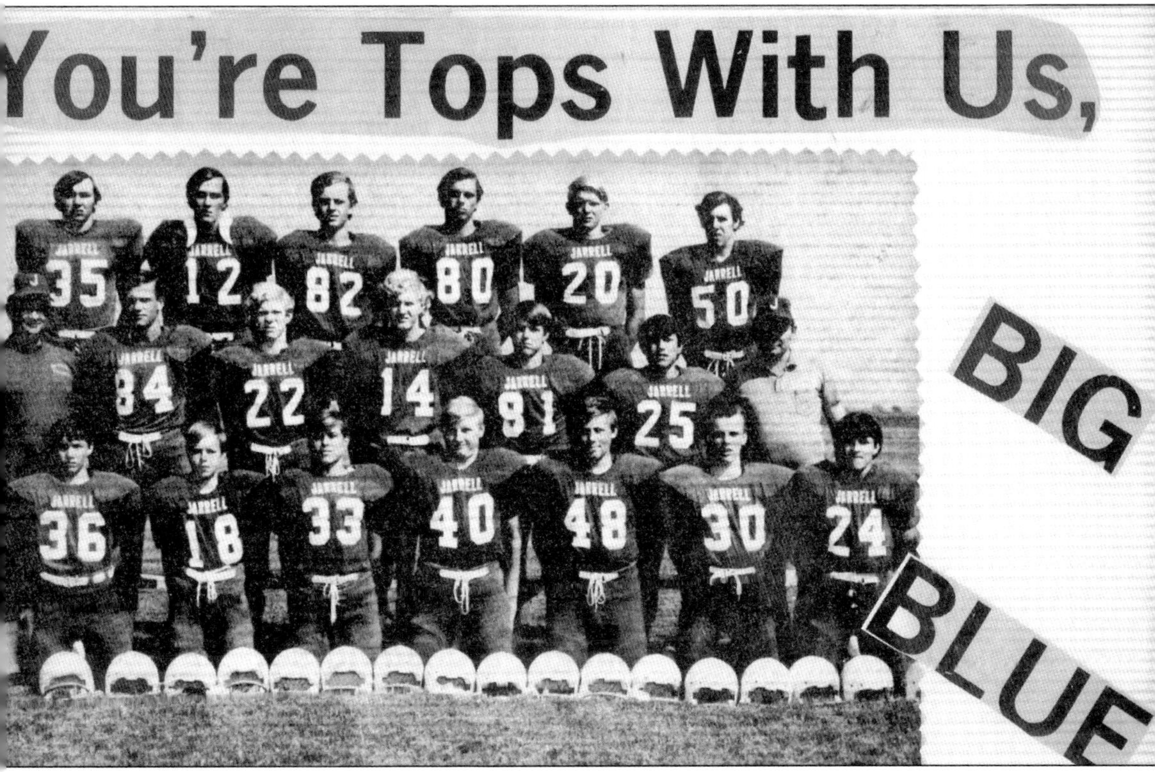

The 1972 Jarrell Cougars Class B six-man football team went to the state playoffs. The team experienced only one loss the entire season. The games leading up to the playoffs were exciting, and the whole town followed the team. The night of the big game, there was no one left in town, as everyone had driven to Coleman to be a part of the excitement. In the end, Jarrell lost to O'Brien 60-14, but only after providing a thrilling season for their fans. Pictured from left to right are (first row) Darvin Bamsch, Raymond Nemec, John Cassens, Calvin Hughes, James Hughes, Gordon Crum, and David Garcia; (second row) head coach Neal Harris, Douglas Bamsch, Jimmy Jones, Patrick Palousek, Bernard Nemec, Joey Jaramillo, and assistant coach Bob Gersbach; (third row) Billy Meyers, Roy Arldt, David Mertink, Gary Smith, David Salyers, and Gordon Stanford.

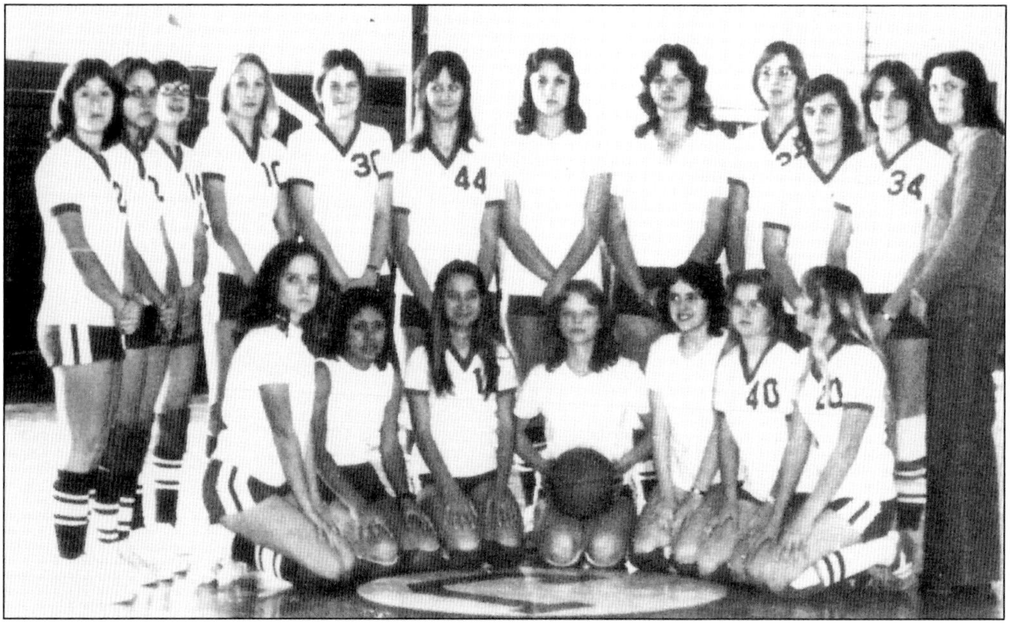

The year 1977 was the first anyone could remember that the girls high school basketball team won the district championships. The regional tournament was to be in San Marcos. The girls almost missed it because the bus driver didn't show up. Coach Susan Goode saved the day and got the girls there, only to lose to Round Top–Carmine 58-50. This was the last year of six-member teams for girls. The following year, teams changed to five players. (Courtesy Kelly and Earline Reichenbach.)

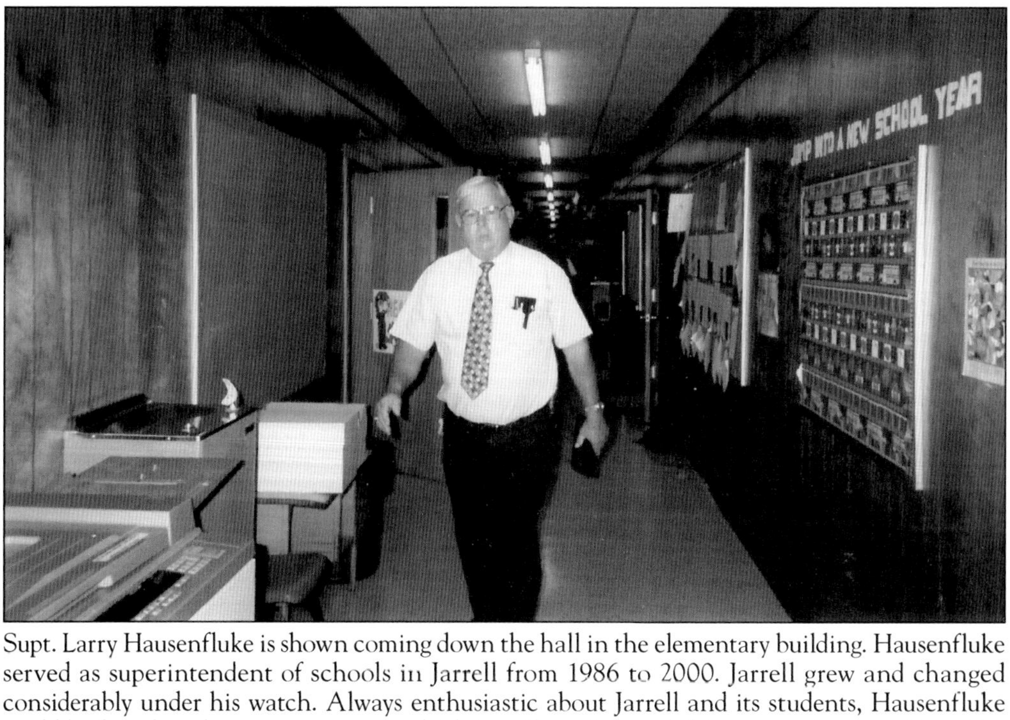

Supt. Larry Hausenfluke is shown coming down the hall in the elementary building. Hausenfluke served as superintendent of schools in Jarrell from 1986 to 2000. Jarrell grew and changed considerably under his watch. Always enthusiastic about Jarrell and its students, Hausenfluke could be found at almost any event in which Jarrell participated. (Courtesy Charlotte Vancil.)

Pictured here are David Harp and Lisa Danek. Harp came to Jarrell in 1990 and served as principal for 17 years. Children may remember visiting him in the principal's office. The first face (and a friendly one at that) anyone saw when entering the school was that of Danek, who served as the sole school secretary for many years. (Courtesy Charlotte Vancil.)

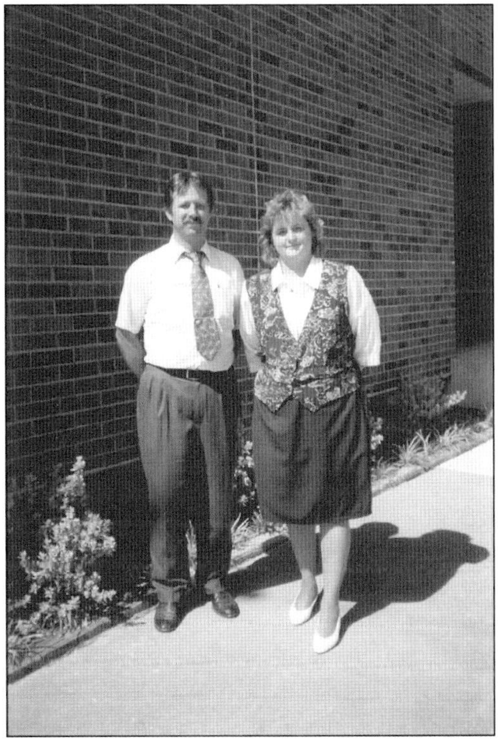

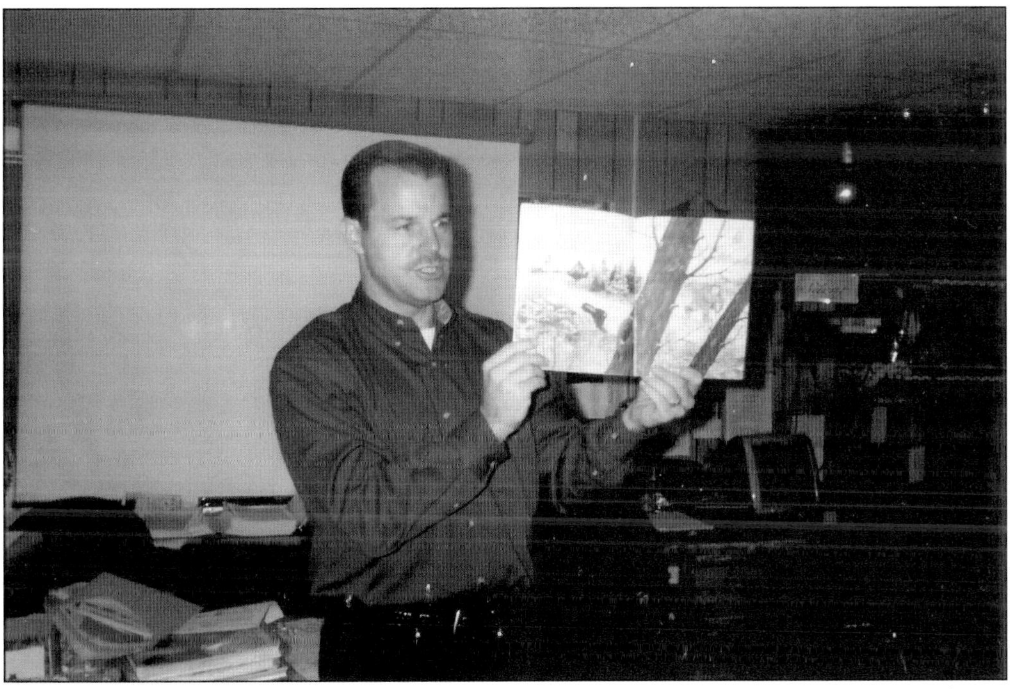

Drew Watkins served as the superintendent of Jarrell Schools from 2000 to 2002. He is shown here reading a book to one of the elementary classes. Watkins made it his personal goal to be at the school each and every morning and to greet each student personally as they arrived. (Courtesy Charlotte Vancil.)

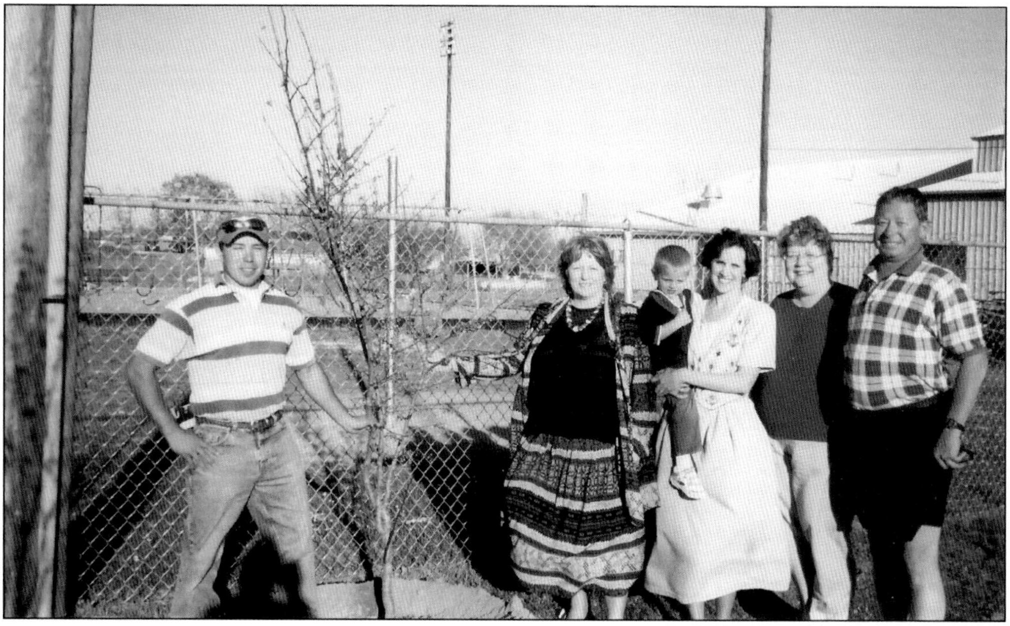

In 2002, the parents of Windy Hill School, a local child-care facility owned by Priscilla King, donated money to have a number of trees planted at the 1916 campus and at the athletic complex. Shown here from left to right are one of the workers who planted the trees; Supt. Jamie Mattison; Jill Sumner and son Garrett; Priscilla King; and landscaper Warren Sefcik. Dr. Jamie Mattison has served as superintendent of Jarrell schools since 2002.

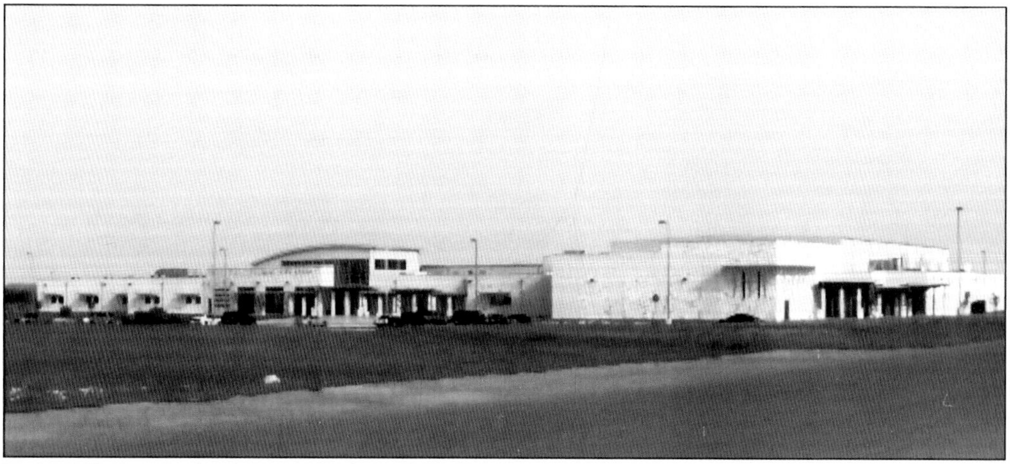

In the fall of 2007, the doors opened on a beautiful new high school for the students of Jarrell. Located on FM 487, the new school provided much needed space and a modern learning environment. Showing community pride, over 800 people attended a dedication barbeque. A vault with meaningful and timely mementoes was incorporated into the new school building.

Five

Down to Business

Businesses moved from Corn Hill to Jarrell were predominantly placed along both sides of U.S. Highway 81, following what is known today as Avenue H. Photographs will chronicle the development of the business district and the various stores and services that have been offered. Forty percent of the farms in the area were still operated by families, who traveled to town for necessary tools, services, and provisions. A local physician, a drugstore, and even an undertaker were all available to residents of Jarrell and the surrounding area. Many of the early Jarrell businesses have come and gone, but a number of them are still in existence today. Photographs of these early buildings stand alongside their modern counterparts. In the 1930s, U.S. 81 was moved a few blocks to the east. Many homes and businesses once again had to be moved. Additional businesses sprang up in the new location on both sides of the highway to meet the needs of travelers and their automobiles. There are lots of colorful stories surrounding the many bars and saloons that were a part of Jarrell. Surrounding towns were "dry," so everyone came to Jarrell to purchase liquor. Even the Fort Hood Officers Club would send a plane to land on U.S. 81, load up with alcohol, and fly back to the base. In the 1960s, U.S. 81 became Interstate Highway 35 and was widened significantly. This completely wiped out the businesses on the east side of the highway. Jarrell was left with what is now referred to as "downtown." Only a few of the wonderful old buildings are left for the current generation to appreciate.

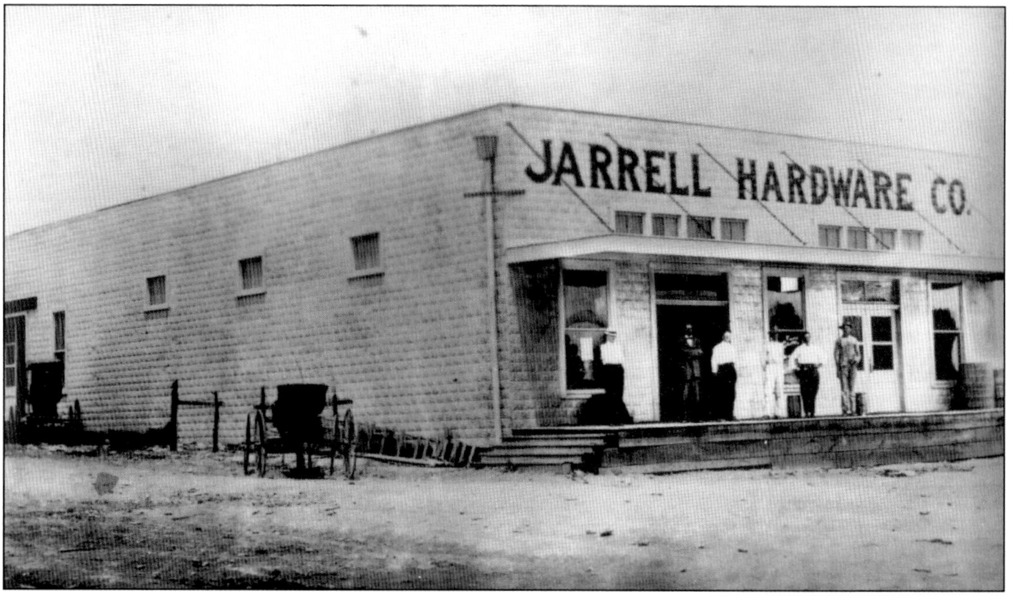

In 1911, E. M. Wilson built a large hardware store in the new town of Jarrell on the corner of Fifth Street and Avenue H. It supplied a wide variety of items that people needed, from hardware to implements and furniture to shelf goods. In 1913, the store was sold to Stokes-Blair Hardware Company of Bartlett, Texas, as shown here. Notice the two buggies parked at the side of the store. (Courtesy Danek Hardware.)

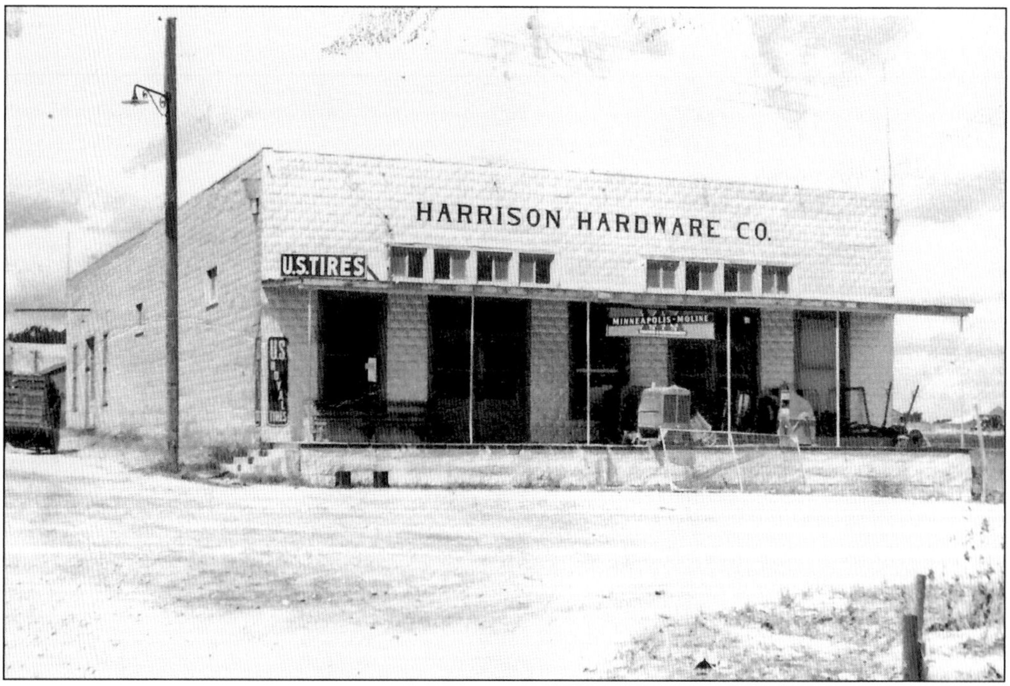

In 1945, the hardware store changed hands once more when it was bought by Fred Harrison. It remained an important part of Jarrell's economy, providing many needed items for residents and farmers from the surrounding area. Harrison owned the business for some years until it was sold to Don Webster. In 1954, it was purchased by John Danek.

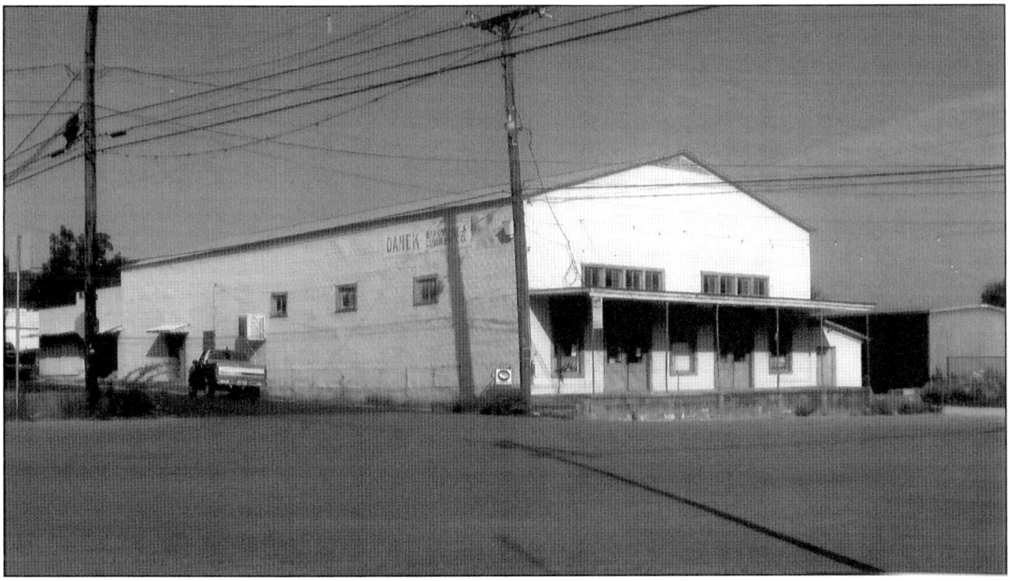

After graduating from high school in 1954, John Danek's son Emil went to work for his father at the hardware store and remains the proprietor today, along with his sons Greg and John. For many years, Danek's has been the place for everything, from hardware to lumber and tools to specialty items. If that's not enough, one can also get an update on the local news. Much of the store remains exactly as it was when it was first built. It is truly a trip back in time for anyone going through the original front doors. Below is Emil Danek in the store office.

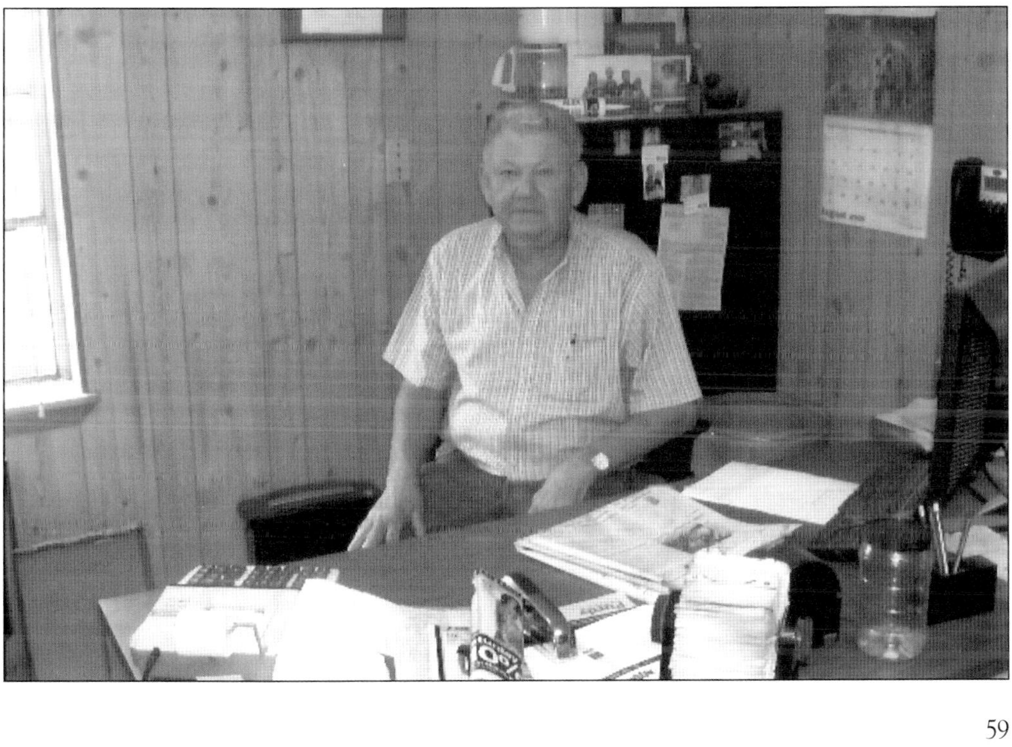

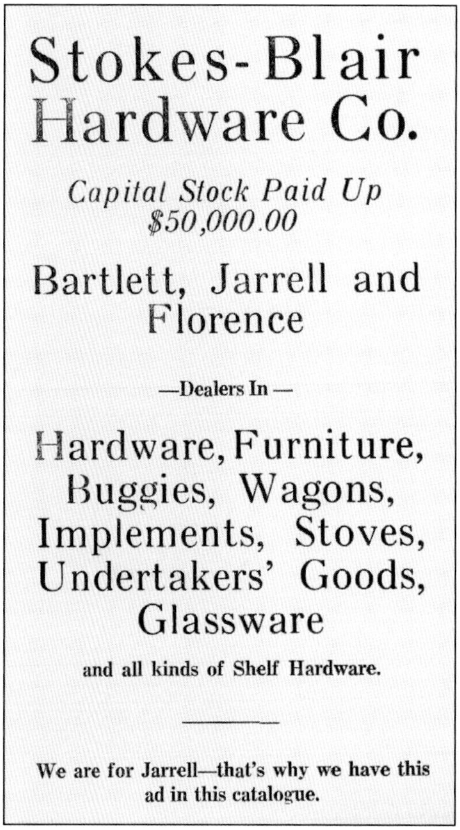

It was common practice for local businesses to advertise in the *Jarrell School Rules, Regulations and Course of Study* book, published each year. This advertisement was taken from the book published for the 1918–1919 school year. It indicates that Stokes and Blair Hardware specialized in hardware, furniture, buggies and wagons, and even woodstoves and glassware. Note they also carried undertaker supplies.

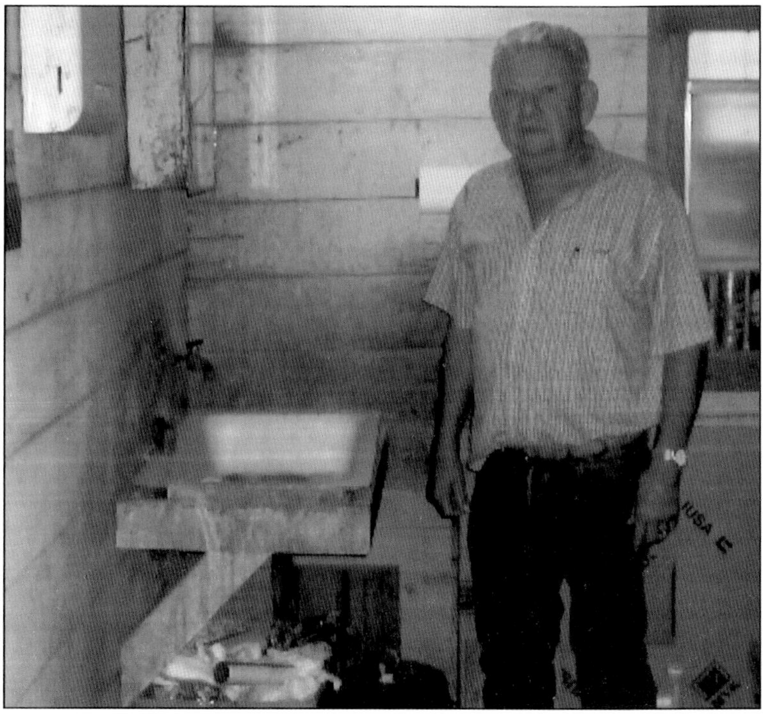

At the back of the Stokes and Blair store was a room used by Grover Young to embalm bodies and prepare them for final disposition. After embalming, the remains would be taken to a residence where people could visit during days before the funeral and burial. The original embalming sink still remains attached to the wall in what is now a storage area. Standing next to the sink is Emil Danek.

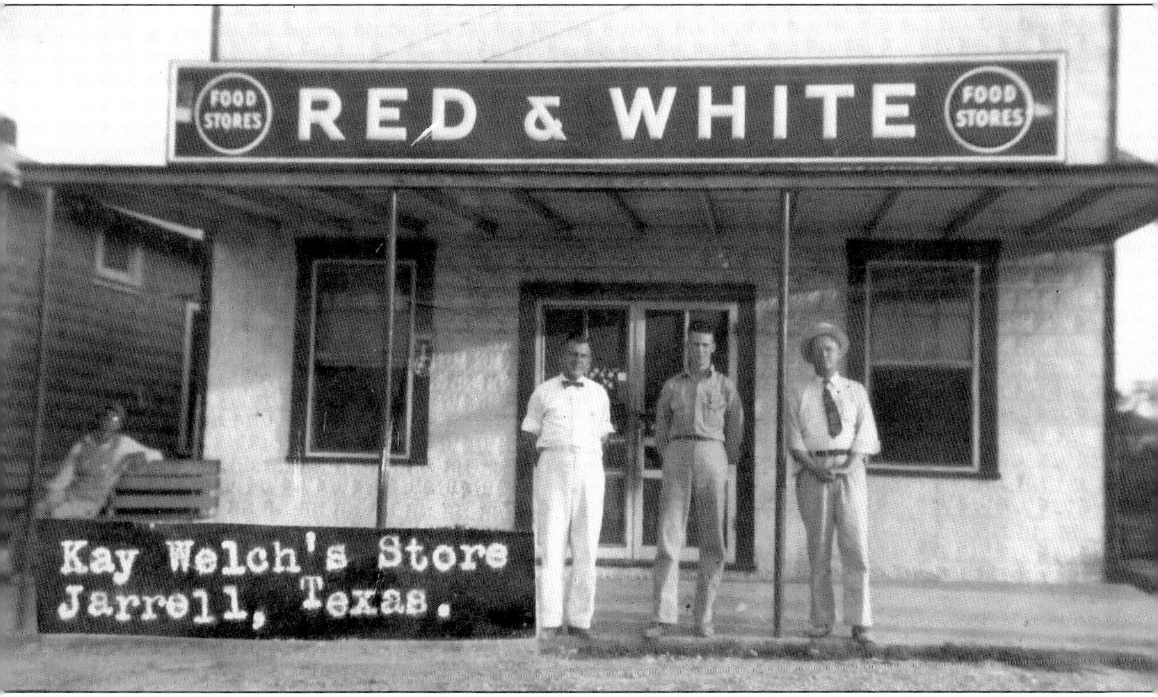

Up the street from the hardware store stood the ever-popular Red and White Grocery. Everyone in town shopped there. It was located on the south side of Avenue H (old U.S. Highway 81) between the Harrison Texaco station and Robert Kalmbach's barbershop. The store carried staples like flour, salt, sugar, and coffee as well as all sorts of canned foods. As money was in short supply, many people brought in eggs and butter to exchange for groceries. The owner, Kay Welch, was very particular about the eggs and butter he accepted to sell. He had a machine with a strong light on it that he used to see through the egg. If there was a spot in it, he would reject it. Here from left to right are Robert Kalmbach, L. R. Smith, and Kay Welch.

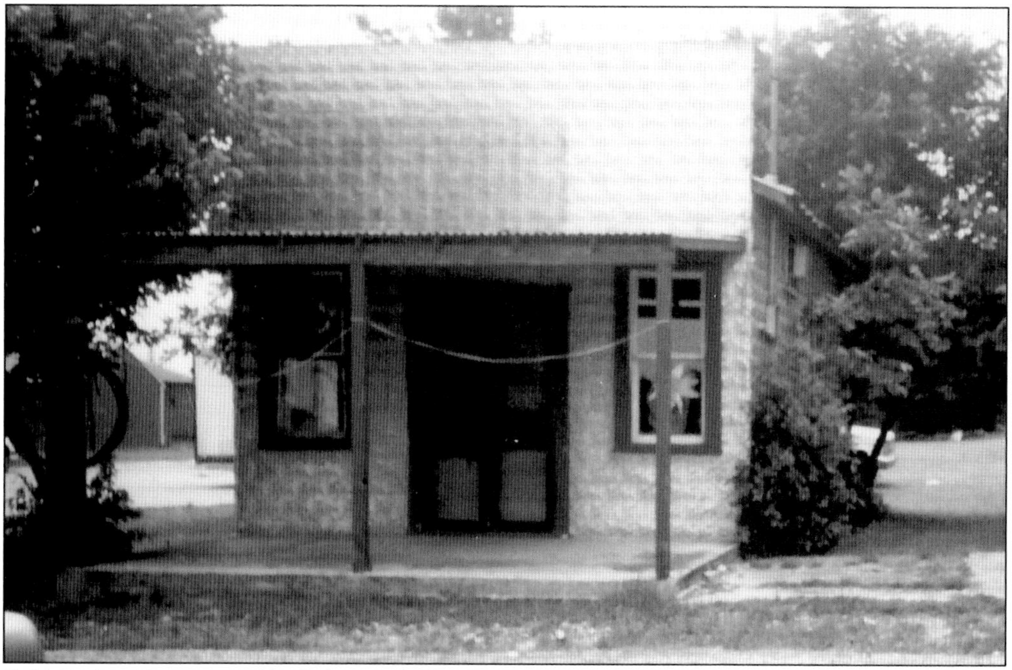

Bob's Barber Shop, owned by Robert Kalmbach, was located on the south side of Avenue H just east of the Red and White Grocery. He took over the shop in 1924. The first barber in Jarrell was Bert Walraven, followed by Walter Dunn, Johnny Hardin, Theo Denham, and Robert Kalmbach. The original building still stands today and has most recently served as the Jarrell Public Library.

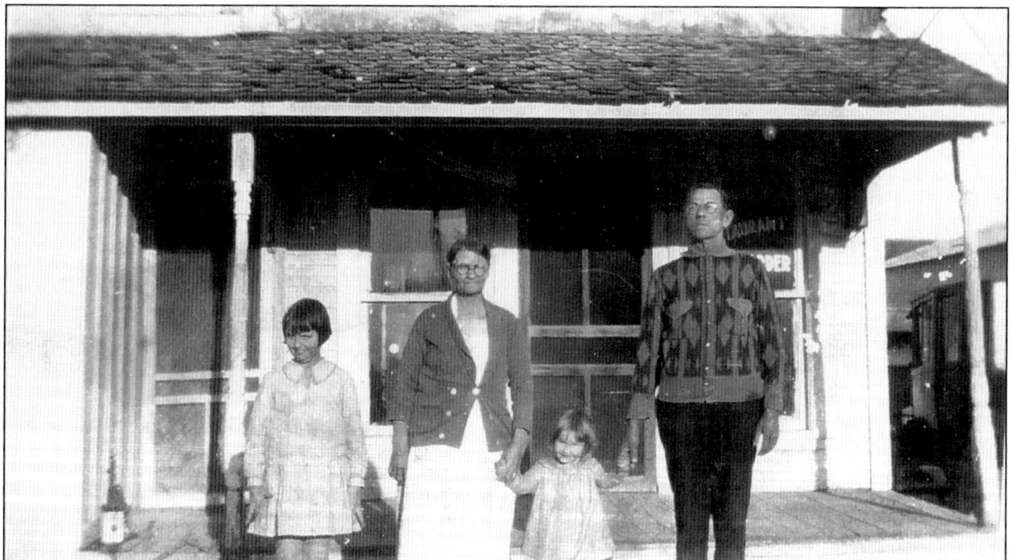

One of Jarrell's first cafés was owned by Jack and Lulu Miles, better known as Uncle Jack and Granny. The café was located in their home at Fourth Street and Avenue H. Granny cooked and Uncle Jack waited on customers. It was a small space with a counter, two stools, a table, and four chairs. The home-cooked food was tasty, and no one ever left hungry . . . even if folks couldn't pay. In 1929, from left to right, are Floy Harrison, Lulu Miles, Mary Harrison, and Jack Miles.

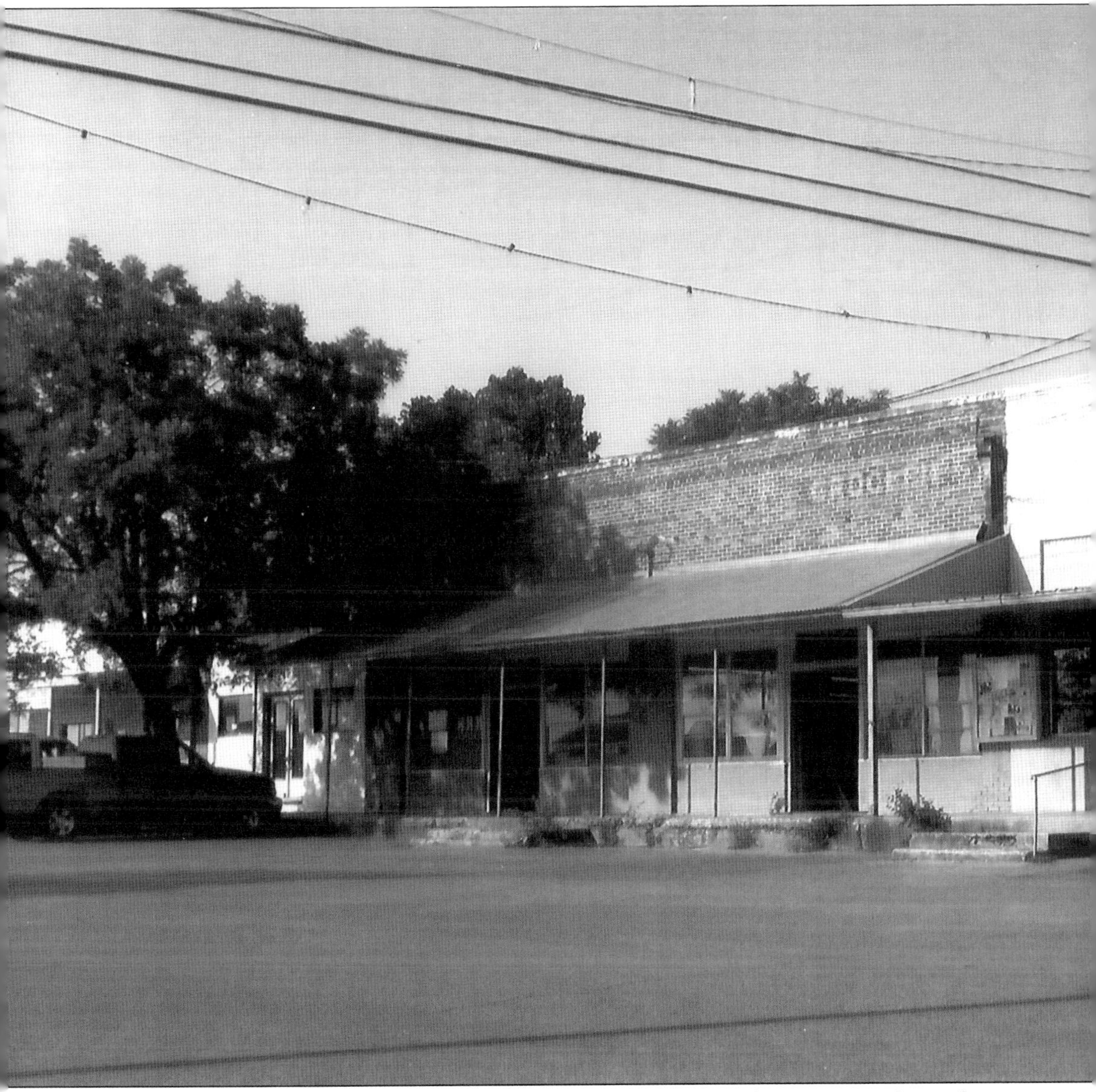

The Jarrell Mercantile Building was constructed in 1911 by E. M. Wilson, a cotton buyer from Taylor, Texas. The building housed both the mercantile and a bank. J. A. Buchanan was general manager of the mercantile store. It had a dry goods department, a millinery shop, a shoe shop, and groceries. Over the years, many Jarrell residents worked at the store, including Fred Buchanan (bookkeeper), Hattie Young, Mary Valenta, Mrs. Will Evans, Myrtle Stinnett, Joe Krejci, Andy Pickle, Mrs. John Vaught, E. B. Watson, Myron Ponder, Frank Kubacek, and W. F. Neeley. In 1940, H. L. Jones purchased the store and operated it until 1973, when he retired. The mercantile part of the building currently houses the HRM Millworks, where custom cabinetry is produced. Originally there were business buildings on both sides of Fifth Street. In 1918, all of the buildings on the east side burned, and in 1927 some of the ones on the west side burned as well. What remained is what is there today.

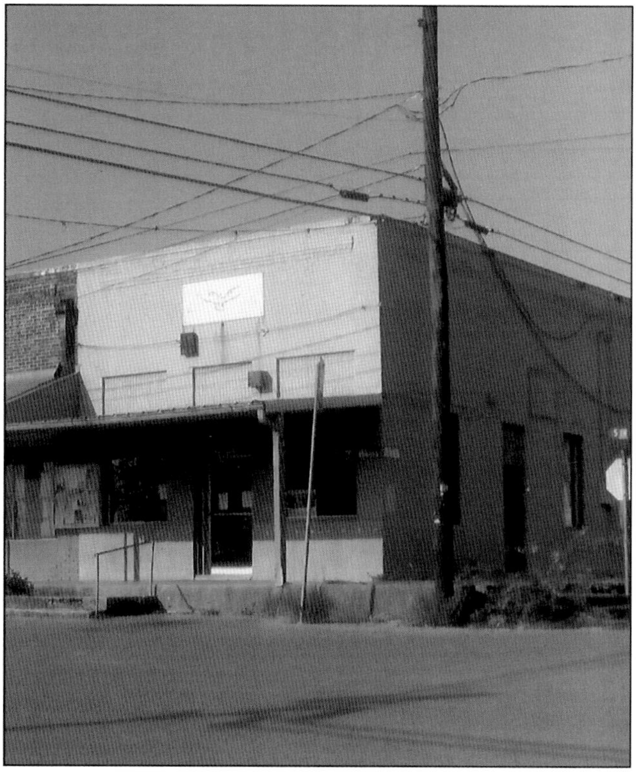

The First State Bank occupied the north corner of the Jarrell Mercantile Building. It opened its doors for business on October 11, 1911. The bank was financed by E. M. Wilson with capital of $10,000. Wilson was president, and W. H. Buchanan was vice president. The bank was a busy place, serving people from Bell and Williamson Counties. The advertisement below appears in a publication printed in 1918.

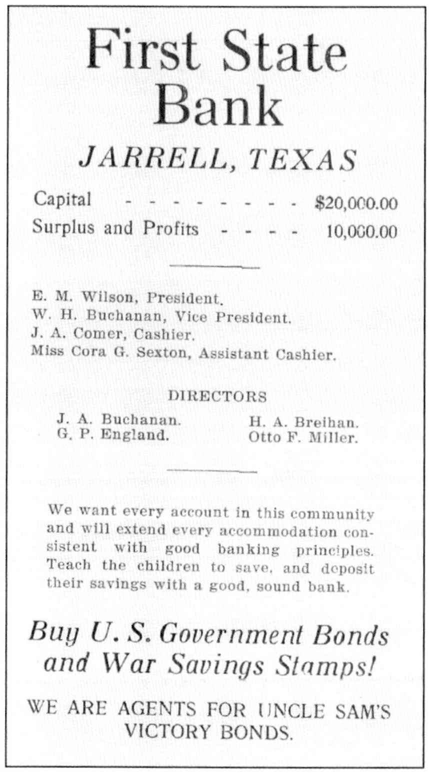

Bank president J. A. Comer is shown sitting at his rolltop desk at the First State Bank. Well respected in the community, he and his wife, Mary, who was disabled, liked to entertain. Neighbors would meet at the Comer home to listen to the radio. Topics might have ranged from one of the fireside chats by President Roosevelt urging Americans to have faith in the banks and to support his New Deal to a boxing match by Joe Louis.

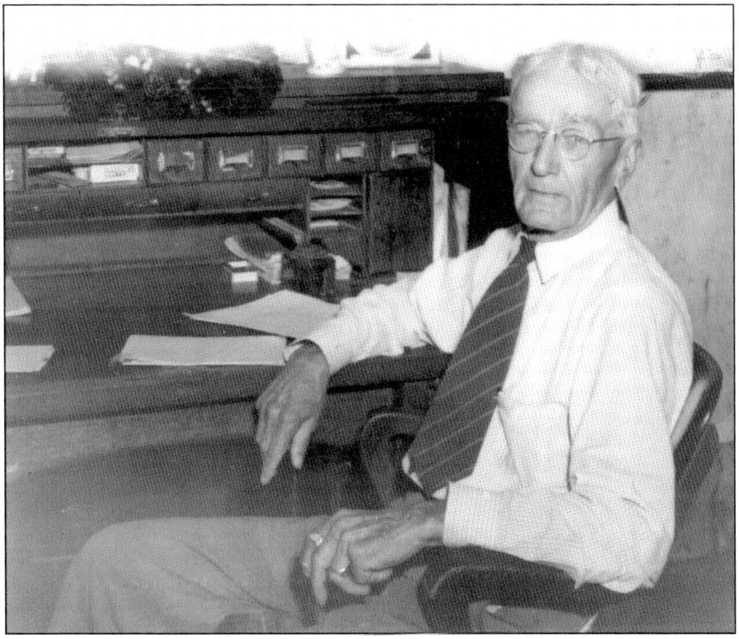

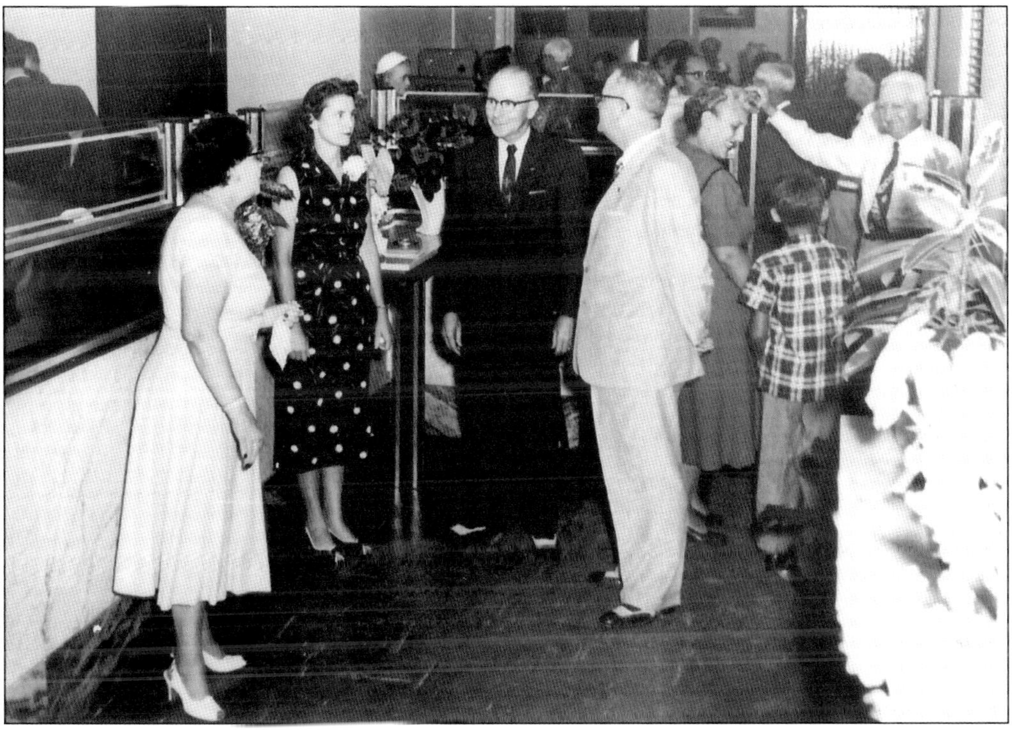

This photograph was taken at the First State Bank during the 1950s. From left to right are Cora Sexton, Claudia Goode, Fred Buchanan, and Grogan Lord. Cora Sexton, better known as "Miz Cora," was the first female bank president in the state of Texas. She prided herself on knowing each customer personally. Patrons of the bank would stick their heads in the front door and holler, "Miz Cora, what's my balance?" Most of the time, without looking, she would holler back with the correct balance.

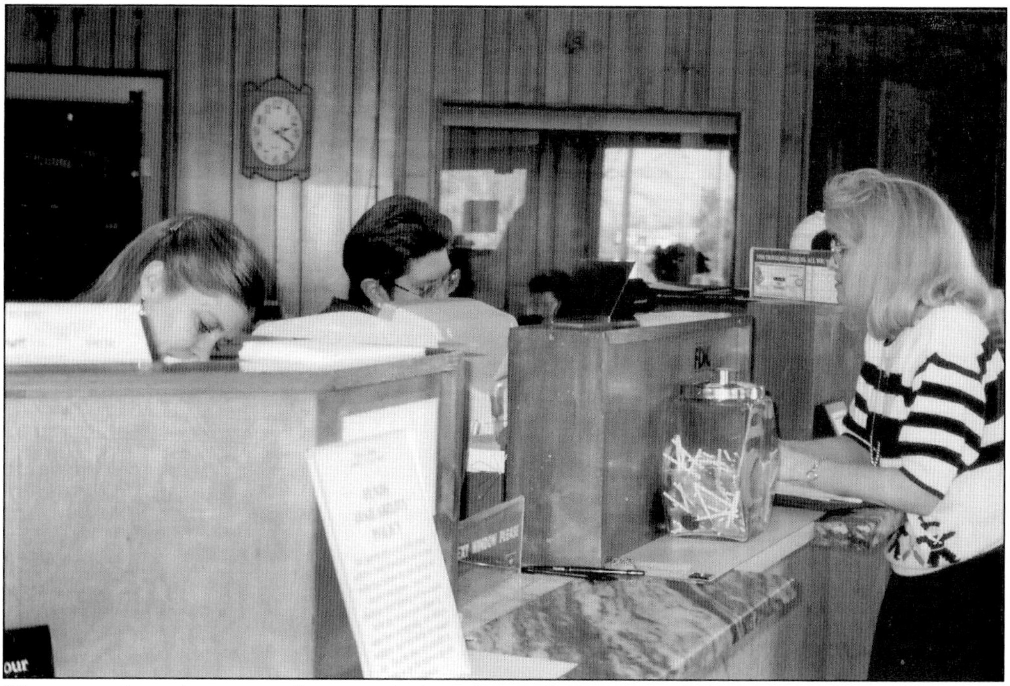

This is a relatively recent photograph that shows the interior of the First State Bank in later years. Cashiers Gwen Hulme (left) and Dorothy Schwerdtfeger (center) stand behind the original marble counter. The bank vault is in the upper left-hand corner. The bank has been in business continuously since 1911. (Courtesy Charlotte Vancil.)

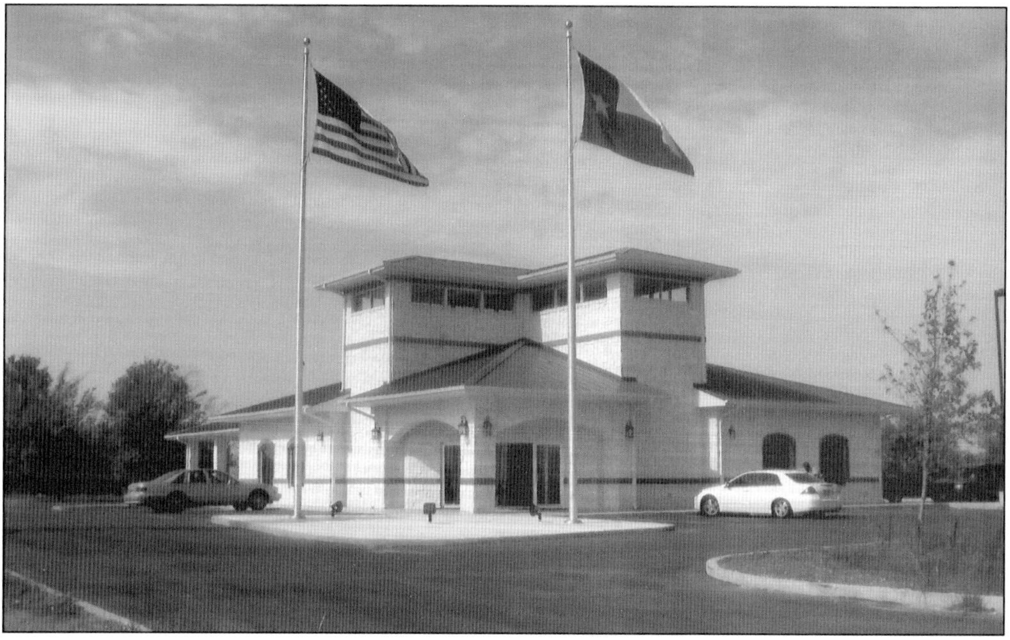

After 97 years in the same location, Eagle Bank moved into its new facility on the west frontage road of I-35. Flags flying, the new bank opened its doors for business on Monday, August 18, 2008. The current president is Tommy Sladecek, who has worked at the bank since 1973.

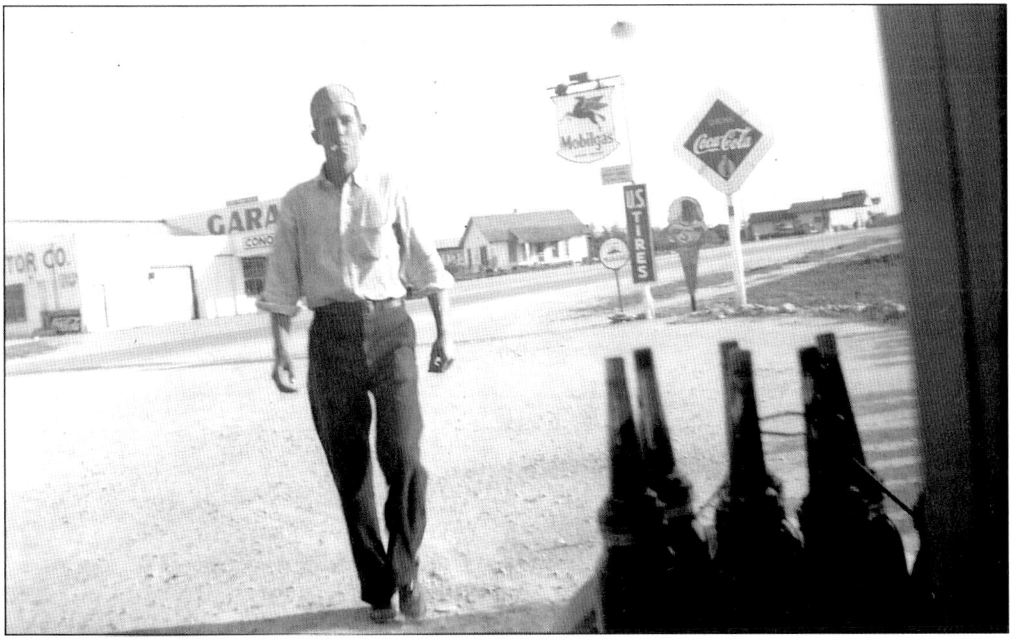

When Highway 81 was moved to the east of its original location, businesses were built to capitalize on the highway traffic. Service stations were in high demand, and three of them were built on the south side of the highway. As Dewey Blackman walks toward the Magnolia station, in the background are Jarrell Motor Company, Garrett Garage, and Conlee's Garage and Ice House.

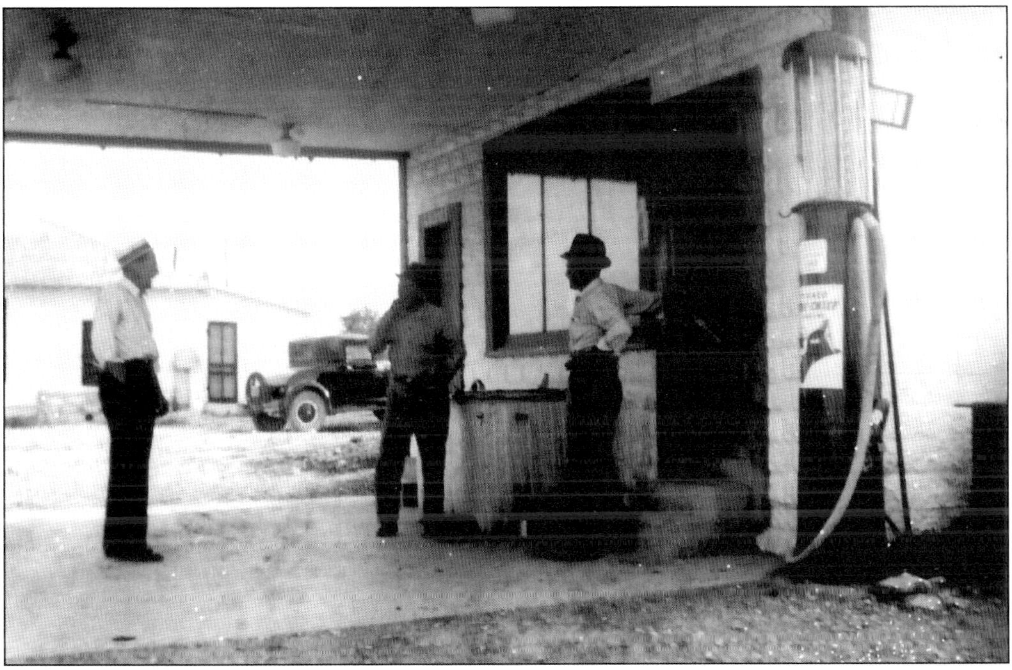

The Texaco station was owned and operated by Marvin and Ethel Harrison. Note the soda water box made from beaded wood. This box was filled with soda each morning and iced down with ice from the Conlee icehouse across the street. In the 1940s photograph are, from left to right, Frank McDougle, Marvin Harrison, and Jesse Sybert. In the background is the Speedway Inn.

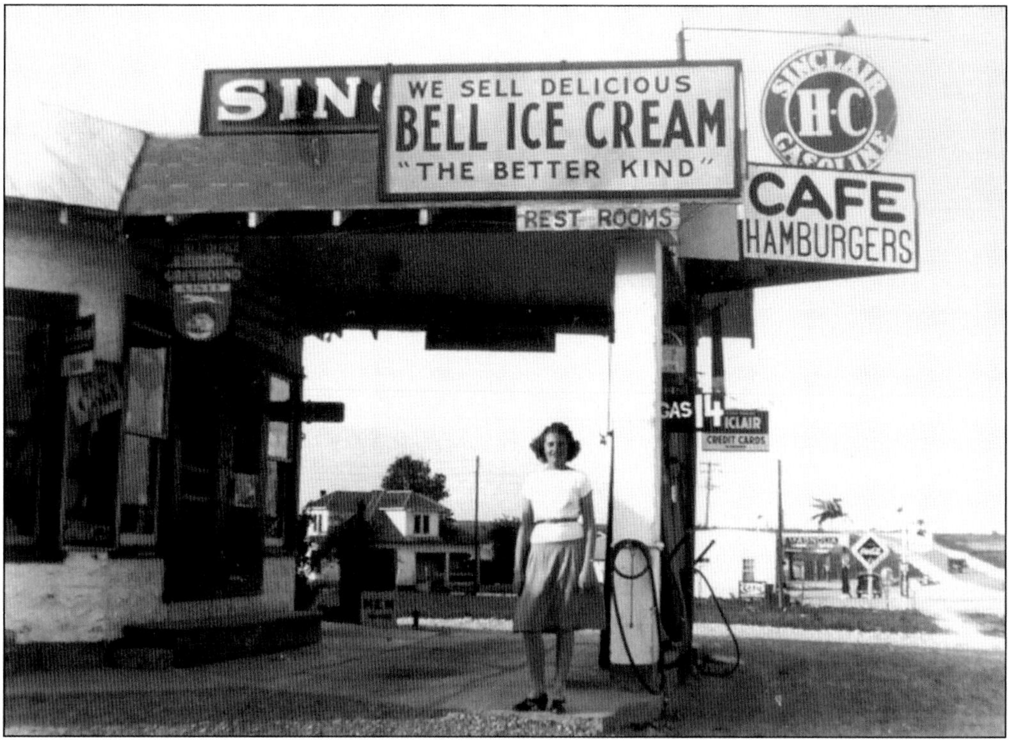

A Sinclair station and café were built just west of the Magnolia station. This served as the Greyhound Bus Station and promised good food and cold drinks. They sold Bell Ice Cream that was made in Temple, Texas. Gas was 14¢ a gallon and could be purchased with a Sinclair credit card. The station and café were operated by Maynard and Vesta Watkins. They lived in a room at the back of the business. The young woman standing above in the driveway is Olga Bozon. The picture was taken by Butch Sybert in the early 1940s. Below is a side view of the café and station taken on a snowy winter day. (Above, courtesy C. B. and Mary Hodge; below, Marcine Bridges.)

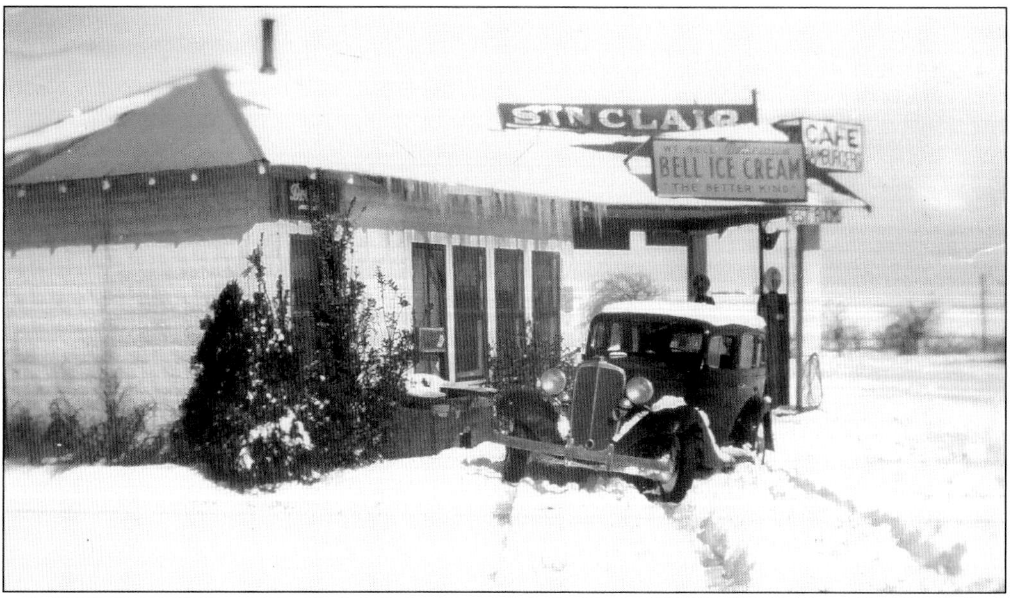

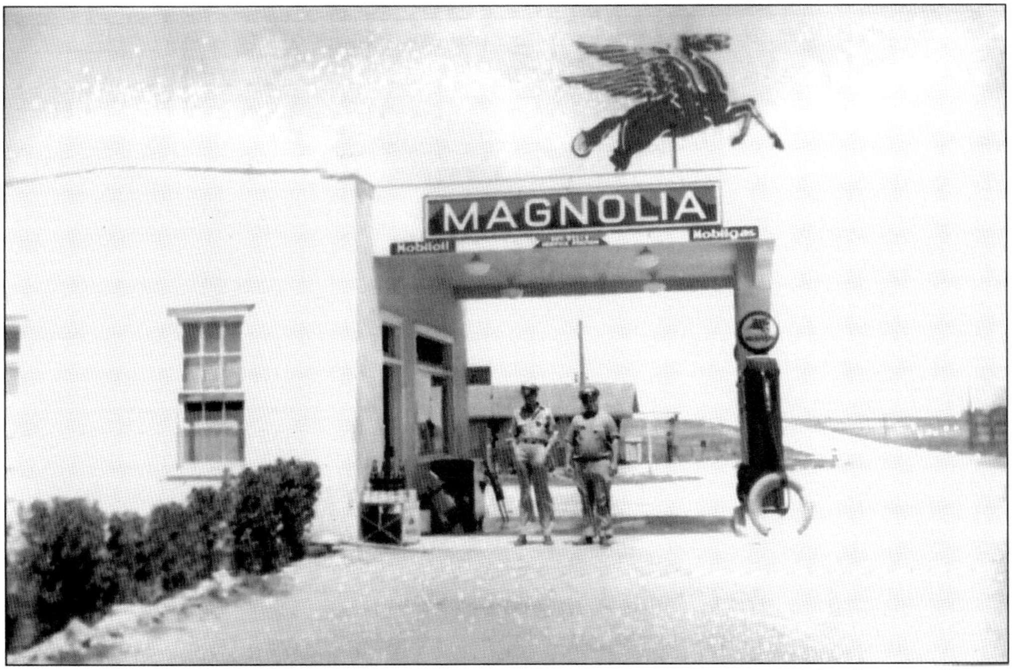

One of the first buildings to be constructed on the new highway was Roy Welch's flying red horse Magnolia service station. Known as a good place to stop for food and gas, it also advertised clean restrooms. This building still stands today and is quite the topic of conversation for travelers stopping in Jarrell. Pictured are B. F. Blanton (left) and Roy Welch. The photograph, taken in the early 1940s, shows the train depot in the background.

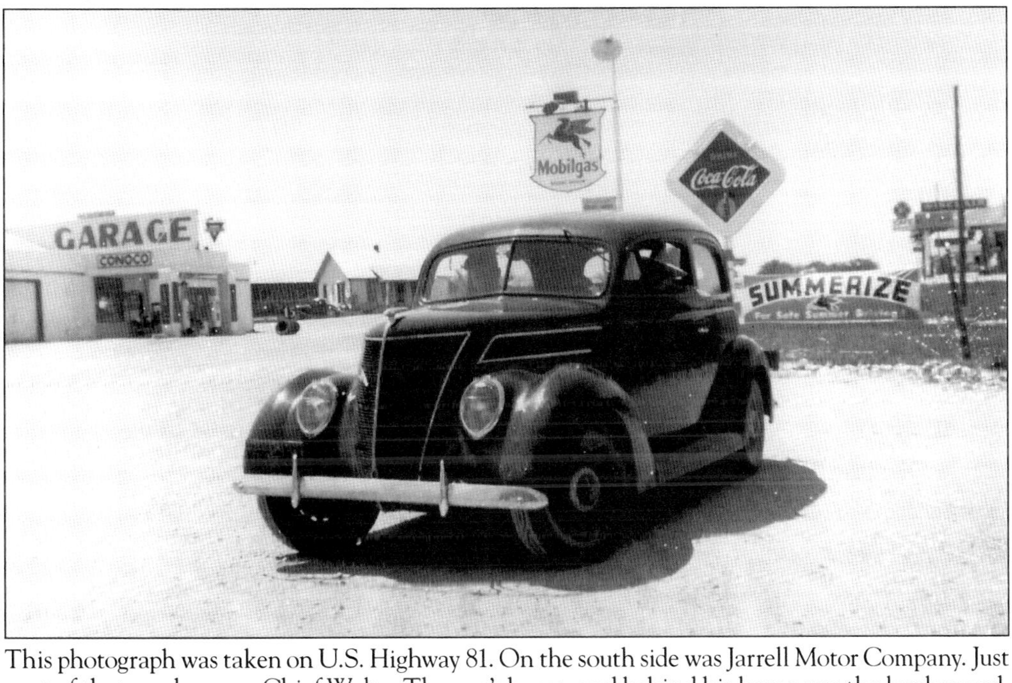

This photograph was taken on U.S. Highway 81. On the south side was Jarrell Motor Company. Just west of that was lawman Chief Walter Thomas's home, and behind his home was the lumberyard. When I-35 was built, all of these businesses were demolished.

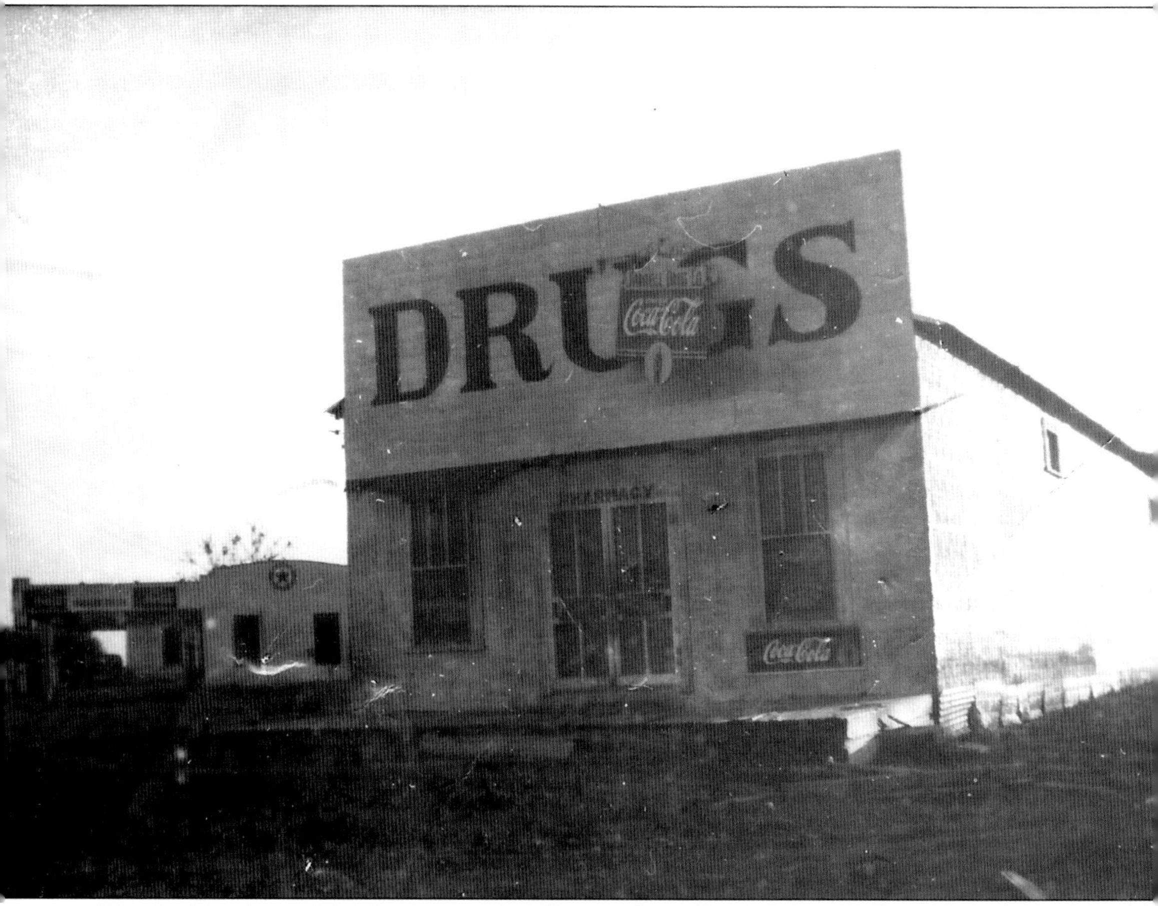

This building housed the drugstore in Jarrell. It was located on Avenue H next to the barbershop. The druggist was Knox Ramsey. It was moved to its current location at the corner of Fifth Street and Avenue I and served as a drugstore for a short time and before moving to the Fireman-Woodsman building. It was known for serving a cool refreshing drink called glass-ade that was available in a variety of flavors. The drugstore also served ice cream. Teens liked to stop by in the afternoons to make plans for the evening. In the back of the store was a doctor's office. Some of the physicians who practiced in Jarrell were Dr. J. E. Willerson, Dr. S. W. Pair, and Dr. C. H. Crawford.

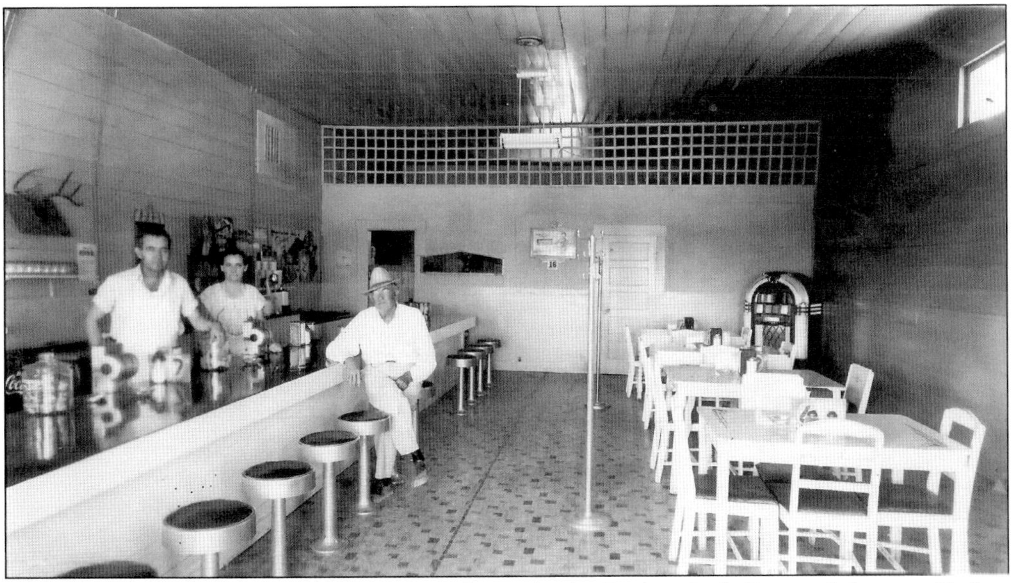

In the 1940s, the drugstore building became home for the Bridges Café. Pictured above and below behind the counter are owners Burnett and Thelma Bridges. They were well known in the area for their lunches, burgers, and homemade pies The lunches sold for 80¢ and were so big that two people would divide a lunch, resulting in a nice lunch for 40¢. The restaurant was a mainstay of the Jarrell business district in the 1940s, 1950s, and 1960s. People came from surrounding towns and didn't mind standing in line for a table. The restaurant was open seven days a week, with Sunday being one of its busiest days. Just mention the Bridges Café today, and those who remember it will immediately start reminiscing about delicious burgers and pies with 4-inch-high meringue. (Both courtesy Marcine Bridges.)

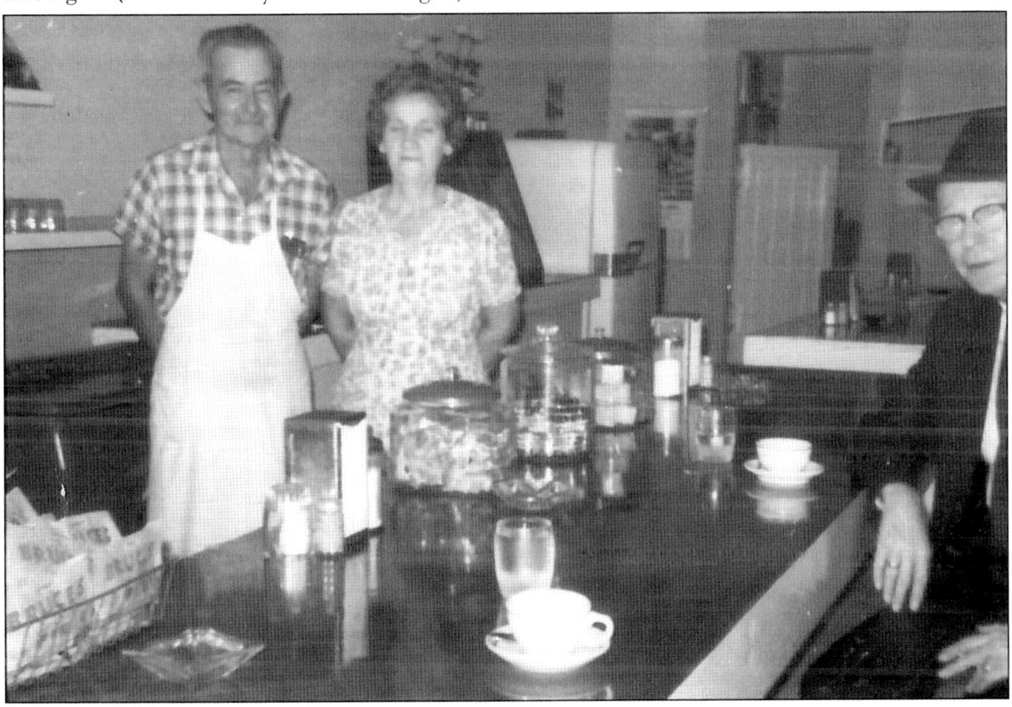

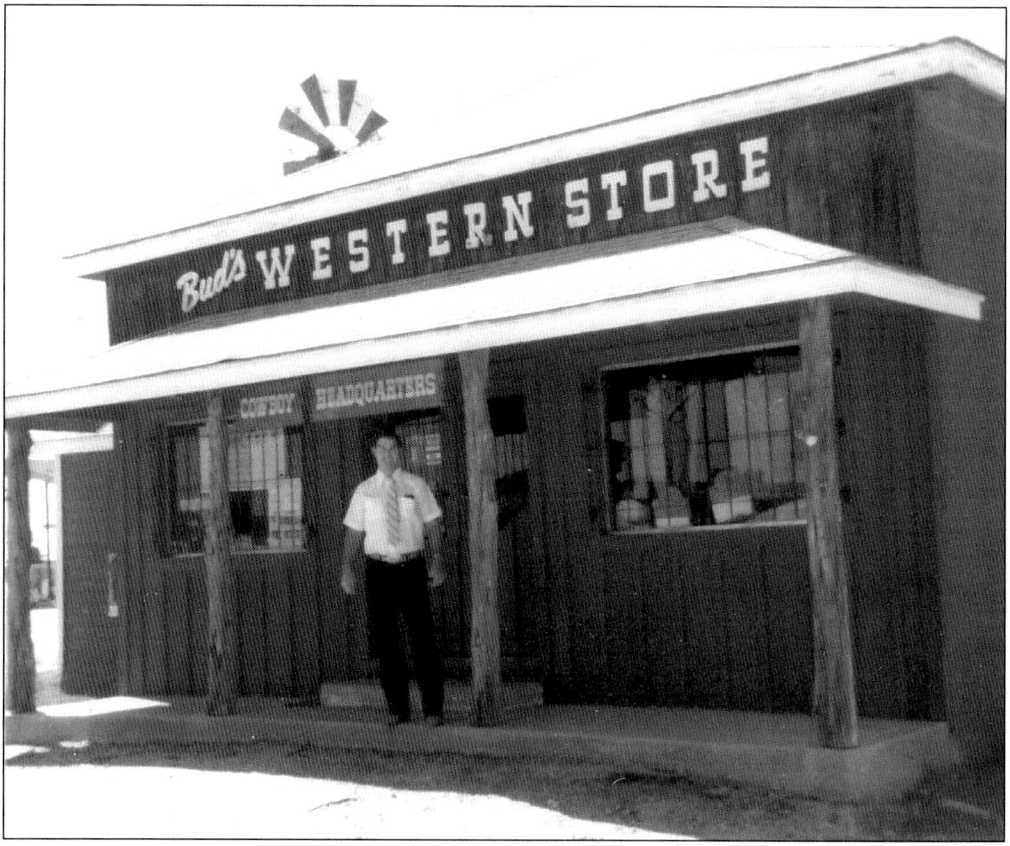

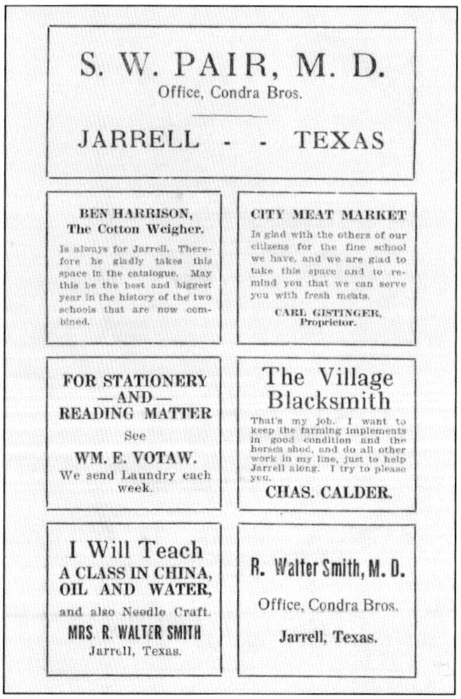
S. W. PAIR, M. D.
Office, Condra Bros.

JARRELL - - TEXAS

BEN HARRISON,
The Cotton Weigher.

Is always for Jarrell. Therefore he gladly takes this space in the catalogue. May this be the best and biggest year in the history of the two schools that are now combined.

CITY MEAT MARKET

Is glad with the others of our citizens for the fine school we have, and we are glad to take this space and to remind you that we can serve you with fresh meats.

CARL GISTINGER,
Proprietor.

FOR STATIONERY
—AND—
READING MATTER
See
WM. E. VOTAW.
We send Laundry each week.

The Village Blacksmith

That's my job. I want to keep the farming implements in good condition and the horses shod, and do all other work in my line, just to help Jarrell along. I try to please you.

CHAS. CALDER.

I Will Teach
A CLASS IN CHINA, OIL AND WATER,
and also Needle Craft.
MRS. R. WALTER SMITH
Jarrell, Texas.

R. Walter Smith, M. D.
Office, Condra Bros.
Jarrell, Texas.

In 1970, C. Bud Stockton, a local real estate broker and developer, opened Bud's Western Store in the old drugstore building. He had a full inventory of Western wear, including hats and boots. He advertised the store as cowboy headquarters—everything the modern cowboy or cowgirl might need. Pictured here is Bud standing on the front porch. The store remained in business until 1980. Through the years, this building has served many purposes. Today the venerable building houses Jeff Stockton's real estate office. (Courtesy Jeff and Kimberly Stockton.)

Jarrell was a busy little town with a variety of businesses and services. The 1918 advertisements here are for two physicians, a cotton weigher, a blacksmith, meat market, bookstore, and even an arts and crafts class. In later years, as the population dwindled, many stores closed and went out of business.

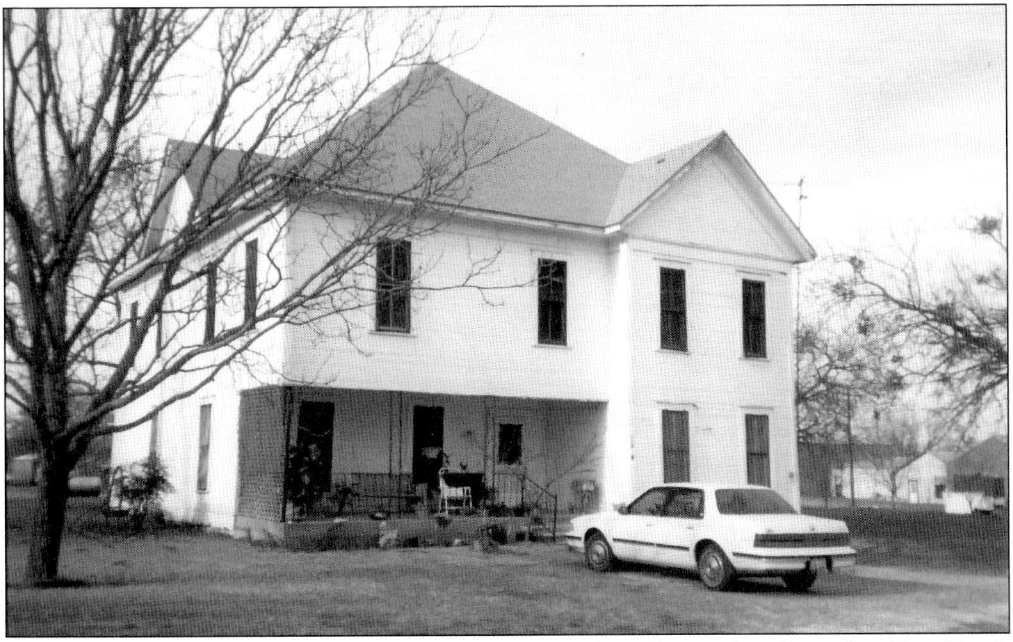

A large two-story building was erected around 1912 and was known locally as the Glass Hotel. Owned and operated by G. W. and Ruth Glass for many years, the hotel was known for its wonderful food and culinary flair. The atmosphere was always cordial, with a warm welcome extended by the Glasses and their daughters, Addie and Nora. Many local businessmen had lunch regularly at the hotel, and people traveling through town could rent a room. It was a popular spot for traveling salesmen called "drummers." These salesmen would gauge their calls so they could end their day with a room and dinner at the Glass Hotel. For many years, the hotel served as a residence for the Dewey Blackman family. Below is a picture of the hotel today. It has just been completely remodeled. (Both courtesy Charlotte Vancil.)

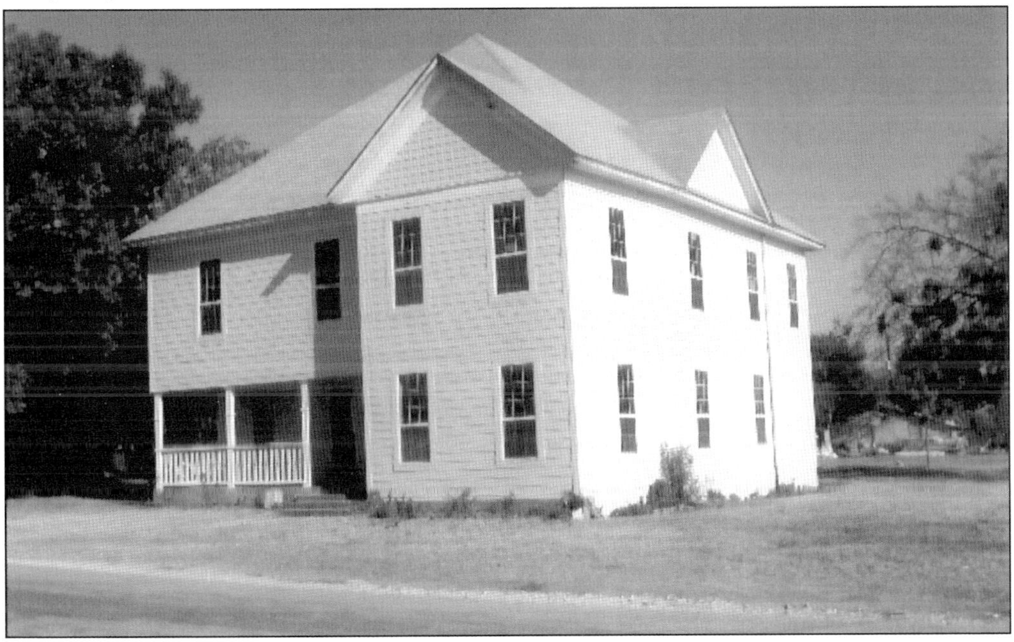

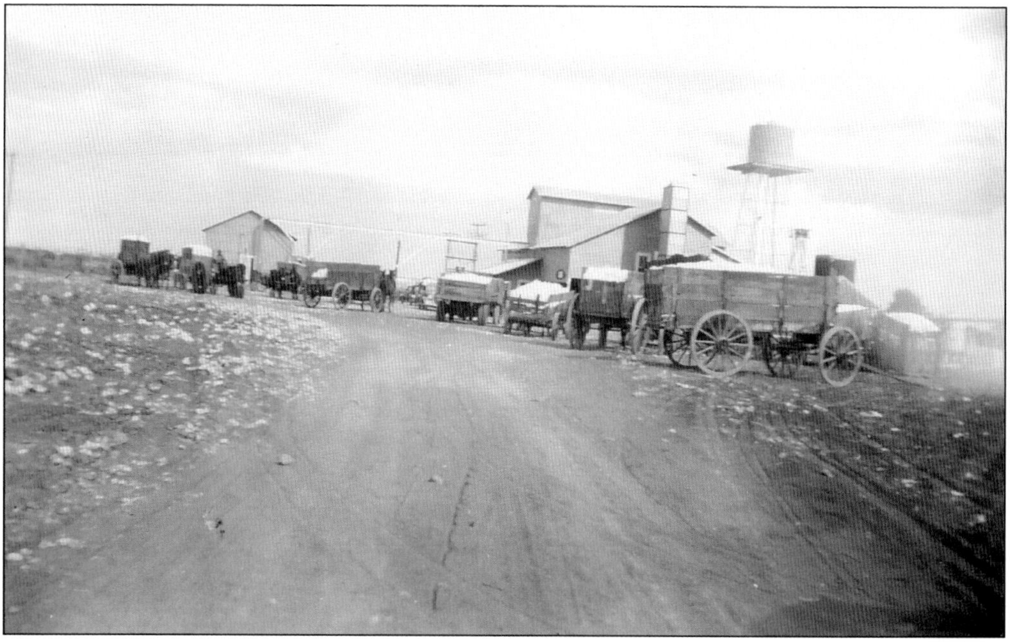

Above is the Harrison Brothers Gin shown in 1920. Volley Killingsworth built the first gin at this location on Fifth Street, but it burned down. Fred and Ben Harrison bought the property and rebuilt the gin shown here. Cotton was still handpicked on family farms at this time, and wagons brought the cotton to the gin one bale at a time. Below is a picture of cotton being brought in by horse-drawn wagons. On the left can be seen a tractor with lug wheels. Even though farming was becoming more mechanized, everyone used what he or she had. Shown in the picture from left to right are (in wagon) Mary Harrison and Claudia Harrison; (standing) Wayne Sybert and Floy Harrison.

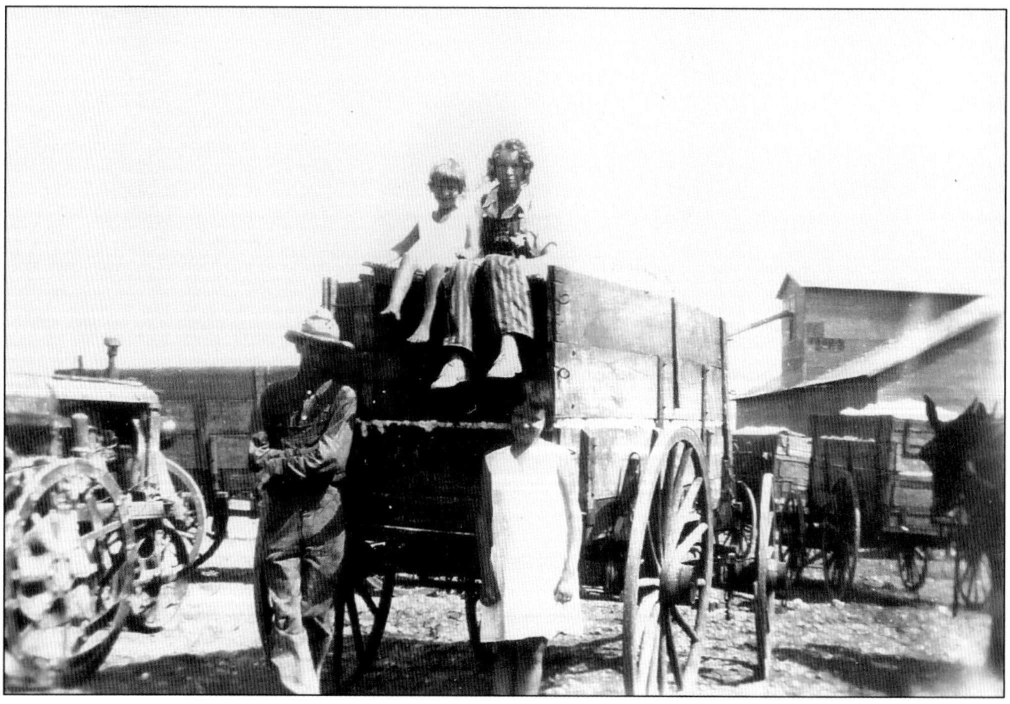

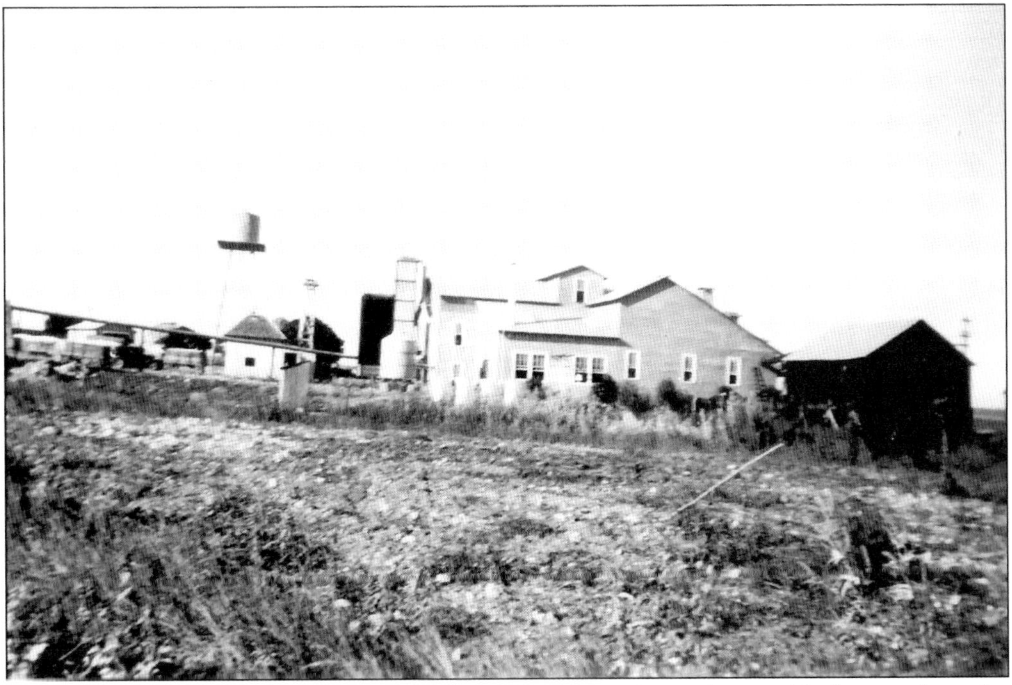

This is a back view of the Harrison Brothers Gin. It was located just a block away from the 1916 Jarrell School building. Notice the dominant water tower, which was a local landmark. The cottonseed house is seen on the right side of the photograph. Times were hard during the Depression, and on winter nights, it was not unusual to find a hobo sleeping in the cottonseed house in an attempt to stay warm. Many meals were given to these destitute folks traveling from place to place either by walking or hitching rides on railroad boxcars. In the picture below, one can see wagons, no longer pulled by horses but rather by cars. Jarrell was still predominantly an agricultural community.

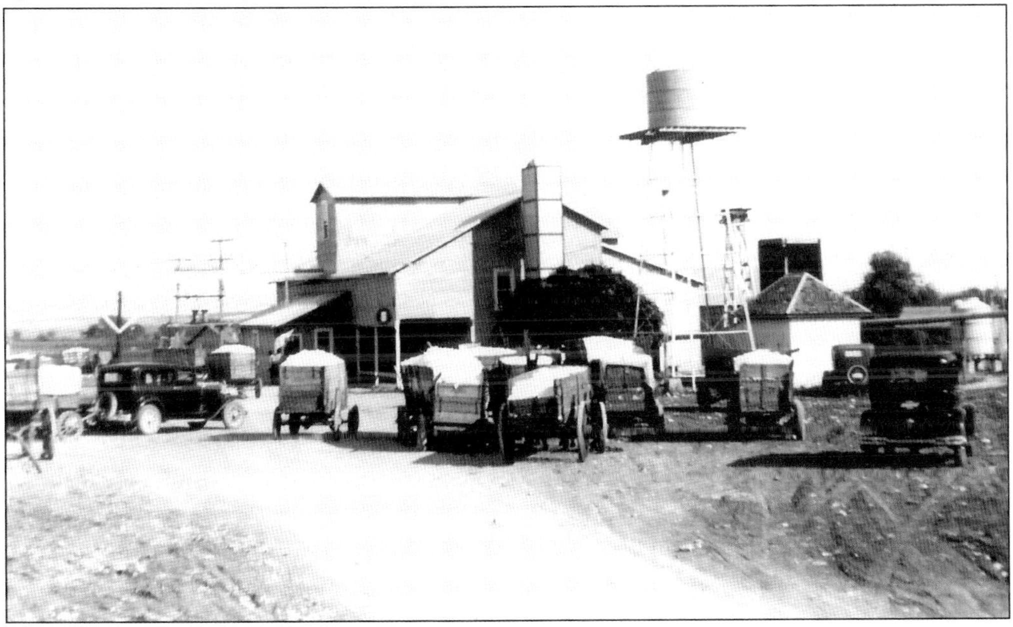

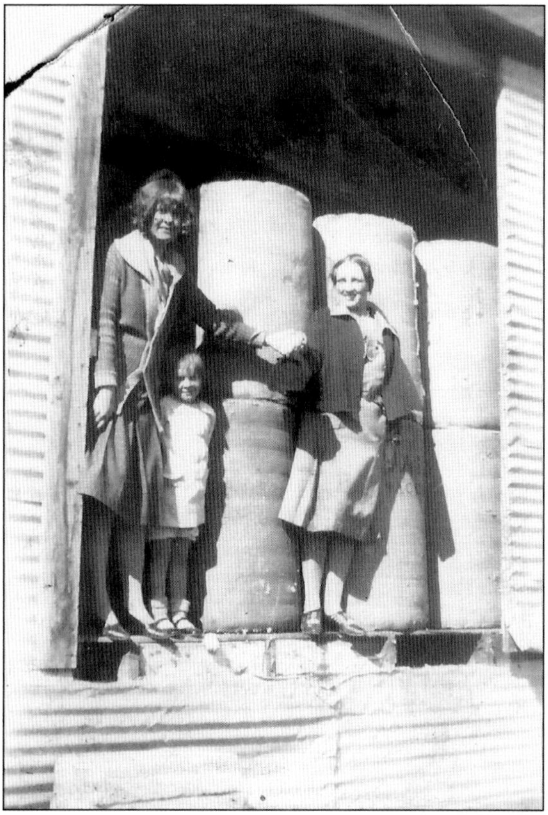

In the image at left are, from left to right, Beaulah McDougle, Floy Harrison, and Lena Mae McDougle. Round bales like those behind the girls were ginned for only a short time. In the early 1930s, Fred Harrison became the sole owner of the gin and sold it to Boyd Goad in 1938. In 1954, B. C. Smith and Jim Sybert joined the Goad Gin Company and in 1960 bought out Mrs. Goad. They operated the gin for several years and then sold it to Jim Sybert's sons, Donald and Jimmy, during the 1970s. When the gin closed, it was dismantled, and some of the property was given to the Jarrell School District. Jim Sybert (left) and Boyd Goad are pictured below in 1926. In the early days, cottonseed burrs were burned near the gin. People remember the whole town being smoky. When a visiting football team came to town, it could hardly play because of the smoke. The Jarrell team was so used to the smoke that its players didn't even notice it and ran right down the field.

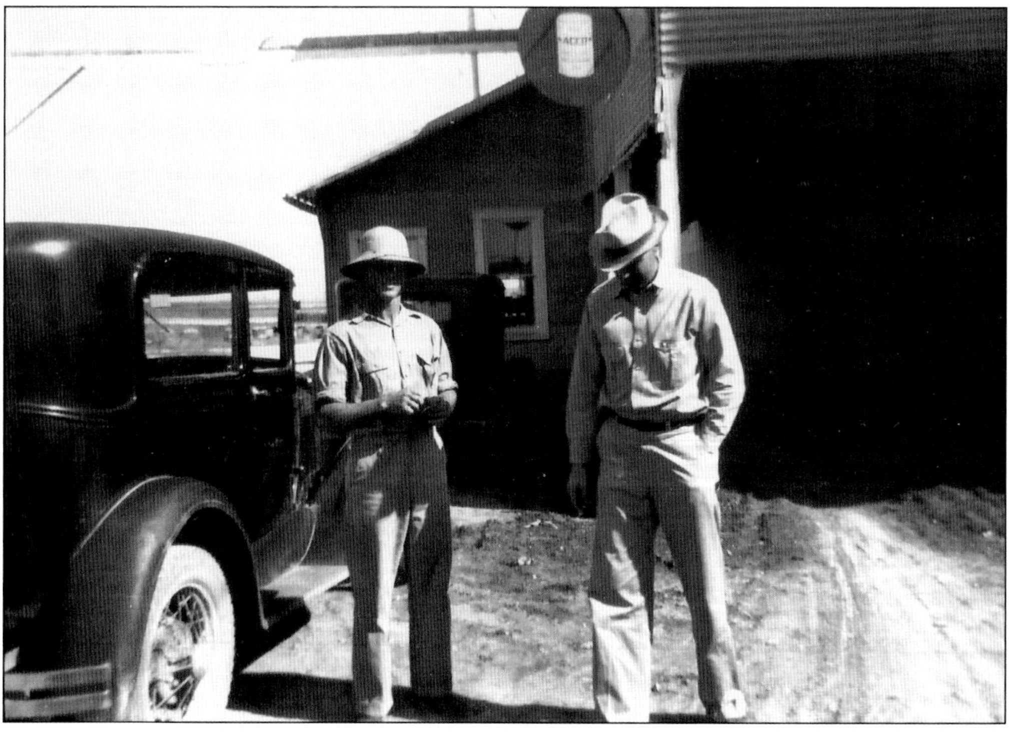

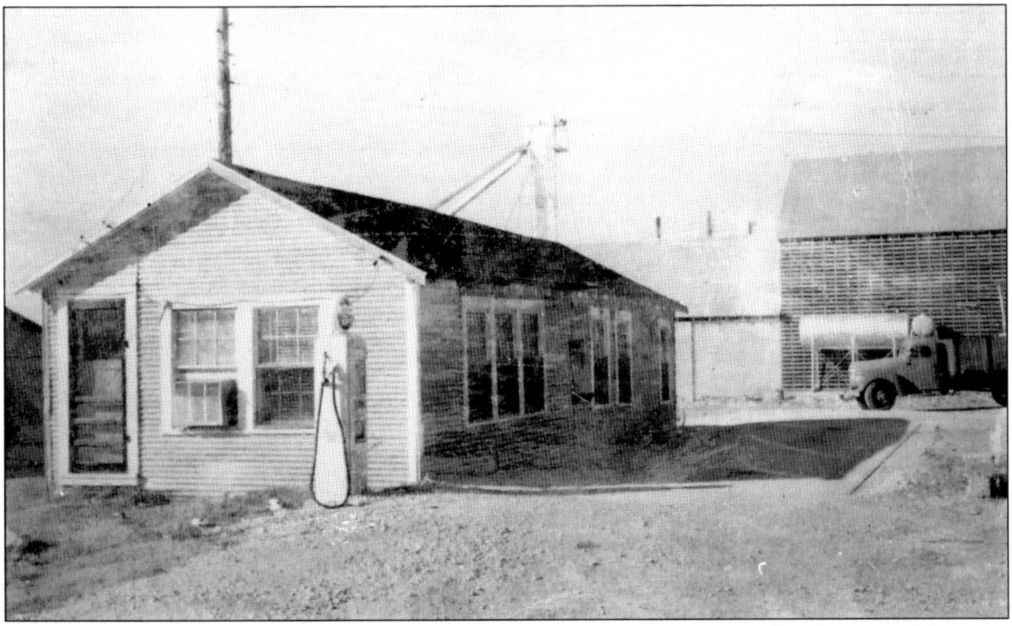

In the late 1930s, many farmers began raising grain instead of cotton. Fred and Eva Lee Harrison saw the need for a grain business in Jarrell and built the above office and storage building in 1939. The building still stands today. The men in the picture below are unloading corn and putting it into the building for storage. The corn came in from the farmer's fields and was shelled and put into 100-pound bags. These bags were then loaded onto large trucks and carried to Houston or Galveston. Some of the Harrison Grain business was destroyed by the Jarrell tornado, but some of it still stands. Locally the business is still known as the "sheller." Over the years, it has provided support and services for the many farmers still operating in the Jarrell area.

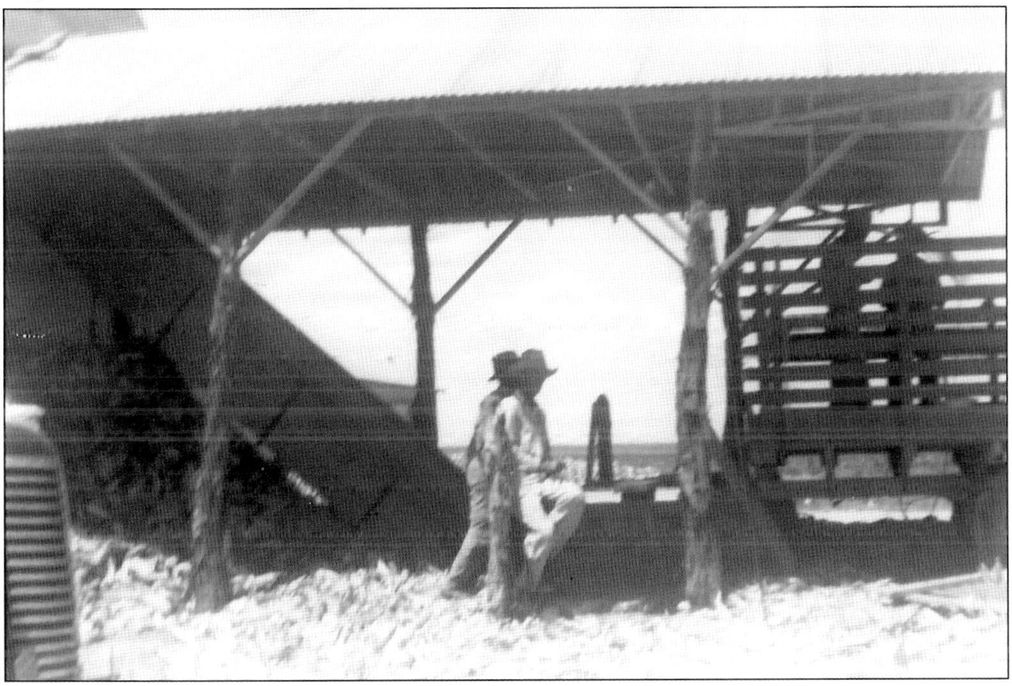

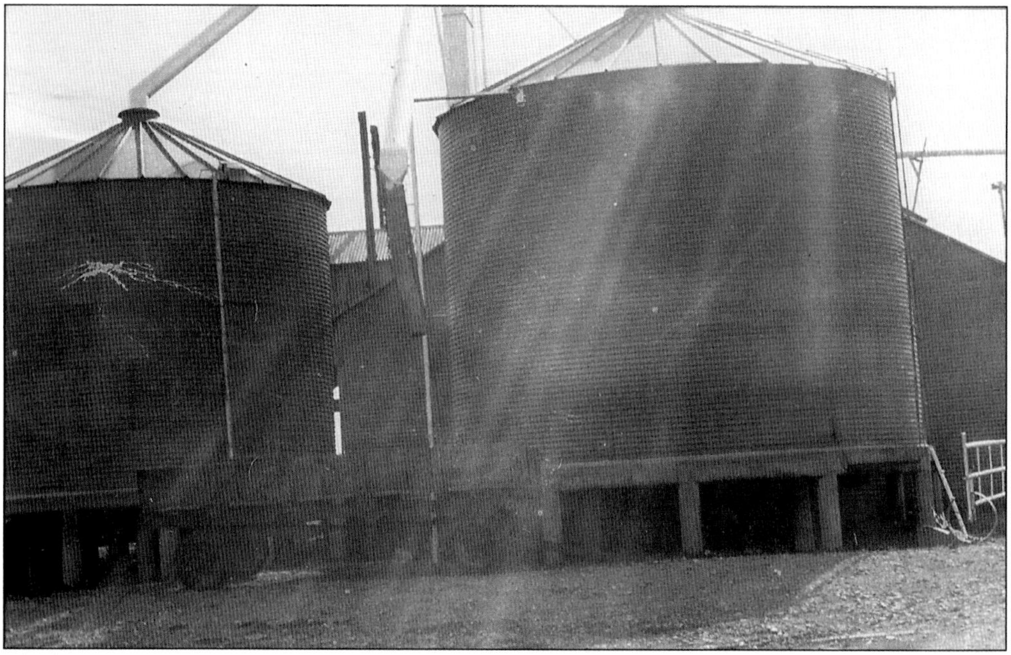

The huge bins seen above at Harrison Grain were used to store ground grain. In the days before commercial feed was available, farmers brought their corn or milo to be sold or ground for feed for livestock on their farms and ranches. A bustling place, the grain business provided employment for many residents of Jarrell over the years. Customers came from all over northern Williamson and southern Bell Counties. Below are some of the employees of Harrison Grain Company. From left to right are Sam White, Bill Mersiovsky, Andrew Blackman, Floyd Goode, Oscar Bohanan, Nick Proctor, Cap Johnson, and, on the counter, little Freddie Goode. Just before the camera snapped, someone stuck a cigar in Freddie's mouth.

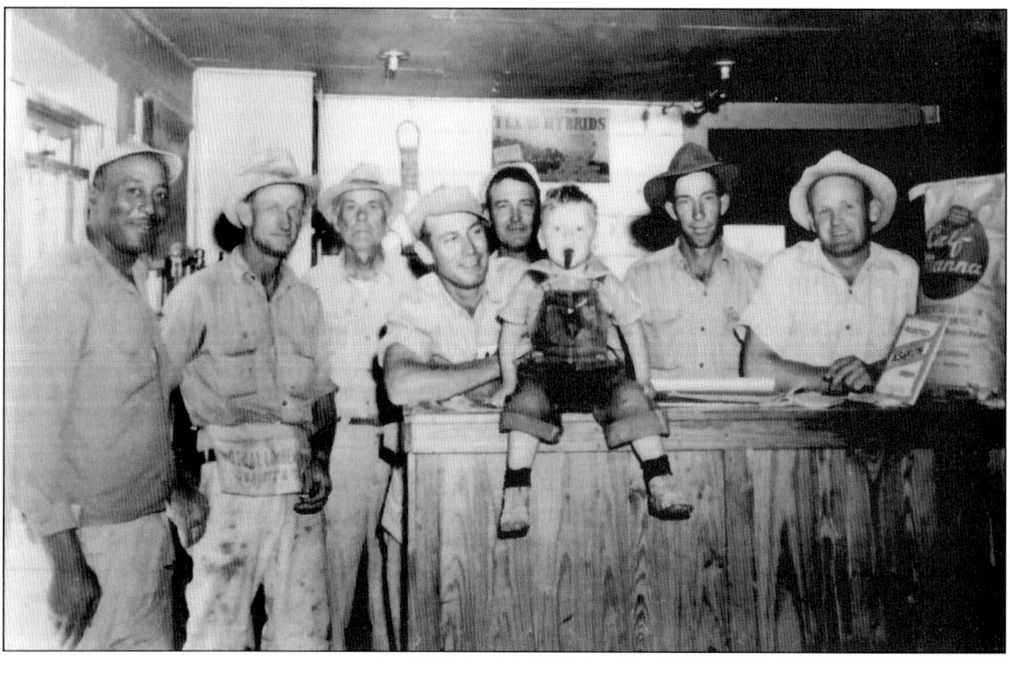

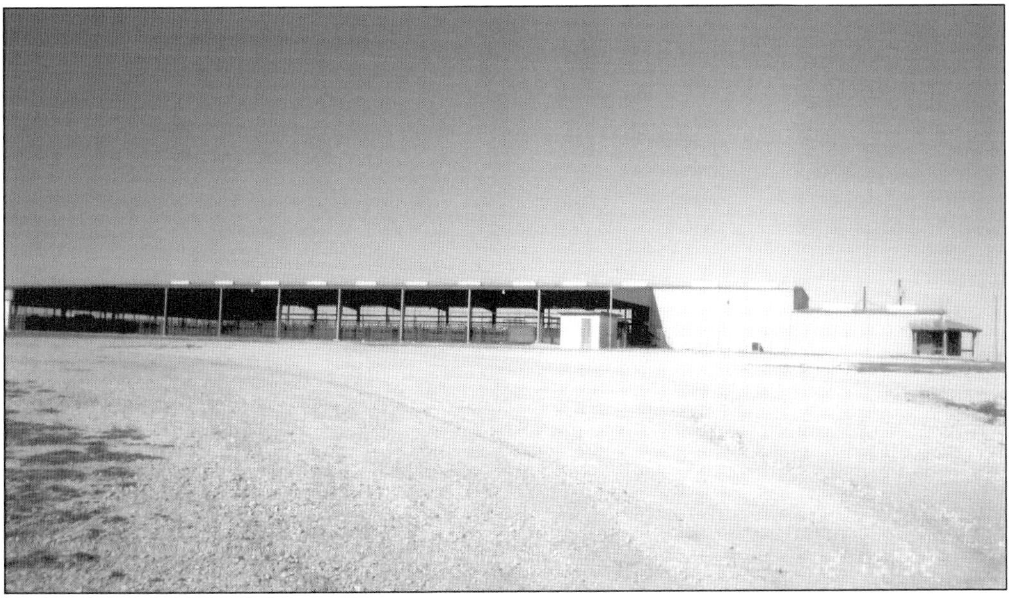

On a hill just northeast of town, Bud and Jeff Stockton built a state-of-the-art livestock auction barn. Just prior to its opening, the 1989 tornado hit and the building and pens had to be rebuilt. It opened in 1990 and remained open until 1996. The auction barn served ranchers from all over Central Texas with sales of cattle, goats, and sheep. Special auctions were held for registered cattle as well as exotic animals like emus, ostriches, and Boer goats. Many of the Jarrell Future Farmers of America boys worked there, gaining hands-on experience in working with livestock. The Auction Barn Restaurant was a popular place, operated by Patsy Goode. Buyers, sellers, and local businessmen made it a point to have lunch there on sale days. Below is the interior of the auction barn on sale day—always a mighty busy place. (Both courtesy Jeff and Kimberly Stockton.)

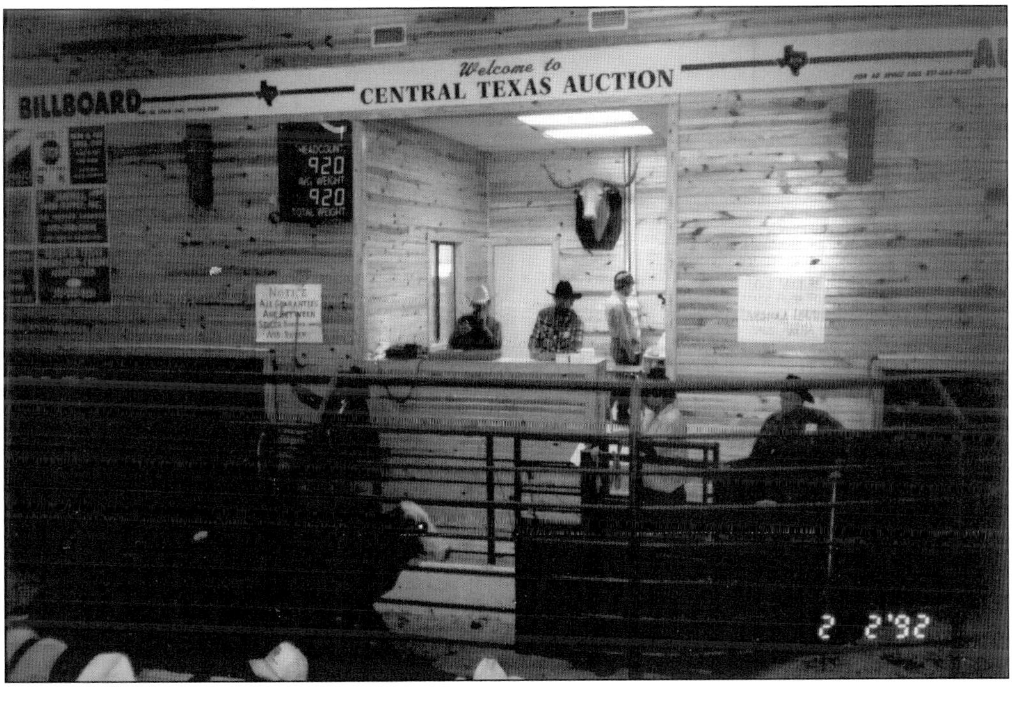

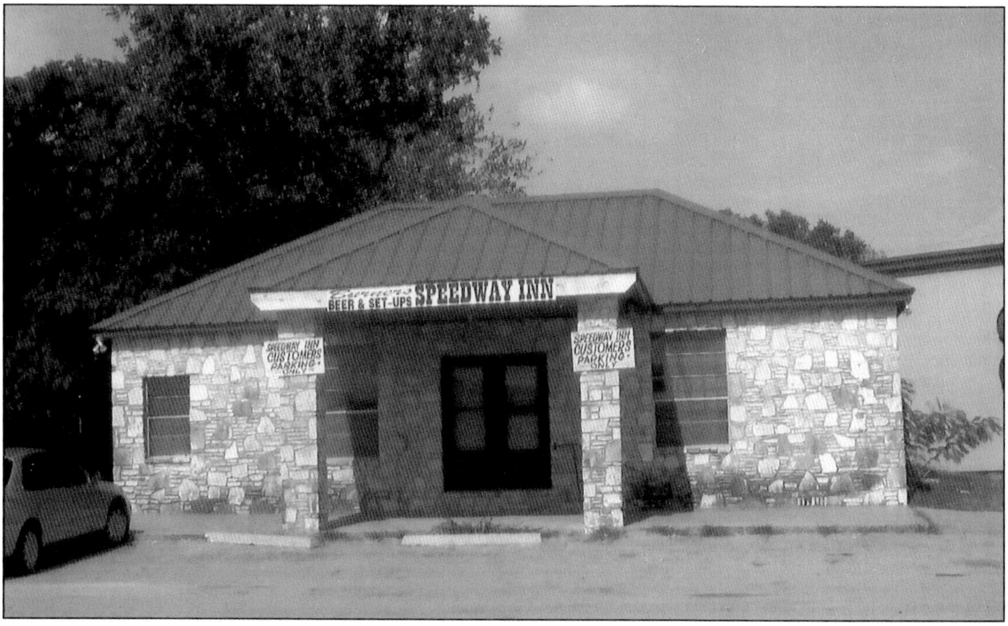

Speedway Inn has been a part of Jarrell for many years. Stories include one that the massive wooden bar originally came from Germany. There was a lot of copper on the bar, but that was sold during World War I because of the need for metal. Then there is the story that during the days when folks carried guns, a man got up on the bar and started dancing. Someone in the bar got annoyed and shot him. The end of the story is a bit vague, but so go the saloon stories in Jarrell.

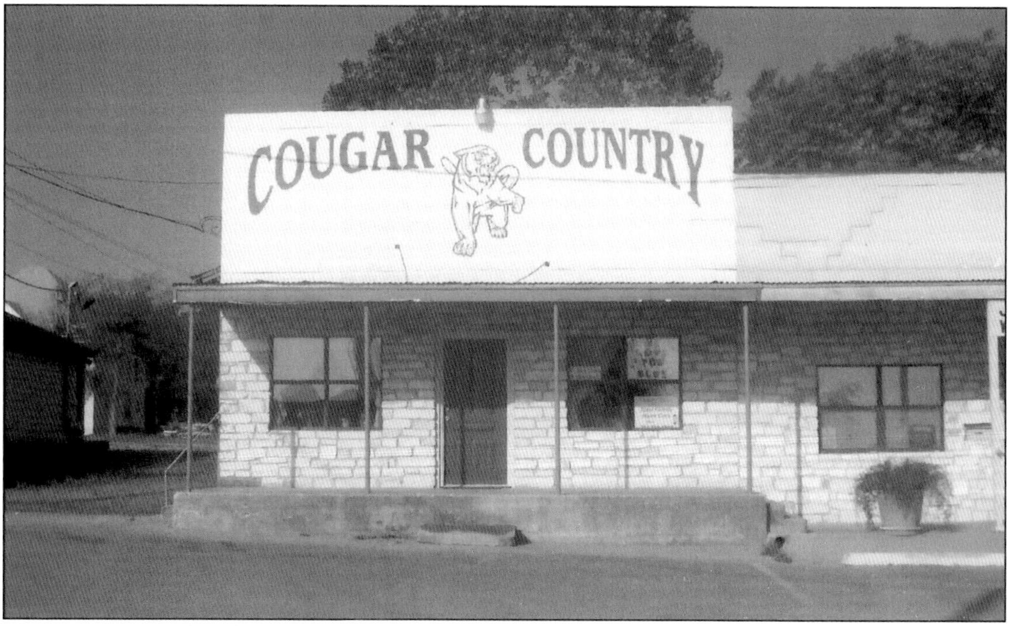

Ginger's Beauty Shop has been a mainstay of downtown for many years. Originally a Jarrell girl, Virginia Lloyd and her husband, Clay, moved back to Jarrell in 1972. Clay opened a garage on Avenue H, and Ginger opened her shop. This building has historical significance as it served as the first post office in Jarrell, although in another location. Ginger's shop is a hub of activity, with people coming and going. It is the best place in town to get the latest news.

Six

Historical Bits and Pieces

Every small town has its own flavor, its own personality, its own uniqueness. Jarrell, Texas, is no exception. It is a town made up of diverse people with diverse interests, a town that has seen its share of tragedy but also a town that knows how to celebrate. Jarrell has its special brand of skeletons in the closet, tall tales, quirky stories, and sometimes questionable verbal history passed down from generation to generation. In this chapter, the authors will try to communicate some of the uniqueness of this community. Stories that may be mostly true, or at least partly grounded in truth, are the things legends are made of. The story of the Salado Creek gold mine is just such a story. According to local lore, early Spanish explorers had stored gold and silver in the San Saba mine. At some point, the gold and silver was moved to a cave on Salado Creek that runs north and west of Jarrell. A picture of the mine entrance in 1933 is included, giving credence to the fact the mine really existed. The authenticity of the stories surrounding the mine will have to be left up to the reader. A chance encounter with Bonnie and Clyde by a young Jarrell citizen is another story related here. There are a few familiar faces, too. The stories of those faces are included as well, the faces of those who have for a long time called Jarrell home.

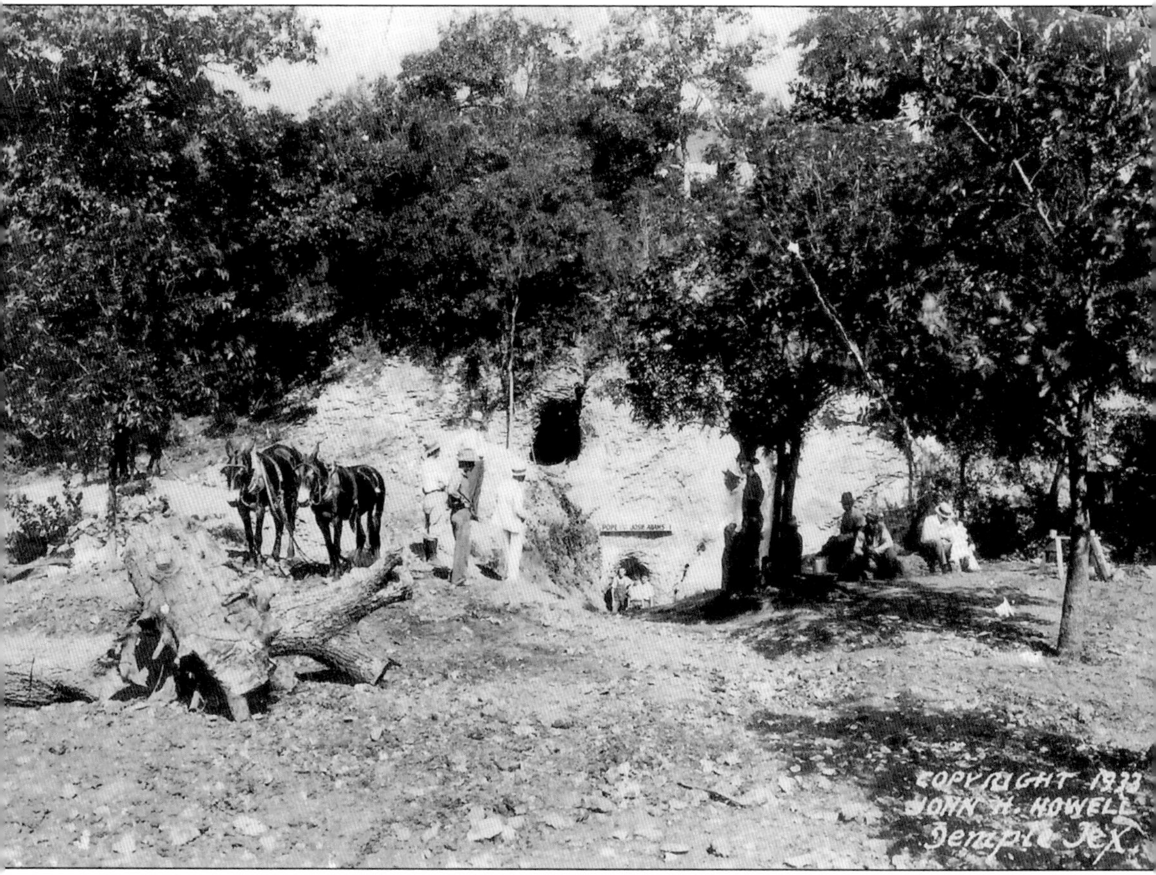

In 1935, a Native American named Hernandez appeared in Jarrell saying his grandfather had been one of the men who helped move the contents of the San Saba mine to a cave near Jarrell on Salado Creek. The treasure was reported to be in a 14-foot-square room, 500 jack loads of it. Named for the owner of the ranch where the cave was thought to be, it was called the Josie Adams No. 1. Stock was sold as far away as New York to raise money to fund the search. Work commenced, and the hunt went on for several months. Because of the springs surrounding Salado Creek, the workers could not keep water out of the cave. As time went on, frustration set in. Workers argued among themselves, and one evening it got out of hand. One man was killed and the others left in the dark of night. This picture shows the cave entrance with the names "Pope" and "Josie Adams 1" above the entrance. Glenn Pope and Glenn Pope Jr. of Temple were some of the promoters of the venture. (Courtesy Varena Blackman.)

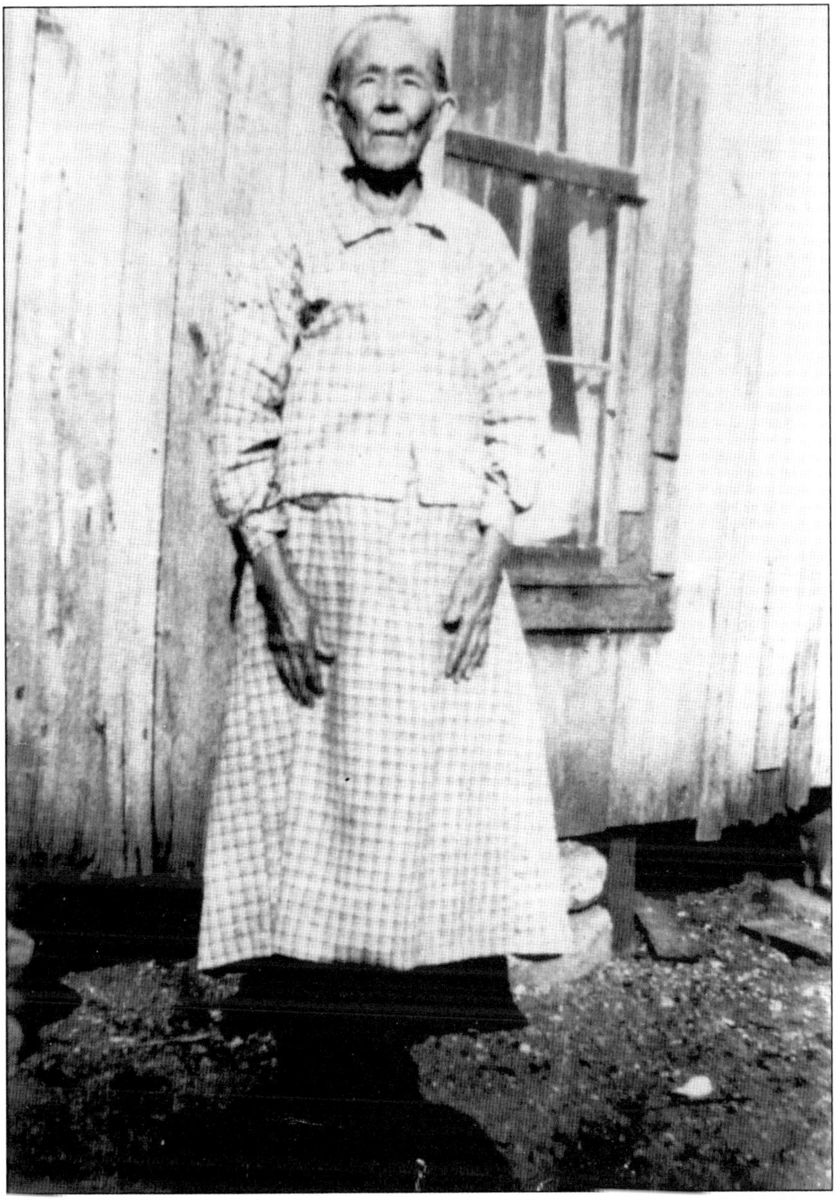

Pictured here is Josie Adams. It was on her land that the gold was supposedly hidden. In 1958, the "treasure hunt" resumed when a man named Guerra claimed he had befriended a Native American who told him about the treasure. After the Native American's death, Guerra found an opening in the creek bank, entered, and got lost. He claimed he spent 48 hours lost in the cave before finding an exit and that he had seen stacks of gold bars and coins along with a life-sized golden bull with ruby eyes. He tried to retrace his steps several times in the next few years but found the tunnels impassable because of cave-ins. Once again in 1965, an attempt to find the cave commenced, and once again nothing was located. Lots of hype surrounded the mine; it was even reported that a skeleton was found somewhere near Salado Creek, and it was assumed to be someone who had gotten lost in the tunnels. The skeleton was brought to town and hung on a wire stretched across Jarrell's main street. Was it all a hoax or does the gold exist? The mystery remains. (Courtesy Varena Blackman.)

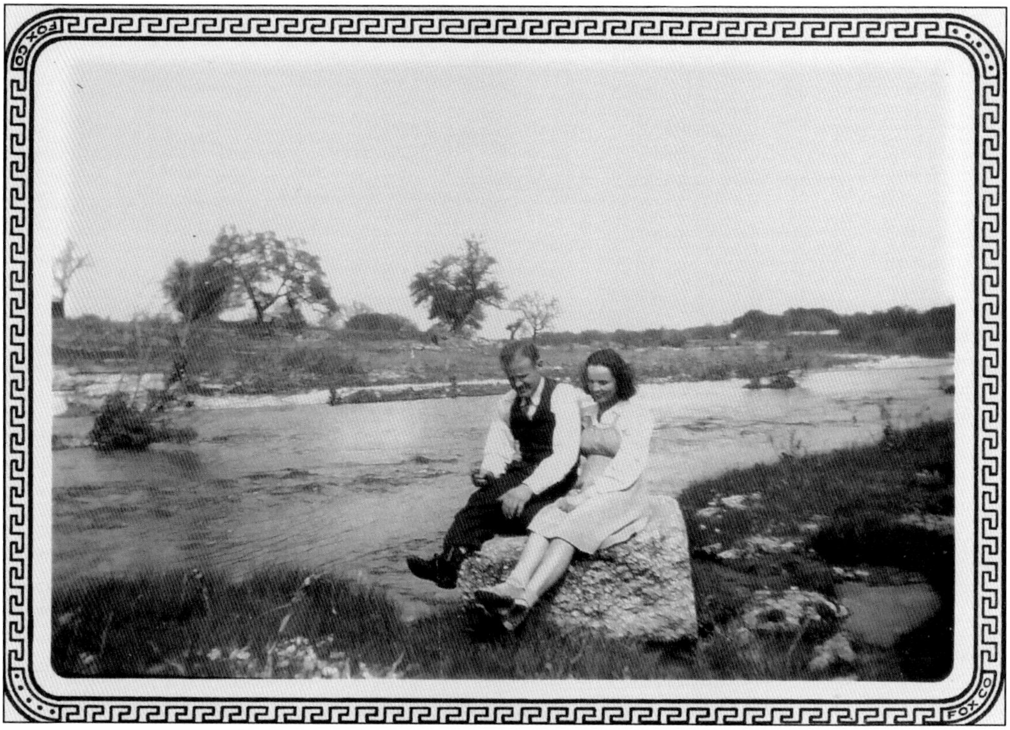

Release of Oil and Gas Lease

Standard Form 26—In stock Olds Press, Tulsa

Know All Men by These Presents:

That the undersigned Harold Reeves lessee in a certain oil and gas mining lease executed by S. J. Seward and wife, Lula E. Seward lessor s and the undersigned lessee dated May 6 1950 does by these presents cancel, release relinquish and surrender unto S.J. Seward and wife, Lula E. Seward all right, title and interest of the said undersigned Harold Reeves in and to said lease covering the following described premises, to-wit:

All that certain tract or parcel of land lying and being situated in Williamson County, Texas, being out of and a part of the James I. Bunker survey, and described as follows:
Beginning N 71 E 90 vrs from the S E corner of the James Roebuck survey; Thence N 19 W 801 vrs a stone mound; Thence S 71 W 90 vrs a stake; Thence S 19 E 1 vr; Thence S 71 W 352.8 vrs to a stake for corner; Thence S 19 E 800 vrs to the south line of the J. Roebuck survey; Thence N 71 E 442.8 vrs to the place of beginning, containing 62.8 acres of land, less, however 1 acre of land conveyed to Otto Bartz by deed dated Jan. 4, 1912, recorded in Book 145, Page 275, also 1 acre of land more or less out of the same conveyed to Bart Zurovetz by deed recorded in Book 145, Page 276 Deed Records of Williamson County, Texas, leaving 60.8 acres of land, more or less. Being the land now owned by S. J. Seward

Section Township Range and containing 60.8 acres, situated in the County of Williamson and State of Texas said lease being recorded in the office of the Register of Deeds in and for said County, in Book 366 of on page 14.

In Witness Whereof, I have hereunto set my hand this 27th. day of September 1951.

Witness:

Harold Reeves [SEAL]

[SEAL]

This picture was taken in front of the infamous gold mine on Salado Creek. It shows the opposite side of the creek from the entrance. Floy and Cap Johnson are in the photograph. The photograph was taken in the early 1940s shortly after the operation of the mine was shut down.

There were dreams of other treasure in Jarrell when certain properties were leased to drill for oil. This lease is signed by S. J. and Lula Seward in 1952. From researched records, there were several attempts to find oil. Minimum amounts were discovered but not enough to make the wells profitable.

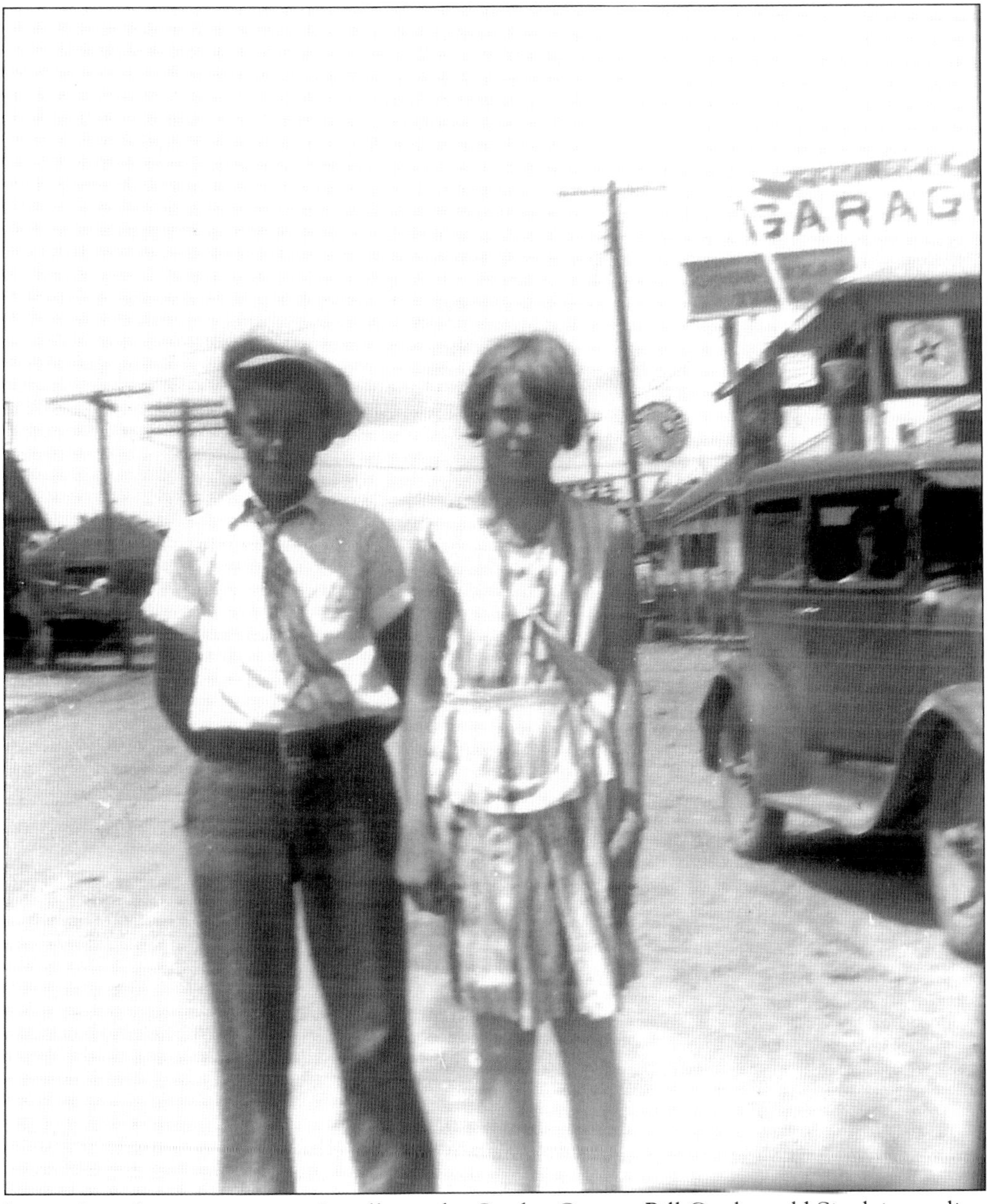

Located on the main street in Jarrell was the Conlee Garage. Bill Conlee sold Sinclair gasoline and Goodyear tires and worked on cars. Directly west of the garage was the Miles Café. One day, Jesse Goode and his six-year-old son Pat were standing outside the garage when a Model A pulled up with a man and a woman inside the car. The man asked Pat if he would run into the café and get them two hamburgers. He promised Pat a nickel for doing this. Of course, Pat agreed and delivered the hamburgers to the window of the car. It was then he noticed the guns lying across their laps. Pat grabbed his nickel and ran. He had just encountered the notorious Clyde Barrow and Bonnie Parker. Folks reported that Bonnie and Clyde came through town quite often, and it was feared they planned to rob the First State Bank. It never happened, but each time they visited Jarrell, it caused quite a stir. Pictured on the right is Claudia Harrison and an unidentified friend with the Conlee Garage in the background.

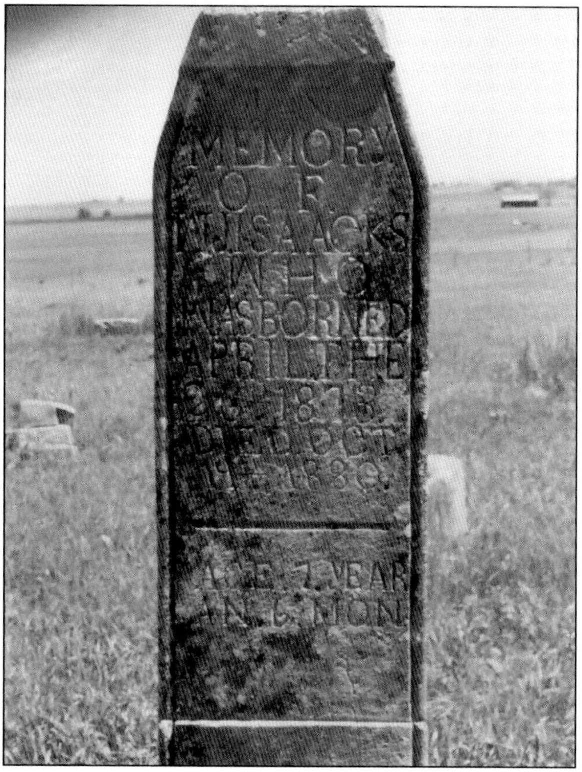

Land Cemetery is the resting place for generations of Jarrell residents. It is located on property donated by Nicholas Land, whose family is buried there. When a family going west in a covered wagon was near Jarrell, their young son died. The boy's father asked if he could bury his son and even stayed long enough to carve a headstone for him. The stone reads, "In Memory of W. J. Isaacks Who Was Borned April the 26th, 1873, Died Oct. 19th 1880, Age 7 Year and 6 Mon." (Courtesy Esther Rosie Conlee Holloway.)

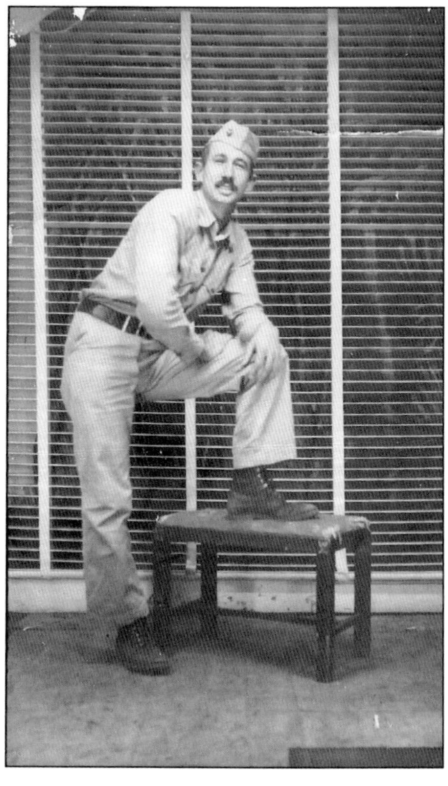

Pictured here is Dewey Blackman in his Marine Corps uniform. This photograph was taken in 1945 just after the Battle of Iwo Jima. Jarrell has had a large population of veterans. Soldiers from all wars in this nation's history, as far back as the Civil War, are buried in the Jarrell cemeteries. (Courtesy Varena Blackman.)

The Conlee family resided in Corn Hill and then in Jarrell for many years. W. A. Conlee and his family are listed in the census of Corn Hill in 1880. Descendants live in Jarrell today. This is a picture of Susan Carolina White, second wife of W. A. Conlee. Shown at her residence on the north side of Avenue A, Susan Conlee is coming to the house from her vegetable garden, shown in the background. (Courtesy Esther Rosie Conlee Holloway.)

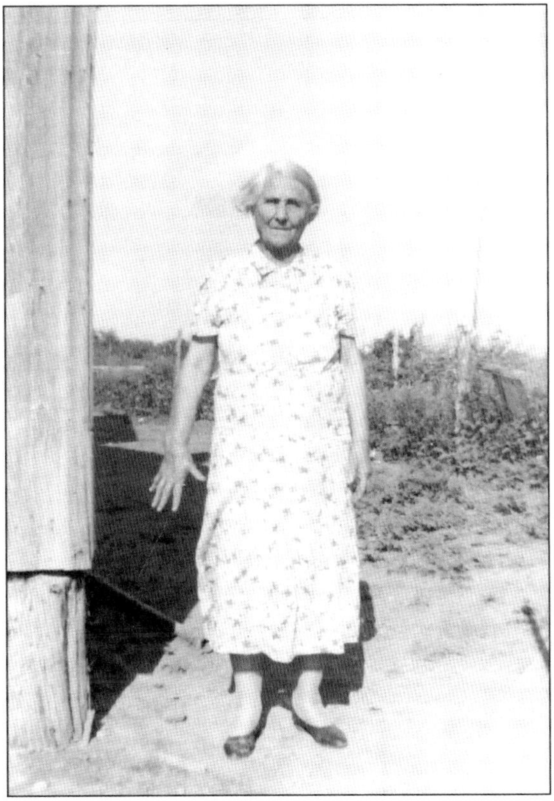

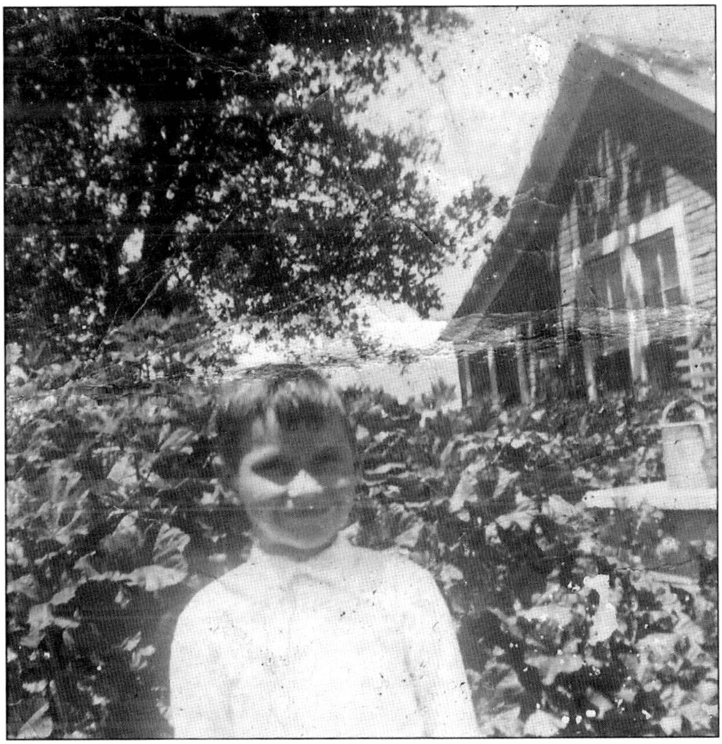

Robert Tschoerner has been a resident of Jarrell his entire life. Like many others in Jarrell, his parents were both born in Jarrell as well. This photograph is of him as a boy in 1966 celebrating his First Communion. (Courtesy Esther Tschoerner.)

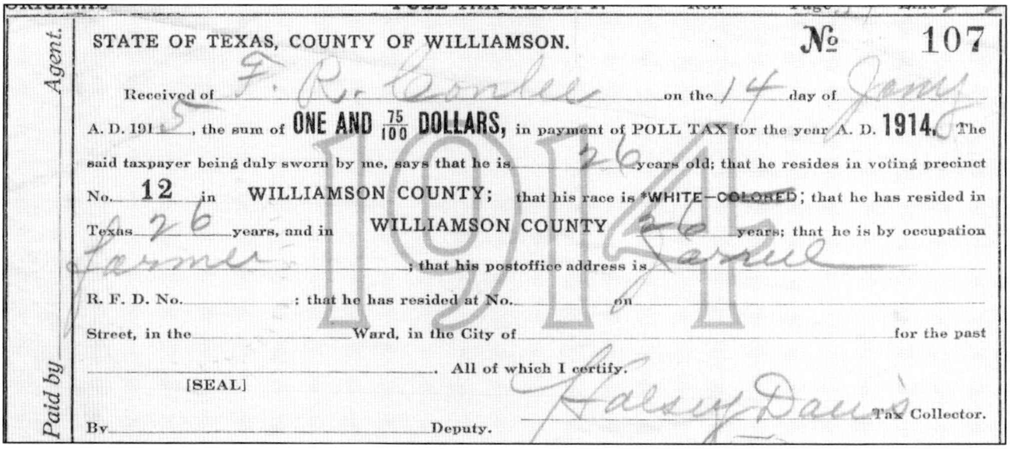
STATE OF TEXAS, COUNTY OF WILLIAMSON. № 107

Received of F. R. Conlee on the 14 day of Jany

A. D. 1915, the sum of ONE AND 75/100 DOLLARS, in payment of POLL TAX for the year A. D. 1914. The said taxpayer being duly sworn by me, says that he is 26 years old; that he resides in voting precinct No. 12 in WILLIAMSON COUNTY; that his race is *WHITE—COLORED; that he has resided in Texas 26 years, and in WILLIAMSON COUNTY 26 years; that he is by occupation farmer; that his postoffice address is Jarrell

R. F. D. No. ; that he has resided at No. on Street, in the Ward, in the City of for the past . All of which I certify.

[SEAL]

Halsey Davis Tax Collector.

By Deputy.

Agent.

Paid by

A poll tax was levied on every adult in the community. It had the effect of disenfranchising many blacks and poor whites because payment of the tax was a prerequisite for voting. This poll tax receipt for F. R. Conlee was issued in Williamson County, Texas, in 1914. It documents that he was 26 years old and had lived all his life in Texas. He listed his vocation as a farmer and his post office as Jarrell. (Courtesy Esther Rosie Conlee Holloway.)

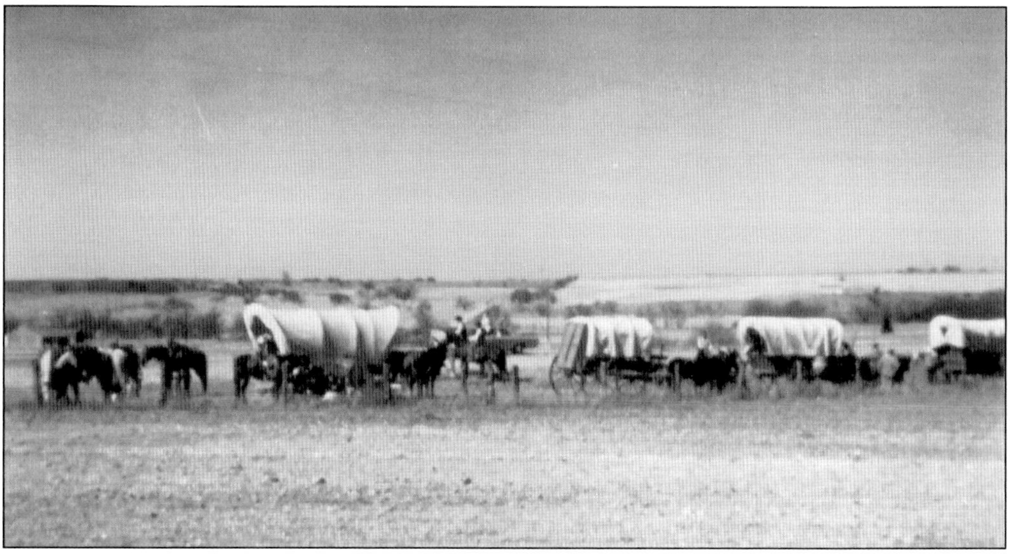

The bicentennial celebration of America in 1976 brought a wagon train through Jarrell, following the Chisholm Trail. As the wagons came through the area, everyone stopped what they were doing and watched. Shown here are a covered wagon and chuck wagon on I-35 just outside town. Wagons like these followed the same trail many years prior to Jarrell becoming a town. (Courtesy Kelly and Earline Reichenbach.)

Seven

Ill Winds Blow in Jarrell

It seems high winds and twisters are a big part of Jarrell's history. Old-timers remember many occasions when the "wind got up" enough to blow over sheds, outbuildings, and things that were not tied down. One of the earliest tornadoes remembered is in 1926, when the Jarrell Methodist Church was destroyed. Frugal folks saved the lumber and used it to build the current sanctuary. The second remembered tornado was in 1955, when there was significant structural damage to buildings but luckily no injuries. On May 17, 1989, things turned deadly when an F-3 tornado struck the north and east side of Jarrell in the early morning hours. Twenty-eight people were injured, and there was one fatality. Thirty-five homes and 12 mobile homes were destroyed or severely damaged. Property loss was estimated somewhere near $5 million. The worst was yet to come. On May 27, 1997, a rare F-5 tornado completely wiped out the Double Creek Estates area west of town. Twenty-seven people were killed, including two entire families. Thirty permanent homes, eight mobile homes, and three businesses were completely destroyed or, perhaps a better word, evaporated. Damage was estimated to be over $40 million. This chapter presents those events, not as a quest for sensationalism but rather as a chronicle of, and a testimony to, the strength of the people of Jarrell. Everyone has his or her own story. Those here are just a small sampling. All will agree the tornadoes in no way define this community. As formidable as the storms have been, the people of Jarrell, along with sadness and a deep sense of devastation and personal loss, have managed to overcome and move on.

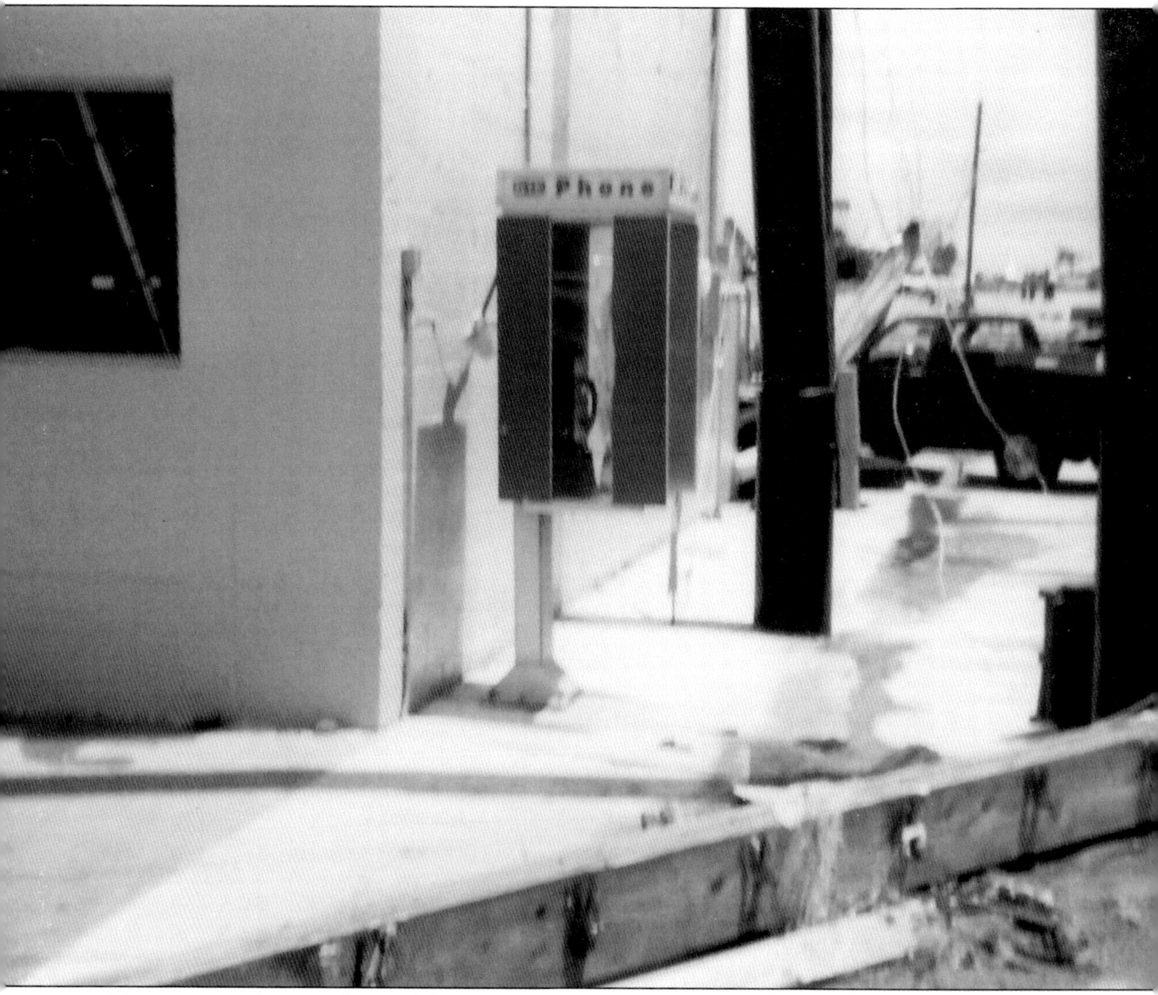

Chris King is the son of one of the authors of this book. Early in the morning of May 17, 1989, he was standing at this phone booth between Bill's Exxon and Doc's One Stop. He had just gotten off work and was on his way home. While he was talking on the telephone, an F-3 tornado with winds of 200 miles per hour hit Jarrell. It was dark, and he had not been aware of bad weather approaching. His car was blown across the parking lot, just a few feet away from him. As he held on to the telephone booth, his feet were lifted into the air behind him. He recalls that the noise was so loud he could hardly stand it and the pressure hurt his ears. A few seconds later, all was quiet. Crisscrossed all around him were huge steel I-beams from Bill's Exxon and large timbers and debris from Doc's One Stop next door. When dawn came, the true realization of what had happened began to sink in.

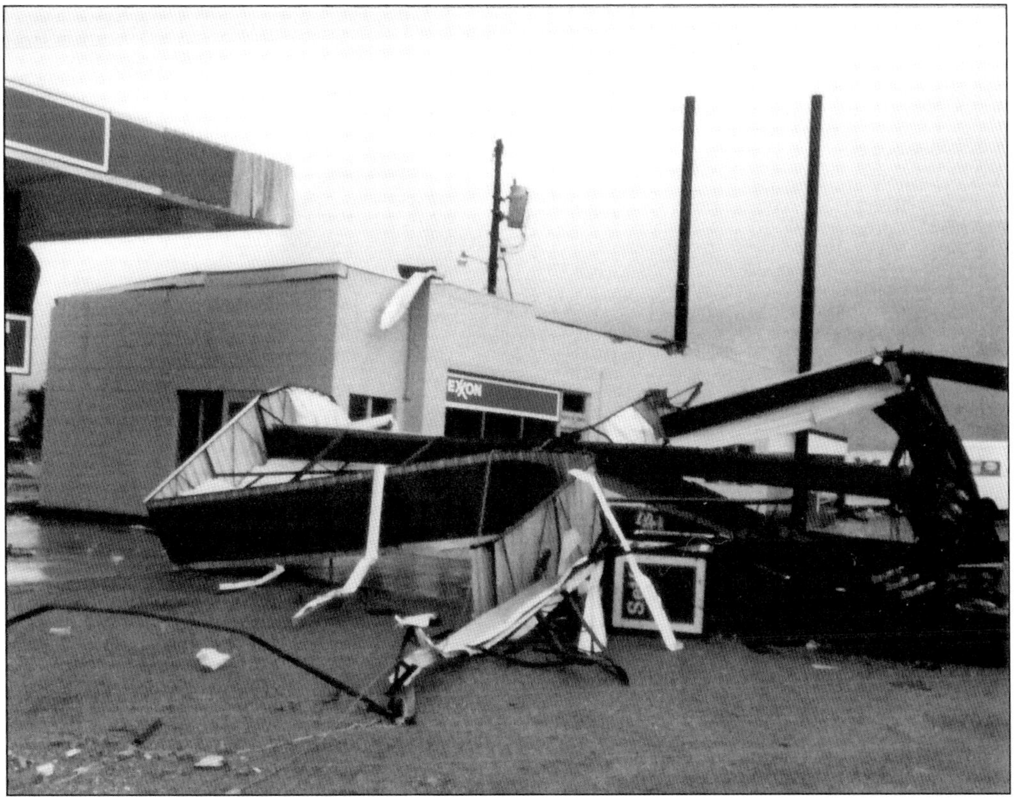

Pictured is Bill's Exxon, owned by the Bill Klepac family. This station suffered extensive damage during the 1989 Jarrell tornado. It was directly in the swath cut by the storm, which took out homes and businesses on the east and south side of the town.

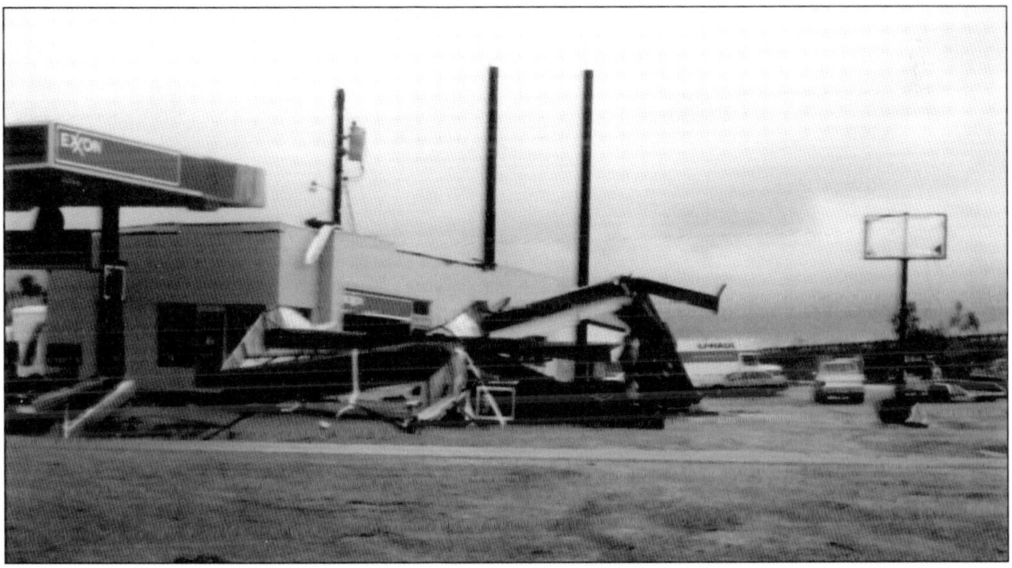

This is a second look at the damage sustained by Bill's Exxon, located on the corner that sustained a direct hit from the storm. The side of this service station is the location of the phone booth mentioned on the previous page.

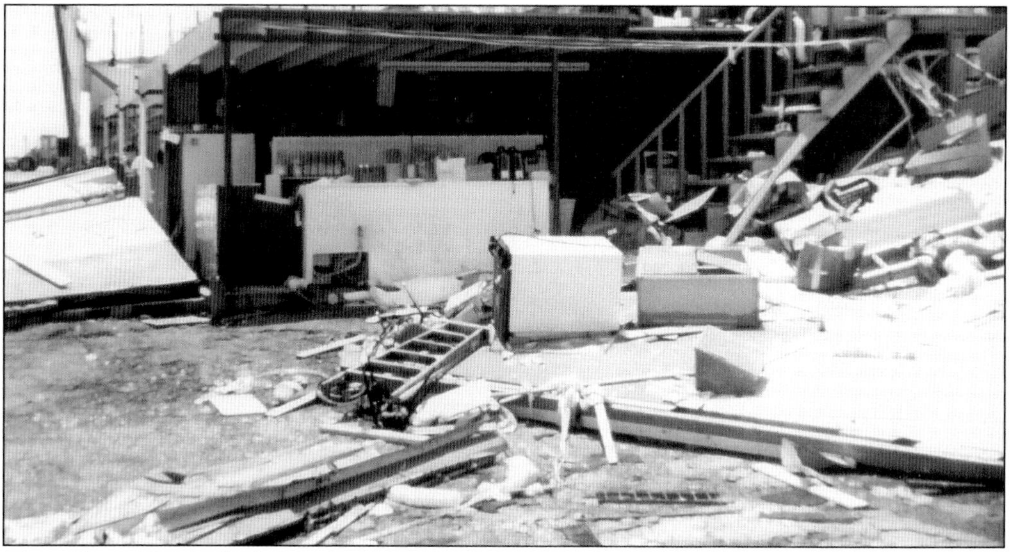

The sights and sounds that early morning in May 1989 were eerie to say the least. Power lines were down, and flashes of electricity could be seen and heard everywhere. The hiss of propane gas leaking into the air lent an alien sound and odor as well. The most haunting sound was that of citizens of Jarrell who had been awakened from their sleep. They began checking the neighborhoods with flashlights, calling to people in their homes to see if they were okay. One of the most dramatic scenes in the aftermath of the storm was Doc's One Stop, a local truck stop and restaurant. Originally a two-story building, it was reduced to rubble. Here are two pictures of the damage to this Jarrell business.

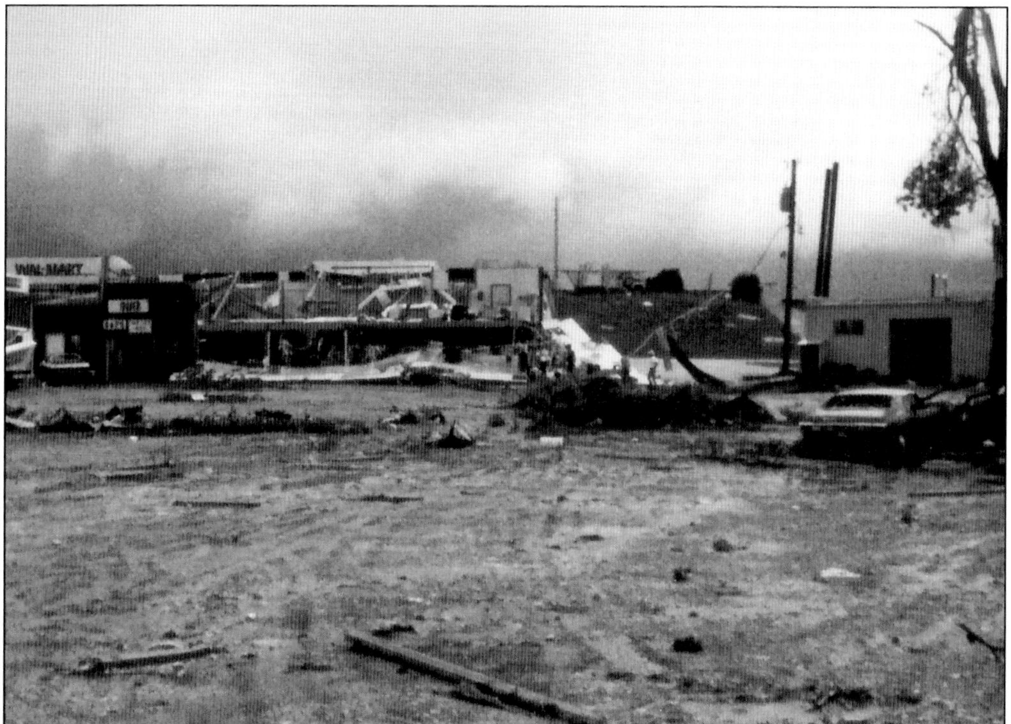

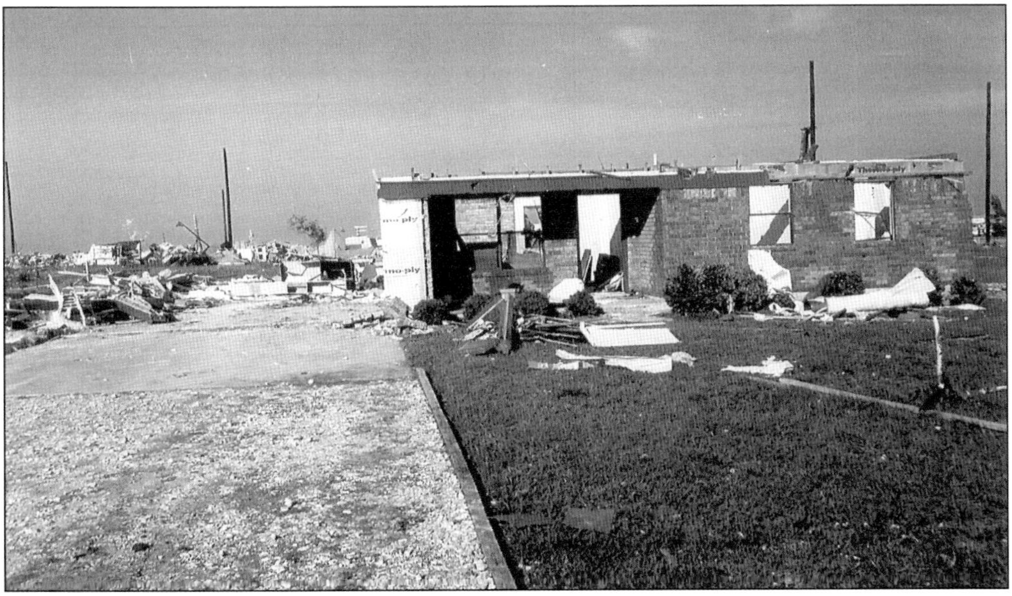

Destruction was rampant. A large swath of homes on the east side of Jarrell had been nearly leveled. With no warning, roofs were blown off, windows were blown out, and walls caved in, all while people slept. These pictures show the damage to Kelly and Earline Reichenbach's home. Notice all the debris in a line behind their home in the above image. The Reichenbachs had a son named Kyle who had just celebrated his first birthday. Early on the morning of the tornado, Earline said she just had a feeling something was going to happen. When the house started creaking, she called for her husband. They got Kyle and went into the hallway. They threw themselves over their baby. As the wind intensity increased, they could feel it pulling Kyle up. They literally held on to his legs with the tornado attempting to suck him up into the air. After the storm passed, he was judged to be unhurt, but with the light of morning, it was discovered that, along with the roof, the mattress of his baby bed was completely gone. (Both courtesy Kelly and Earline Reichenbach.)

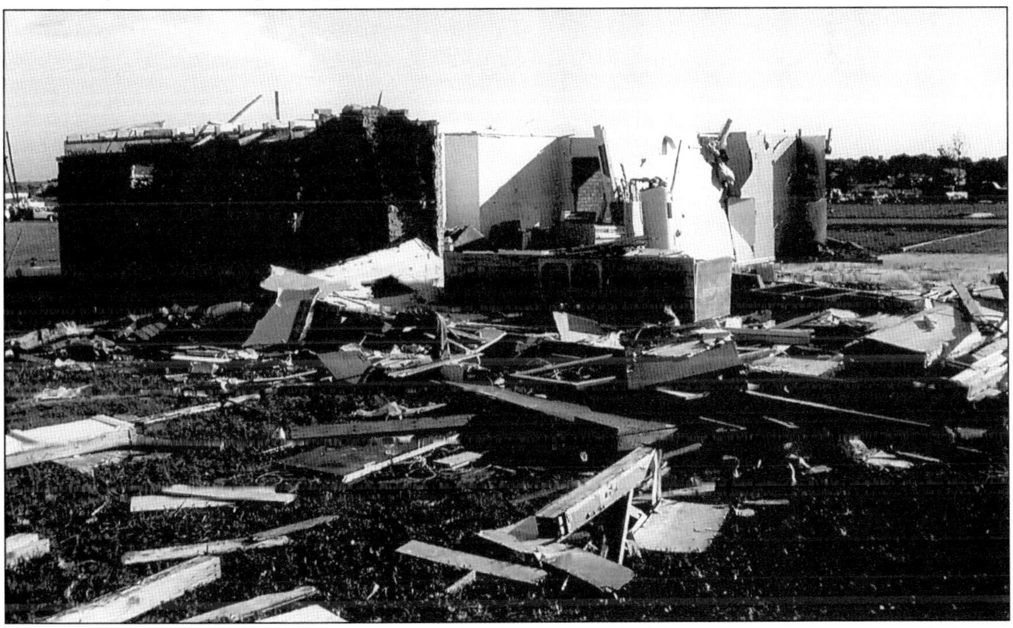

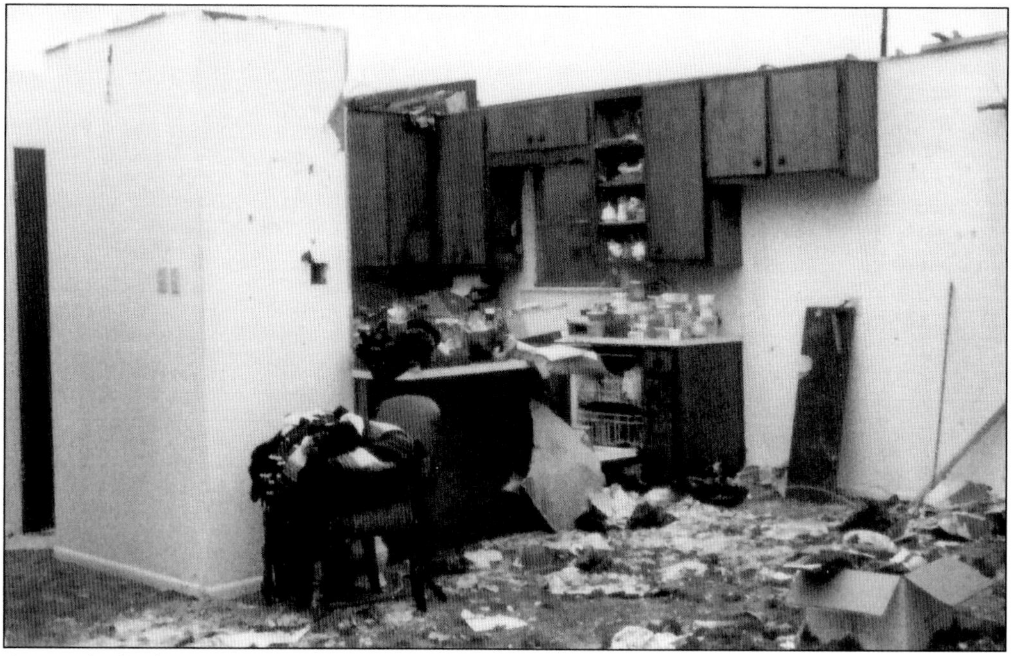

Across the highway was F. G. and Martha Mihlberger's home. This picture shows the extensive damage to the kitchen area. Note that the roof is totally gone. As the tornado hit when it was still dark, there was no preparing for it. People were taken by surprise and were totally unprepared. With the power interrupted, they were left in total darkness and had to wait for daylight to assess the damage.

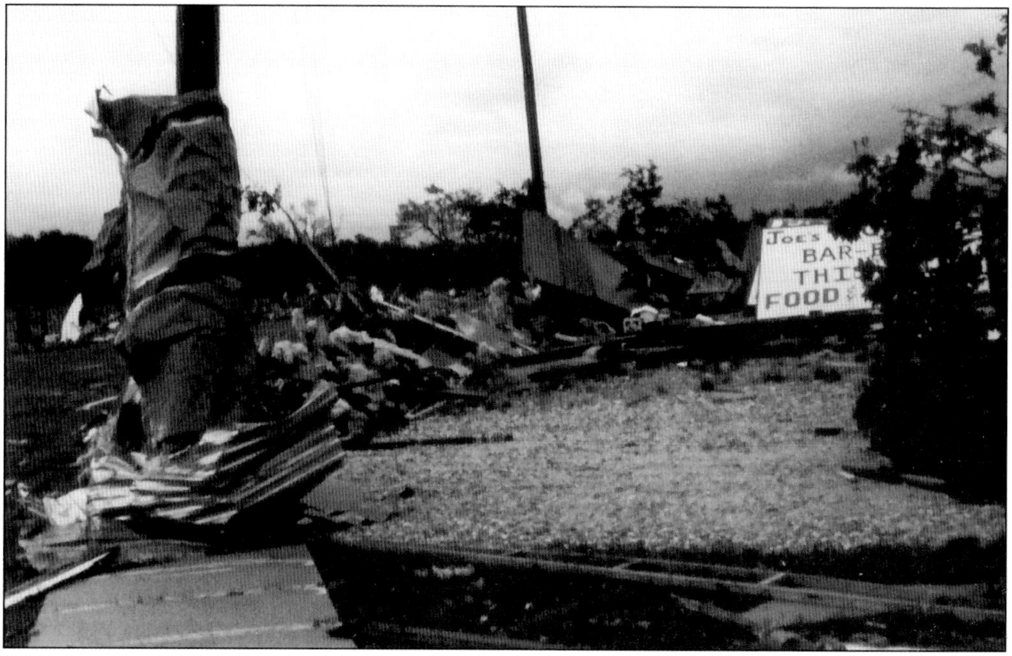

Just a short distance away was Joe's Bar-B-Q, owned by Joe Hoes. His home and business were completely destroyed. Personal items were strewn all over the ground, and the building was hardly recognizable. Joe and Louise were okay but had to totally rebuild their home and their lives.

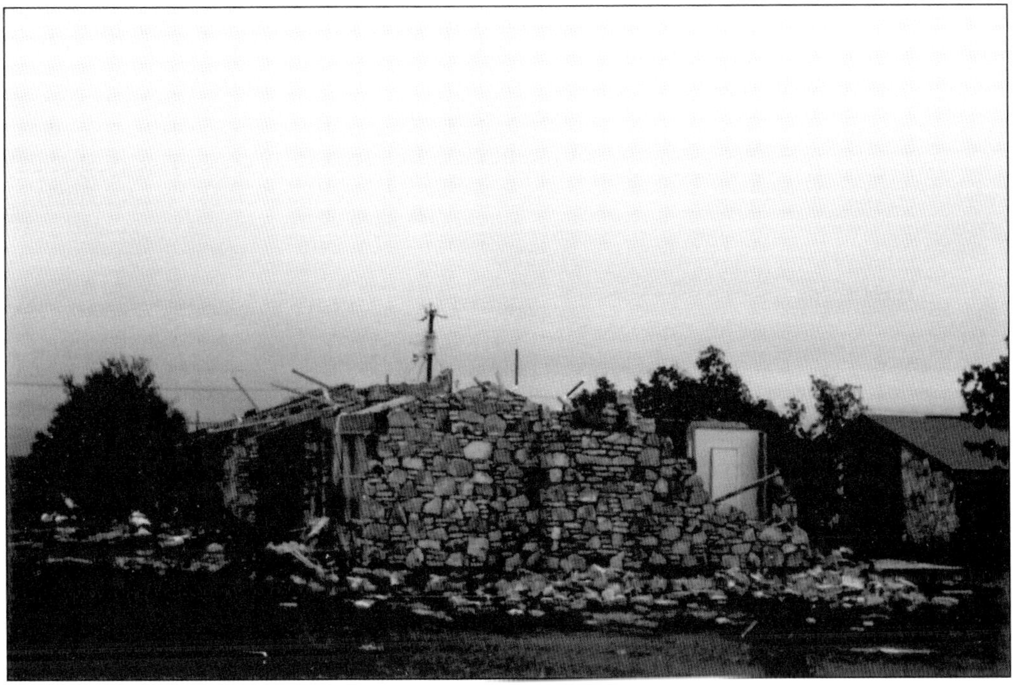

In the one apartment complex in Jarrell, Rock Terrace, people were planning on getting up in a couple of hours. This is what the apartments looked like when the sun came up and there was enough light to see the destruction. There were injuries here but no fatalities.

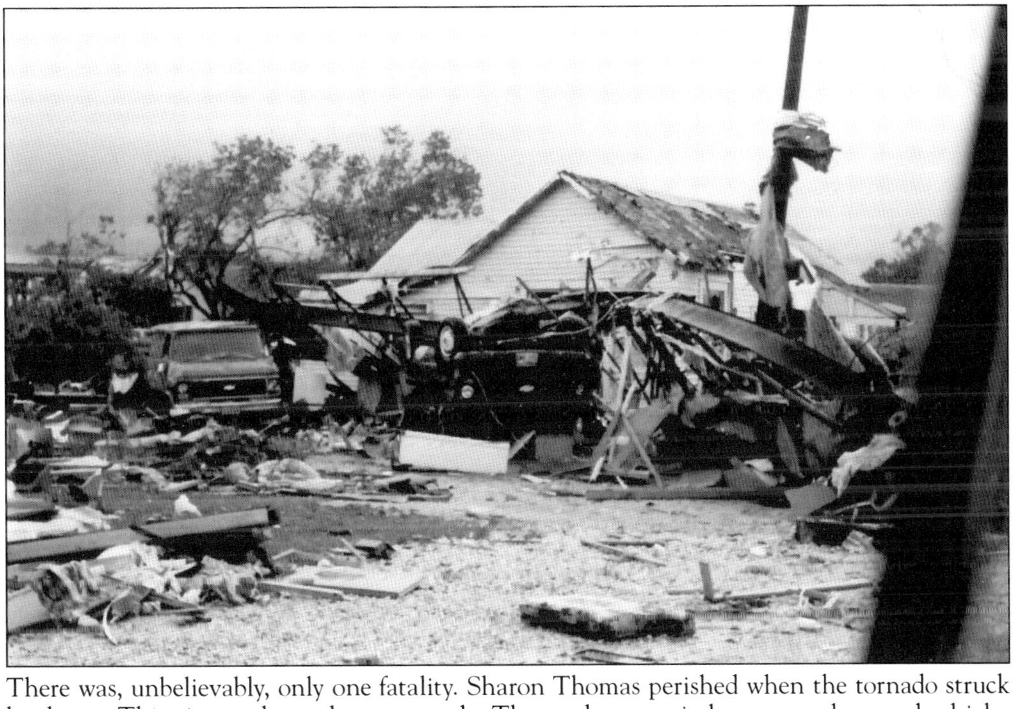

There was, unbelievably, only one fatality. Sharon Thomas perished when the tornado struck her home. This picture shows the scene at the Thomas home—timbers everywhere and vehicles tossed like toys.

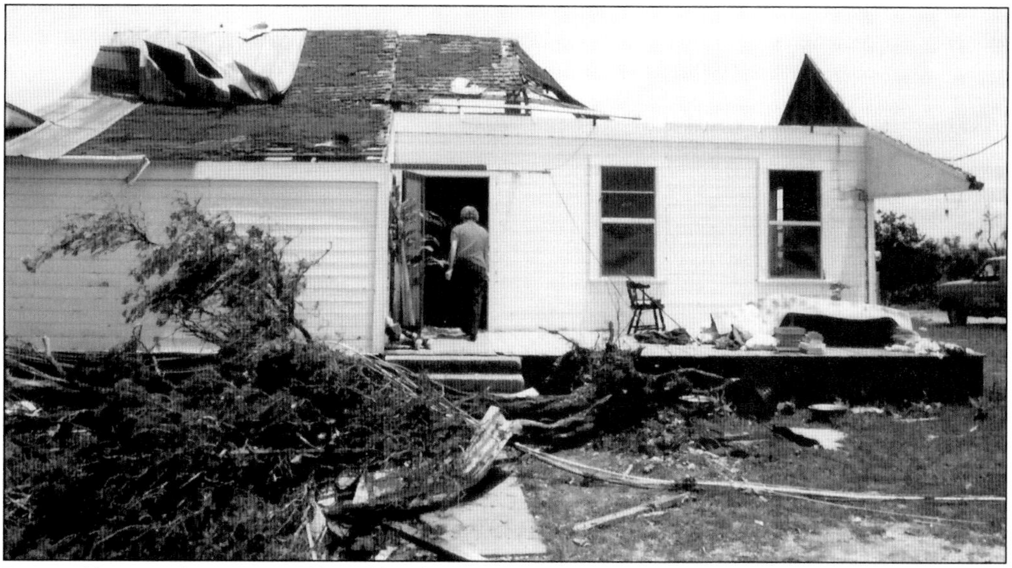

Pictured here is a home owned by Bill and Dorothy Klepac. This is the home rented by Chris King and some of his friends and was his destination when he stopped to use the phone as mentioned earlier. Damage to the home was extensive. Trees were blown down and much of the roof taken off. Chris's grandmother, Alice Schneider, is shown in the picture.

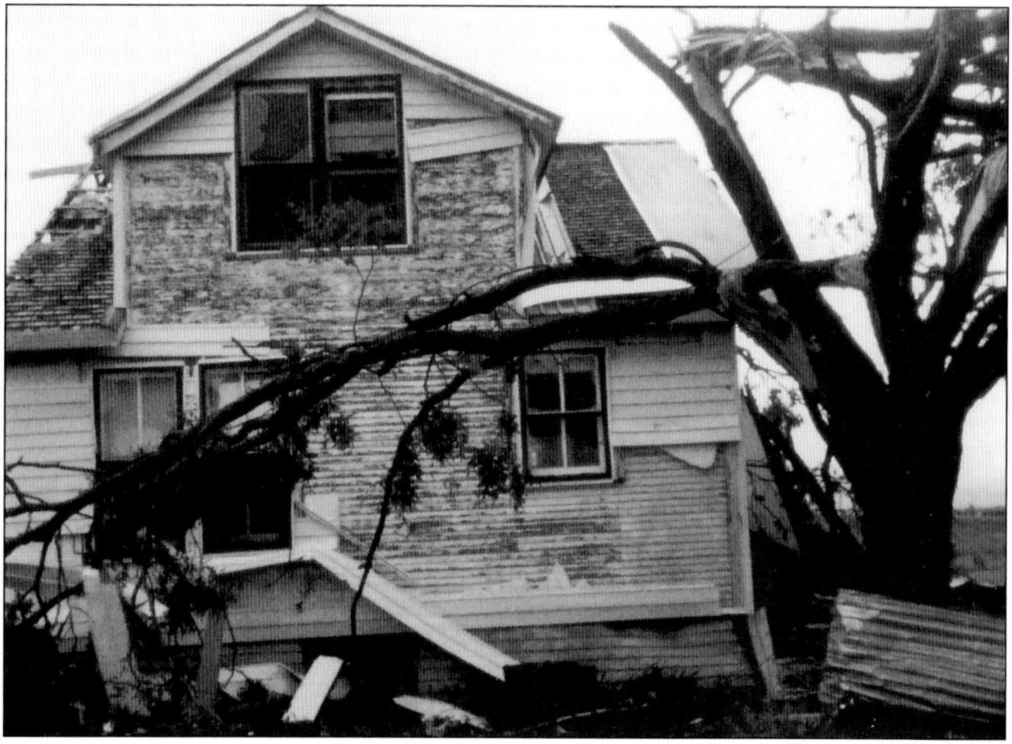

The scene at the Jerry Sladecek home was dismal. The home had been there for many years and was solidly built, but it was so badly damaged it had to be dismantled. Mr. Sladecek had files in his home with cancelled checks he had written. Pieces of these checks were found as far north as Temple, Texas, some 30 miles away.

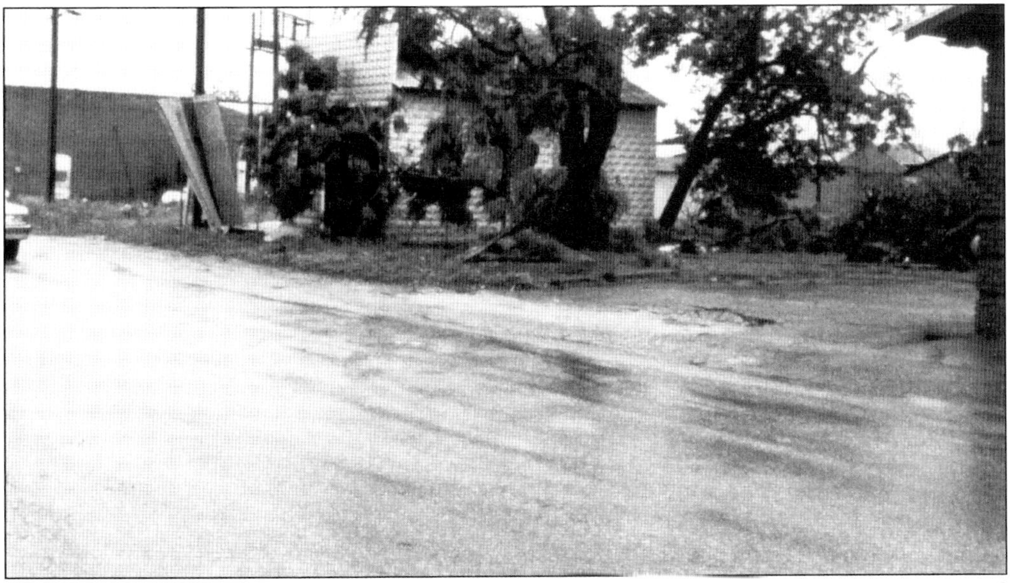

Huge trees were uprooted by the storm. Pictured is the old barbershop, which sustained minimal damage. This building is featured in an earlier chapter. It has seen a lot and still survives. As the old saying goes, "If walls could talk."

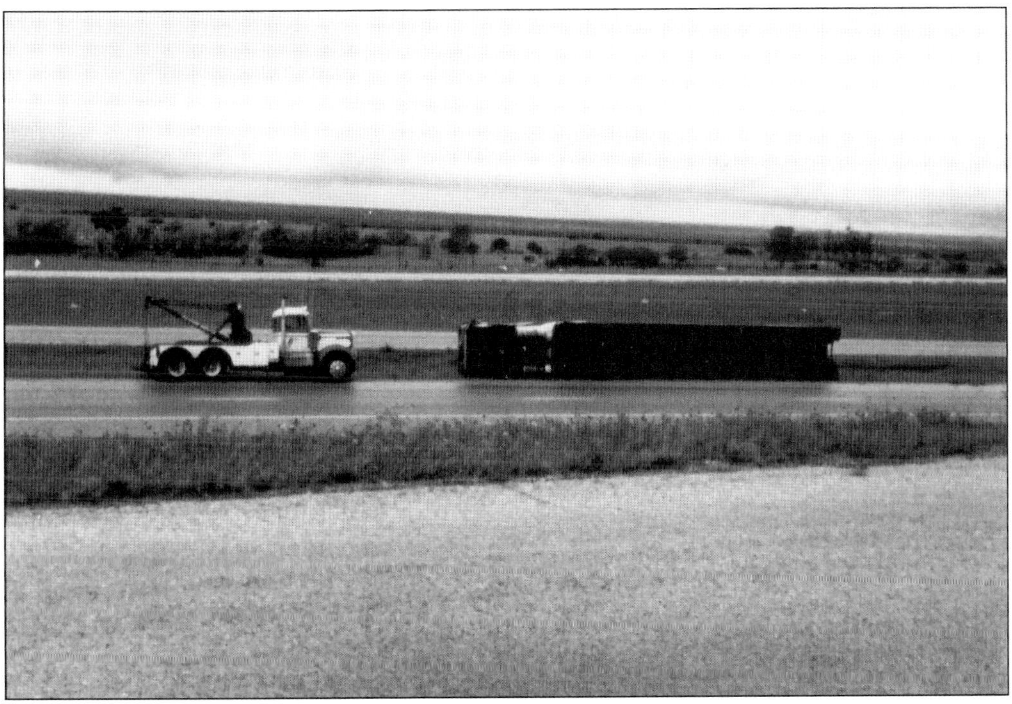

Traffic on Interstate Highway 35 ground to a halt as 12 tractor trailer rigs were overturned by the F-3 tornado. Trucks were strewn along the highway like matchsticks. Drivers of the rigs reported that the wind was so strong it literally picked up the trucks and turned them over. Again, miraculously, no one was seriously injured.

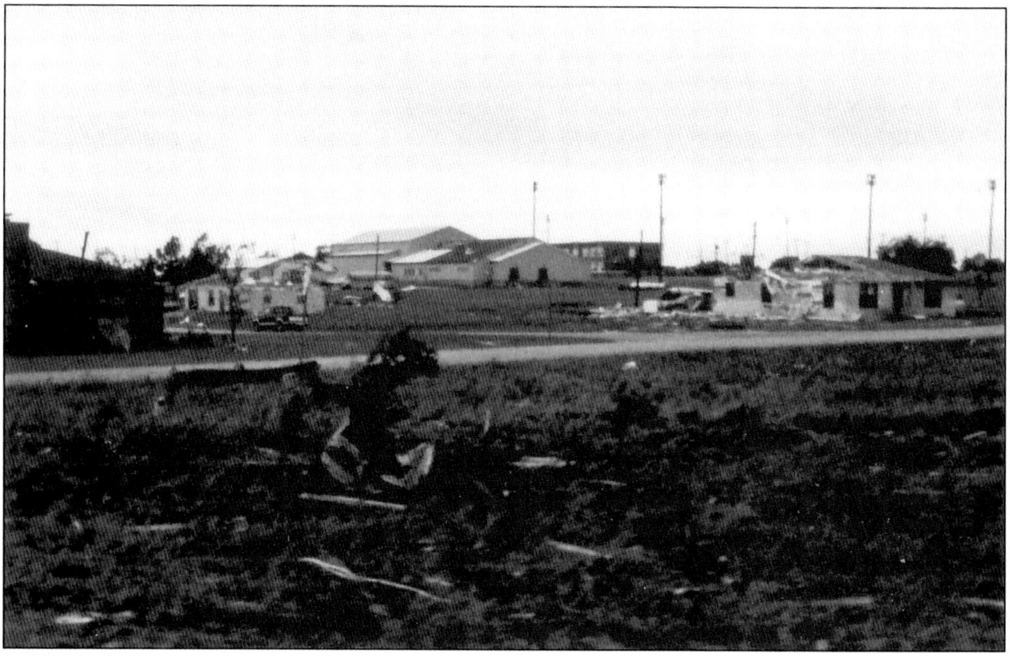

Looking north from I-35 is the Jarrell School campus, seen above. There was some damage, but most of the wreckage was to the nearby neighborhoods. The community of Jarrell came together quickly to meet people's needs. There was no electricity, but the American Legion offered its gas stoves so food could be cooked for anyone who was hungry. The First Baptist Church opened its doors as a shelter along with the Catholic Cursillos de Cristiandad Center, which provided cots and mattresses for those who had no place to sleep. Below is Fifth Street in town the morning of the storm. Volunteers are already beginning to roll up their sleeves and clean up the mess.

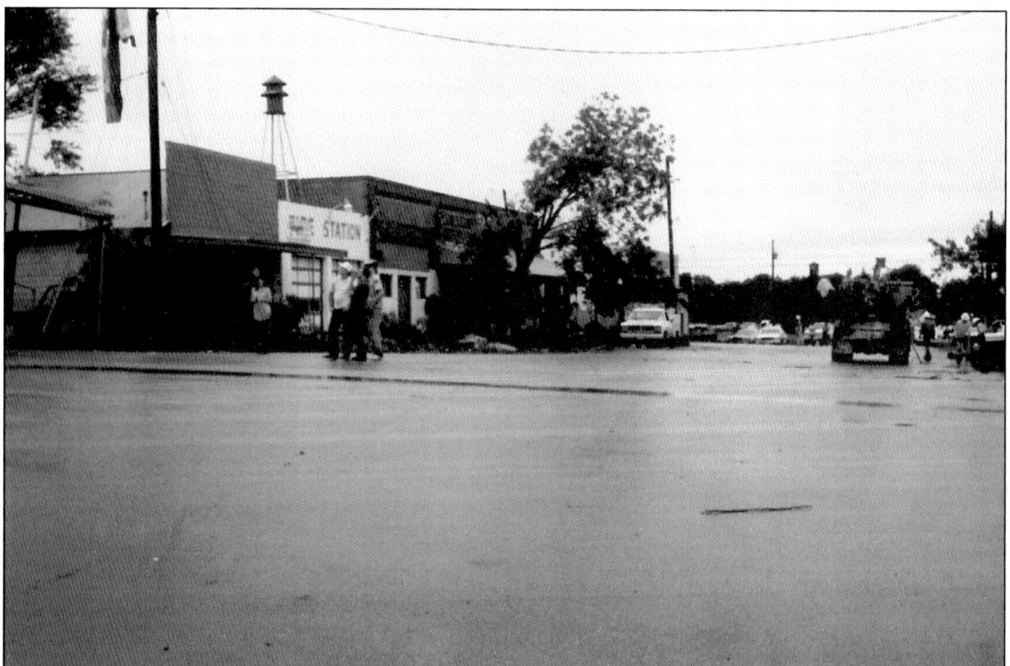

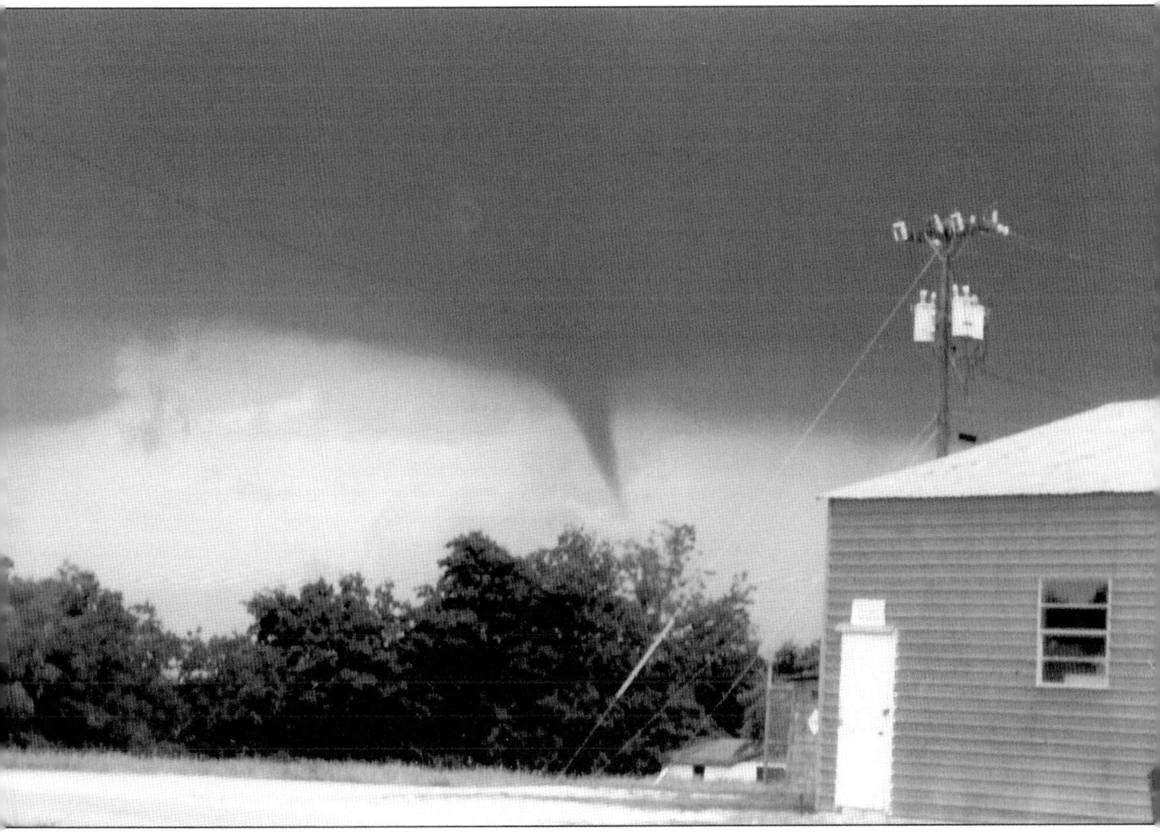

On May 27, 1997, Jarrell, Texas, was just settling in for summer vacation. School had just let out a couple of days before. Charlotte Vancil, one of Jarrell's veteran teachers, was paying close attention to the weather. The forecast had included thunderstorms with locally heavy rainfall and possibly strong winds. Tornadoes had been spotted in McLennan and Bell Counties some 60 miles to the north of Jarrell. Tornadoes traditionally move from southwest to northeast, but not this time. These storms continued to skip down I-35 into Williamson County with Jarrell directly in their path. Charlotte grabbed her camera and shot this picture (and the two on page 100) from her home on First Street. She is looking to the north across the vacant lot that sat at the corner of Avenue G. The Jarrell Schwertner Water Department building is shown at right. (Courtesy Charlotte Vancil.)

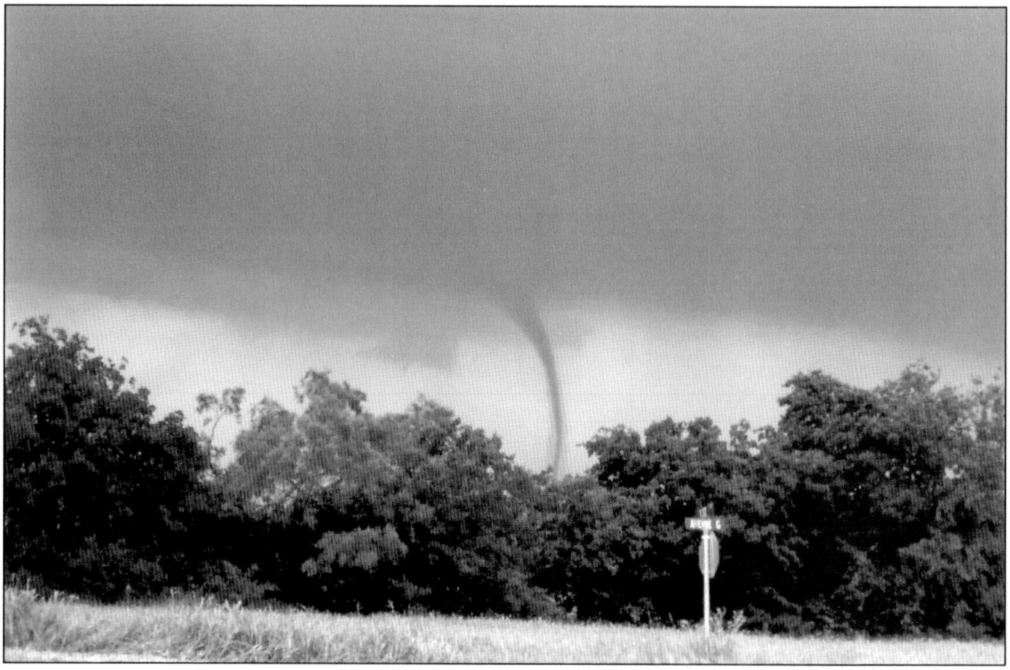

More than one tornado hit Jarrell the afternoon of May 27. The above photograph shows the pencil-like vortex of the first approaching storm. Shown below is the F-5 tornado that followed two smaller funnels. Seen from the same vantage point on First Street as on page 99, the tornado is moving from the right to the left of the picture with the Double Creek subdivision its target. No one had any idea the strength or voracity of this tornado as it marched across the Jarrell landscape. Life in the quiet hamlet of Jarrell would change forever. (Both courtesy Charlotte Vancil.)

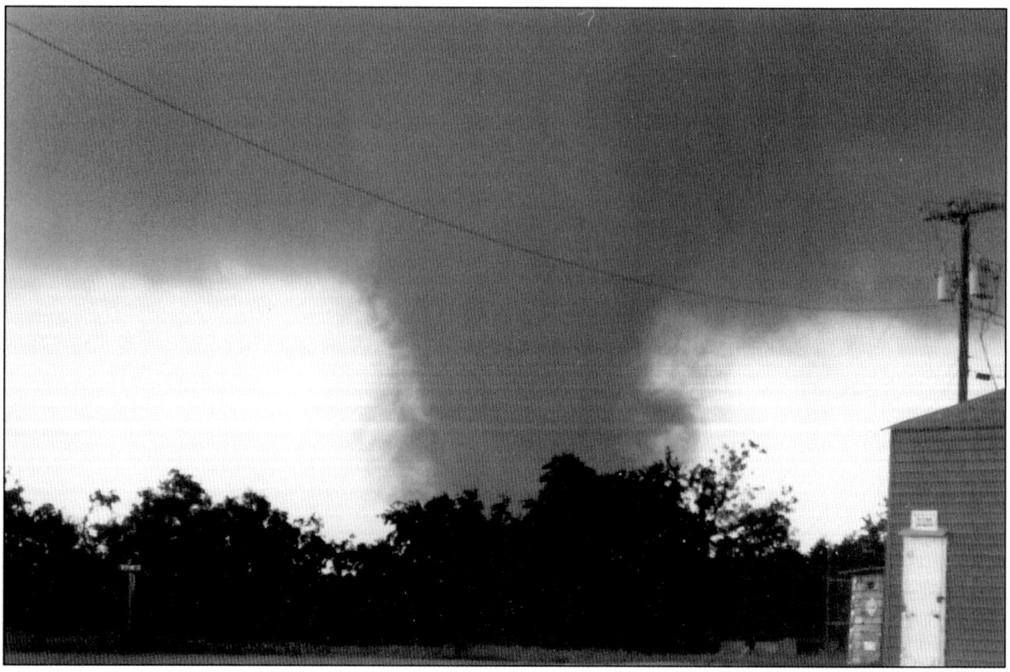

Scott Beckwith worked at the Jarrell Farm Supply. On this particular day, he had been keeping his eye on the weather. He captured the progression and intensity of the storm in the following remarkable series of pictures. (Courtesy Scott Beckwith.)

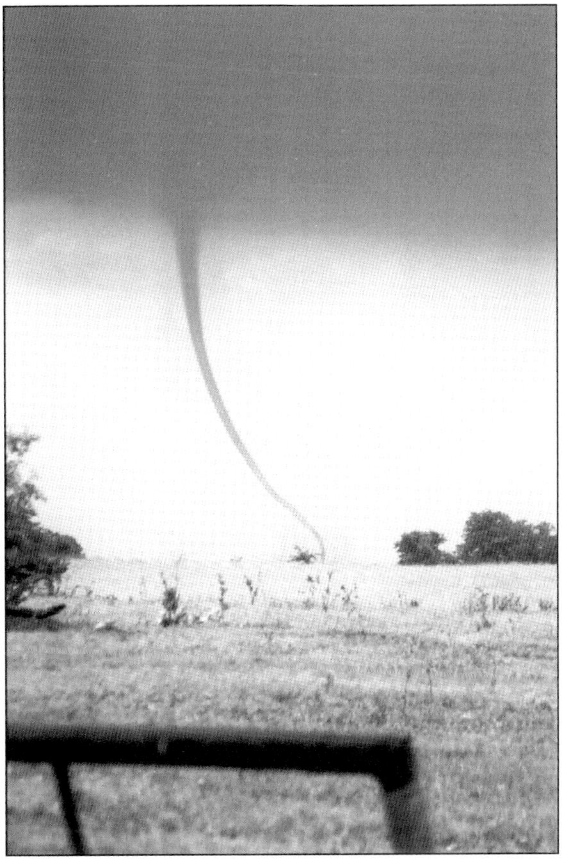

Looking out across a pasture, the size of the first funnel grew larger as it approached. It remained fairly high off the ground, with a long rope-like vortex skipping along the ground. (Courtesy Scott Beckwith.)

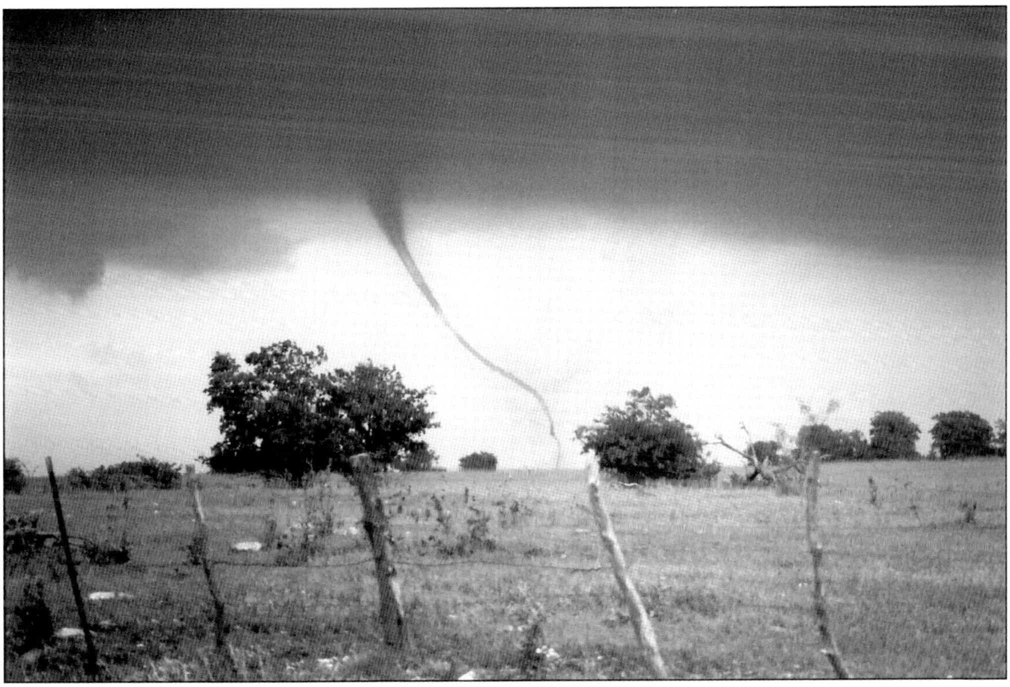

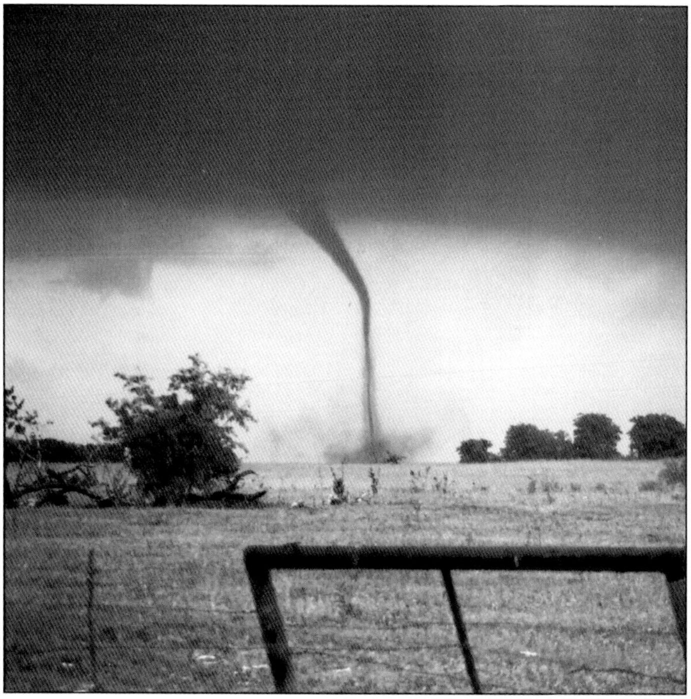

Now a fully formed tornado with destruction on its mind, the storm moved directly toward the west side of Jarrell. The fire department siren was sounded, not to warn the public but to summon the firemen. Experience with the previous tornado indicated they needed to be ready. (Courtesy Scott Beckwith.)

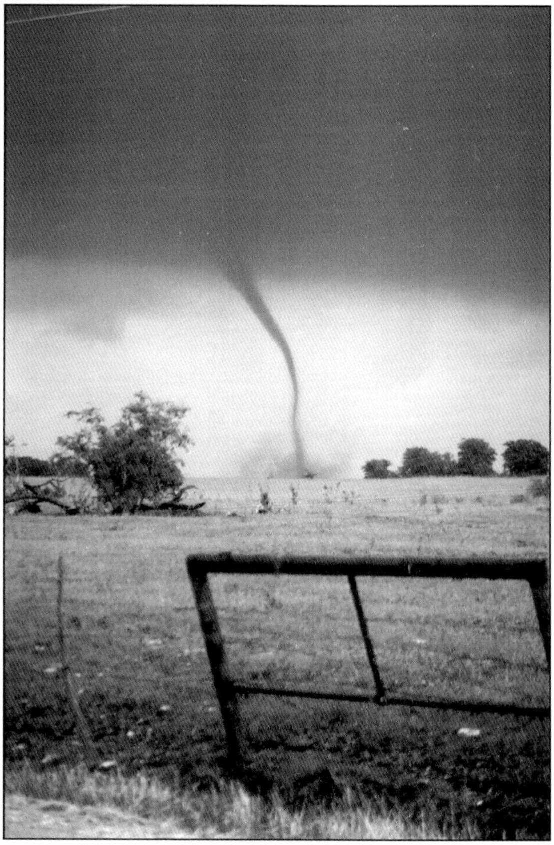

Look carefully and one can see the debris being kicked up at ground level. Citizens at this point were taking cover. This pencil-like funnel did a lot of damage but was only a precursor of what was to come. (Courtesy Scott Beckwith.)

Once the funnel cloud disappeared, everyone took a deep breath. Perhaps Jarrell had been spared. Those watching the horizon, however, noticed a strange formation. It was cloud-like but close to the ground. There seemed to be no real organization to it at first, but slowly the cloud started to take shape. At right is the first preview of the larger storm that was approaching. Below, the wall cloud is now visible and the storm a bit more organized. One of the authors, Priscilla King, was viewing this same storm from about 4 miles to the south. Her child-care facility had been in lockdown for several hours. When the first tornado came and moved off to the west, she remembers saying to a fellow teacher, "Boy that was close," quickly followed with, "What is that? It looks like a vertical cloud." A few seconds later, everyone recognized what it was: a huge multi-vortex storm. Fortunately for the 100-plus preschool children, this storm followed the path of the first one, veering off to the west just before reaching the school. (Both courtesy Scott Beckwith.)

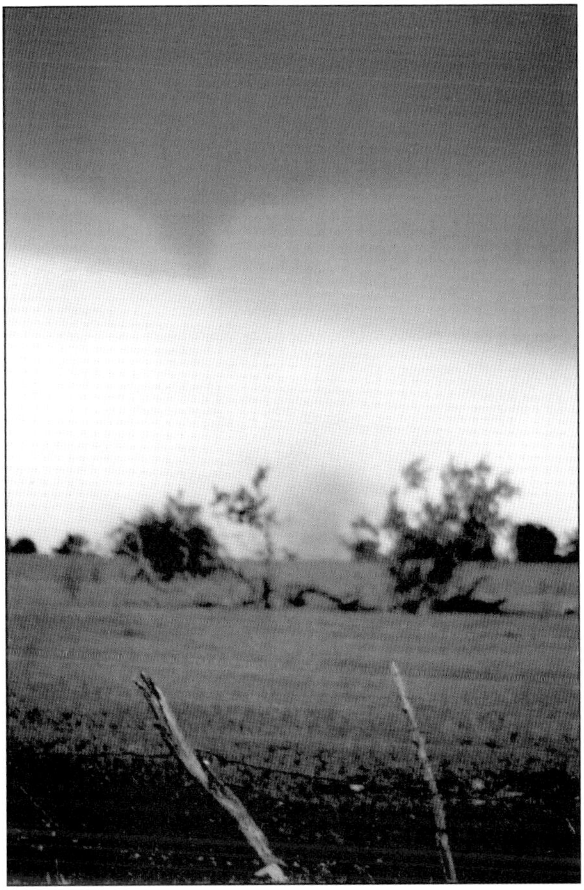

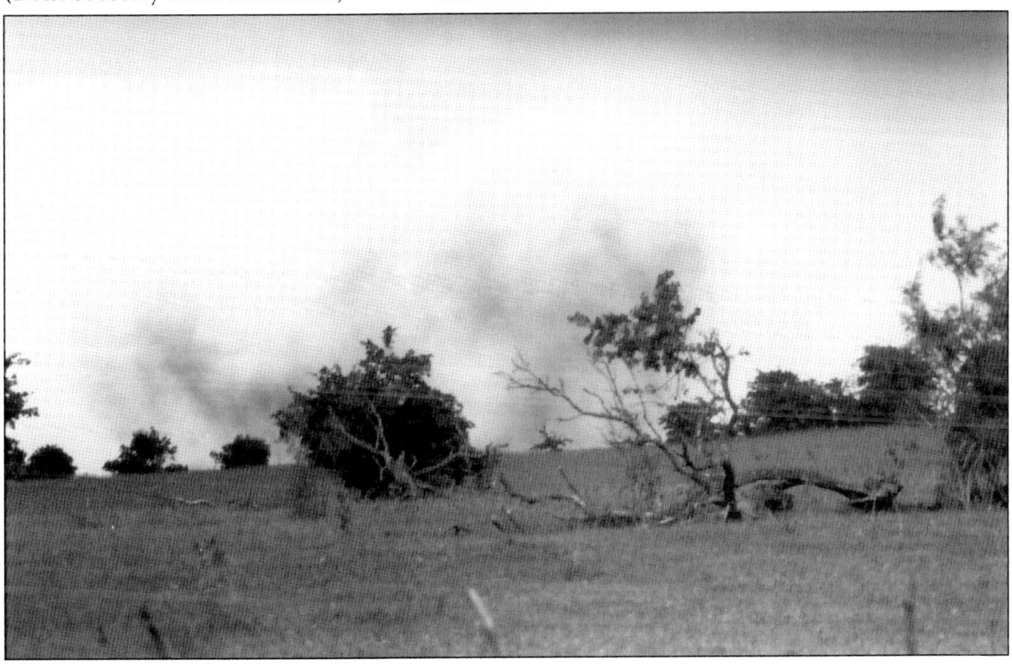

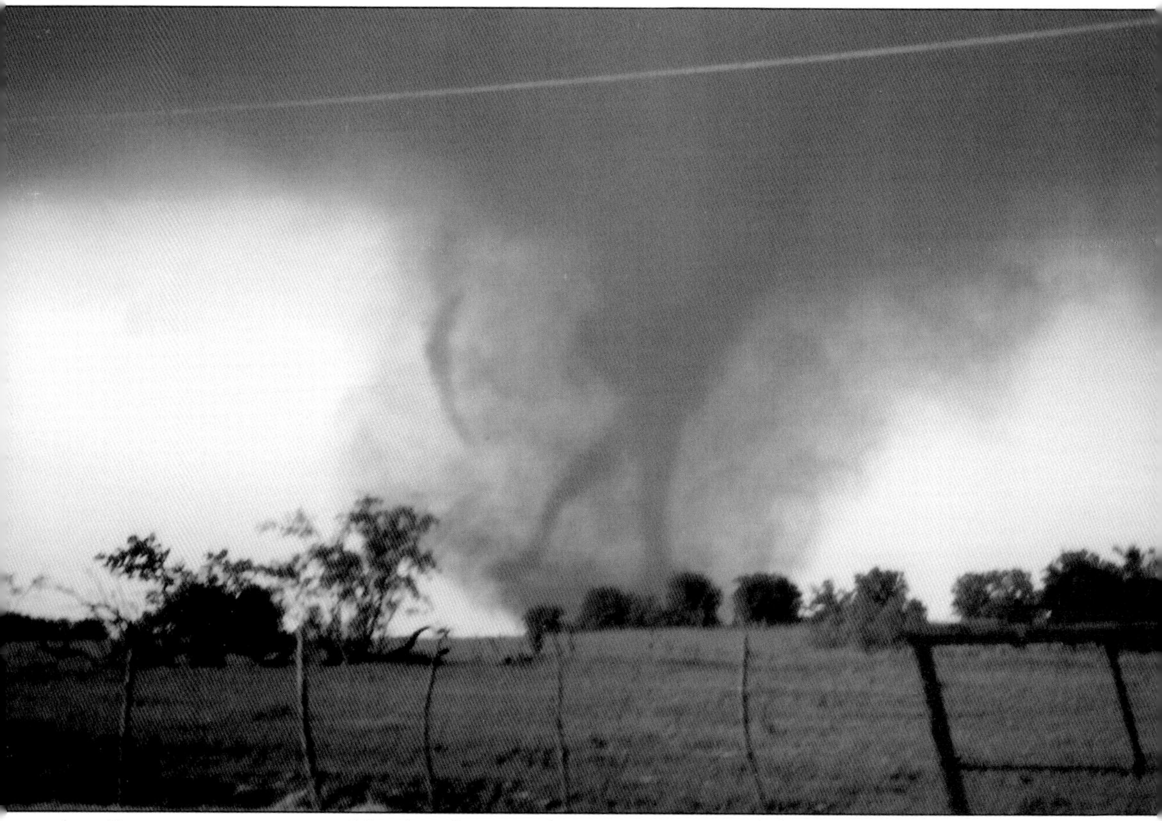

Snapping pictures quickly, the photographer was unaware of the unbelievable images he was capturing. After developing the film and viewing the photographs, everyone was utterly shocked. This now-famous photograph was among those taken as the deadly tornado approached Jarrell. Verbally passed down for generations, Native American legends tell the story that if someone sees a dead man walking in the sky, people are about to die. The photograph clearly shows the dead man walking, and the prediction was accurate. Three tornadoes were combining to form a multi-vortex storm. This storm was estimated to be almost half a mile wide and to have contained winds in excess of 261 miles per hour, perhaps as high as 310 miles per hour. Man was completely at Mother Nature's mercy. (Courtesy Scott Beckwith.)

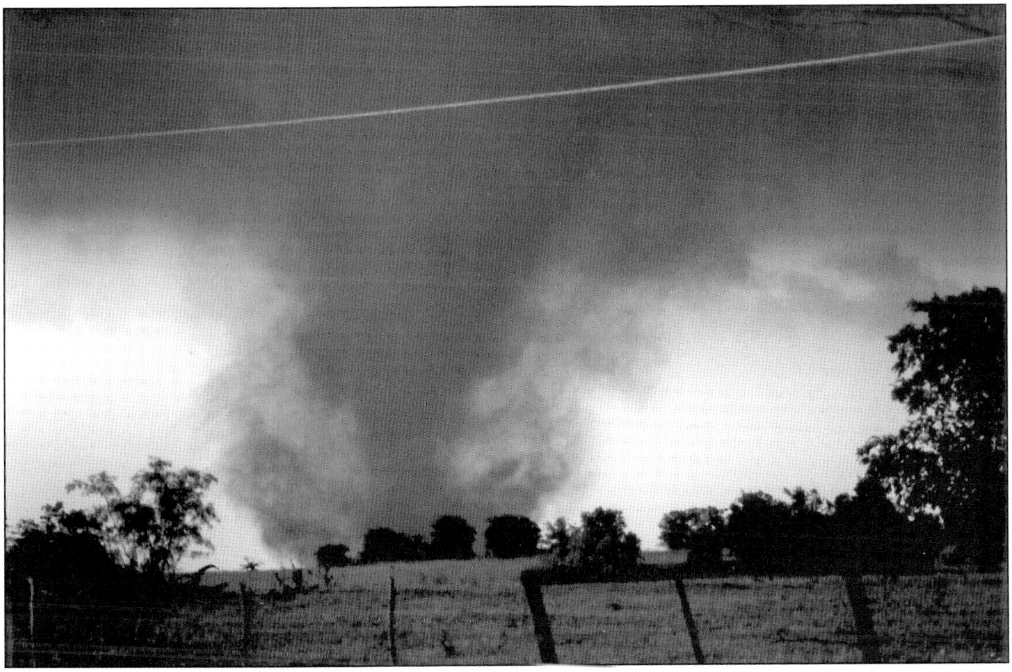

Not to be reckoned with, the storm continued to increase in size and intensity. As it marched across the various farms and pastureland, it literally ground up everything in its path, including homes, windmills, crops, trees, and barns. (Courtesy Scott Beckwith.)

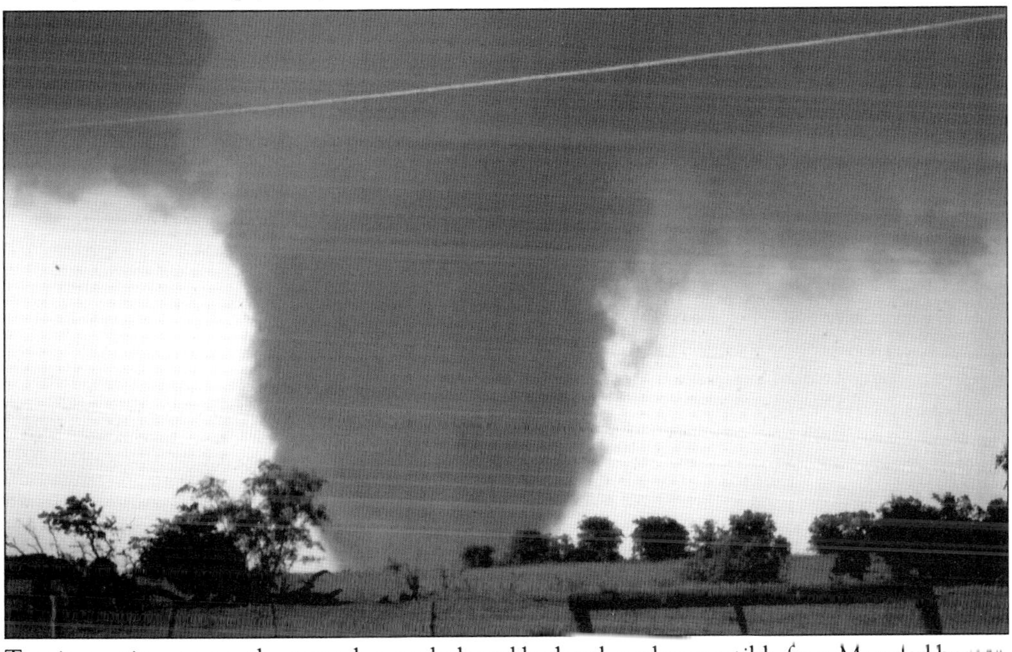

Turning ominous now, the tornado was dark and had gathered perceptible fury. Mangled homes, farm equipment, and livestock could be seen in the debris the storm was carrying. There were reports of wheat impaling farm animals and cattle and sheep being picked up, their hides completely stripped by the wind before being slammed to the ground. Whole herds of livestock completely disappeared with no trace left behind. (Courtesy Scott Beckwith.)

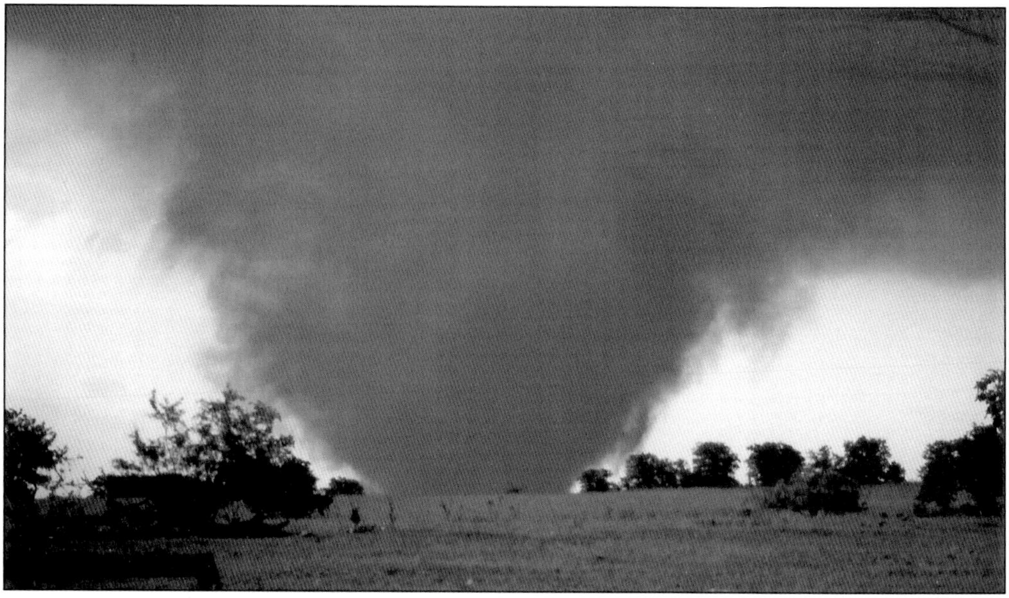

Continuing to bear down, the tornado traveled directly toward County Road 305. Double Creek Estates subdivision was now sporting a bull's-eye directly on its back. No words could describe the fear generated by a storm of this size. At this point, the storm slowed down considerably, which made matters worse. A slow-moving tornado, with a mind to staying on the ground, is the most dangerous kind. Tornadoes of this size and wind speed are extremely rare. In fact, less than one percent of all tornadoes are rated F-5. Experienced researchers who studied this particular storm's aftermath estimated it to be the most powerful and violent storm they had ever encountered. Double Creek residents were now in their bathrooms or in their hallways, holding on to each other . . . waiting . . . waiting . . . waiting. Juanitta Petersen remembers, "People tell you these things don't take long to pass through, but when you are lying in a bathtub covering two little babies, it seems like forever." (Both courtesy Scott Beckwith.)

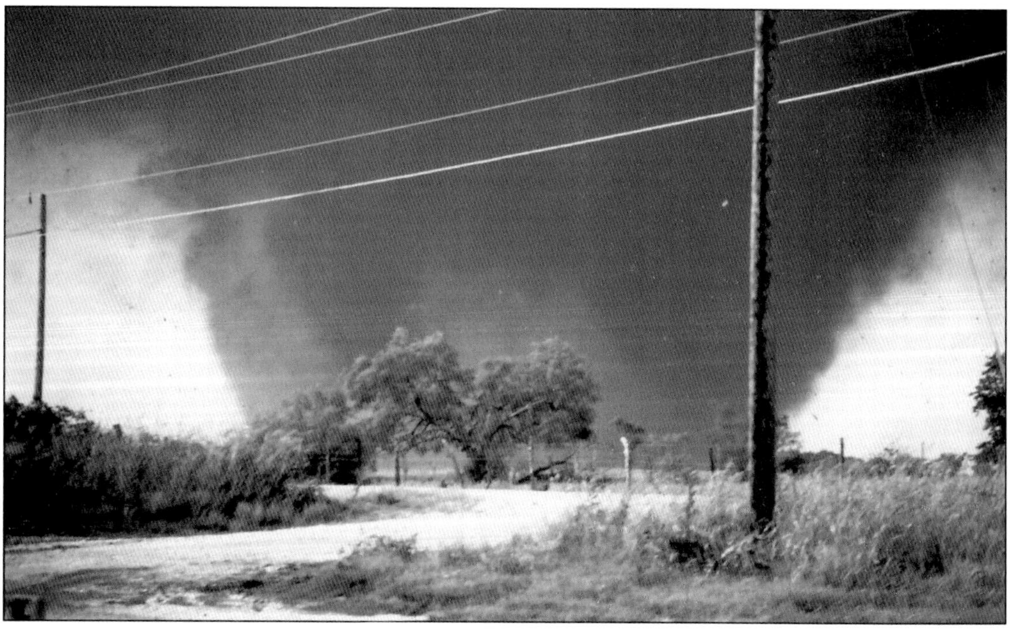

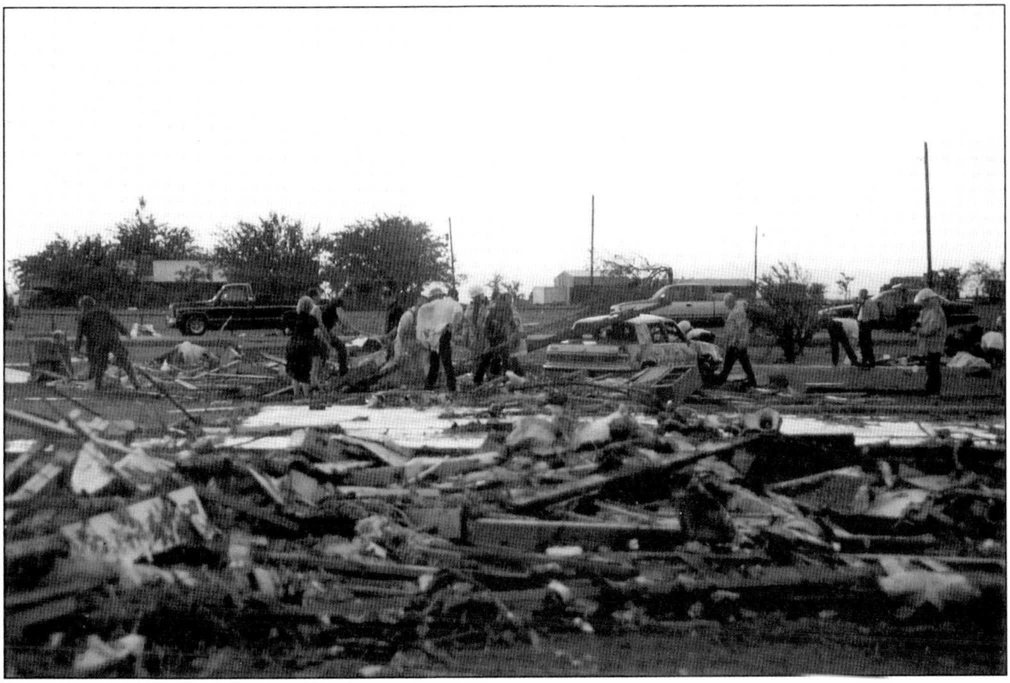

In post-tornado scenes, one usually sees destruction in the form of roofs gone, walls down, trees uprooted, and cars turned over. The debris field of this storm was completely different. About 40 to 50 structures were completely destroyed, but there was little rubble. Everything had literally been ground up and carried away. The homes in the background were somewhat spared while those in the foreground were obliterated. (Courtesy Scott Beckwith.)

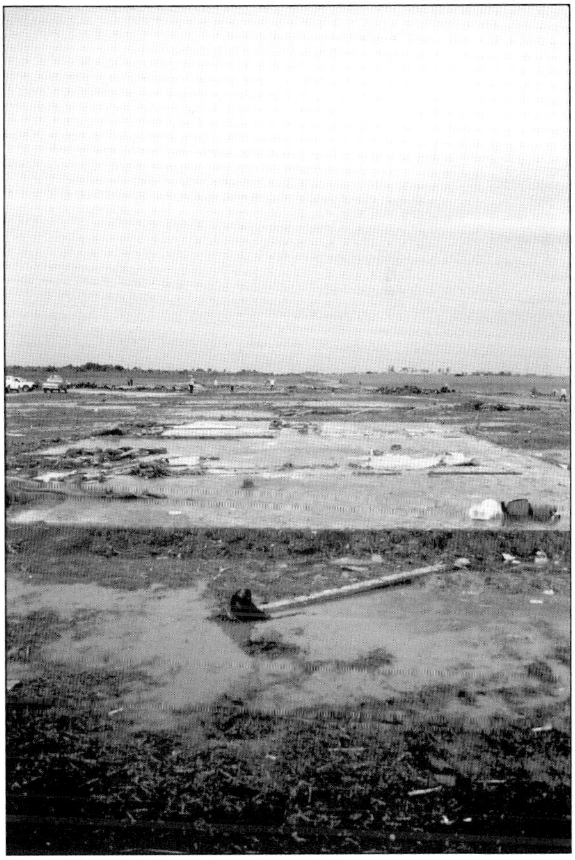

A few foundations were visible, but even some of those were gone. Roofs were torn off storm shelters, and water was sucked out of deep wells and septic tanks. Everything was destroyed, leaving no recognizable remains. Emergency crews found the work extremely dangerous, especially as evening approached. Where once had been storm shelters, wells, and septic tanks were now large gaping holes in the ground. (Courtesy Scott Beckwith.)

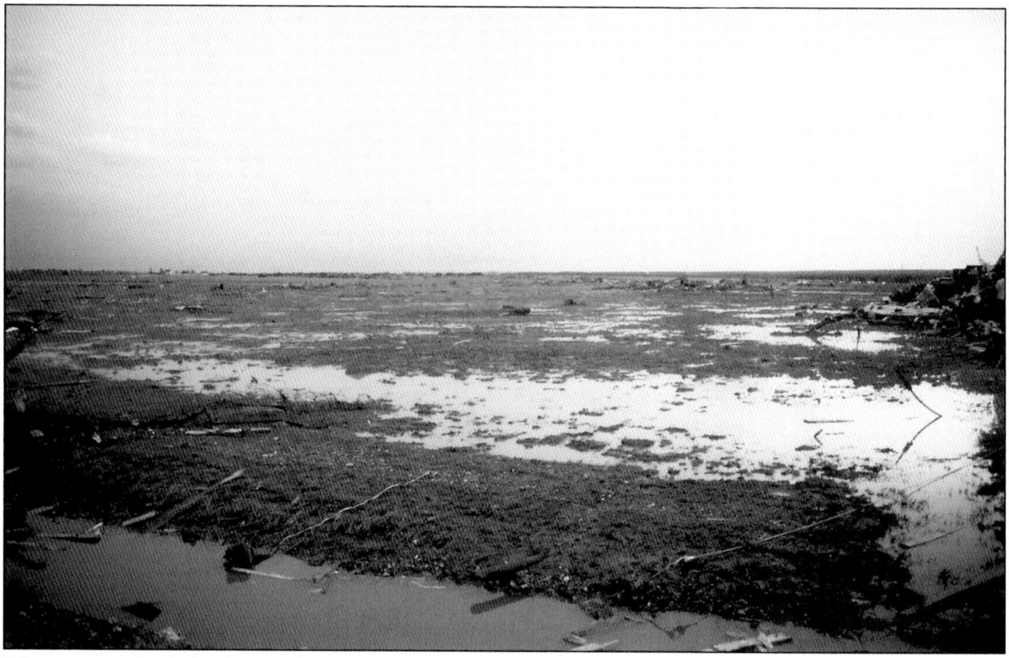

The storm, which had moved ever so slowly, penetrated the earth to a depth of 18 inches. It pulled out all grass and plants by the roots, picking up dirt as it churned. This produced a mud storm, the likes of which is hard to describe. Asphalt on the county road was completely peeled up as if there had only been a gravel road. (Courtesy Scott Beckwith.)

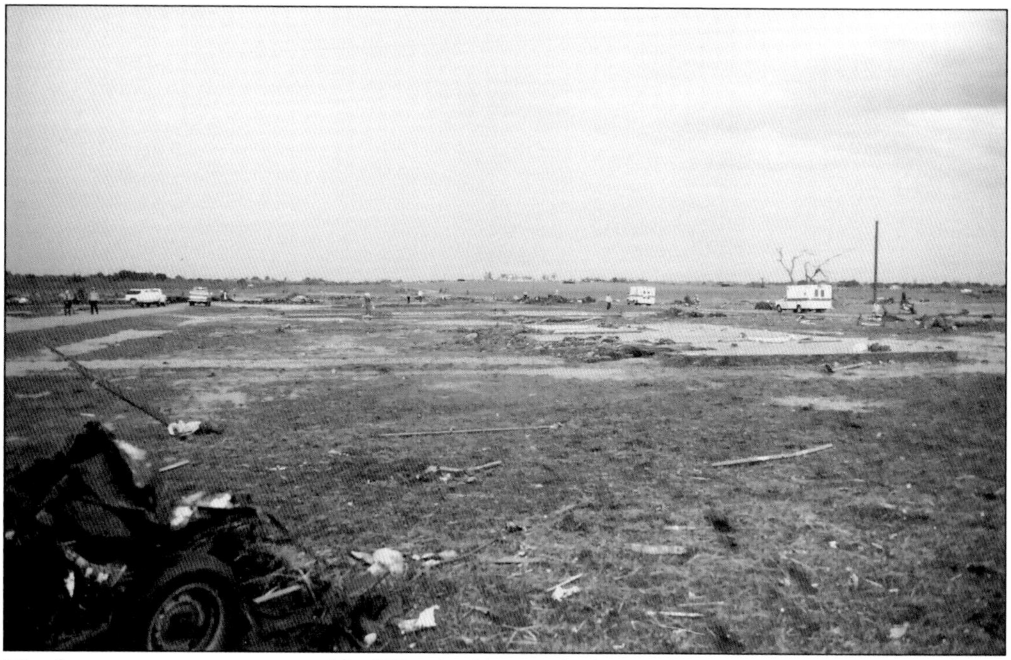

The devastation was unimaginable. What had been a fairly populated neighborhood was reduced to a water-filled field of mud. All evidence of homes, and the families who lived there, was gone. In this photograph are the remnants of an automobile with several ambulances in the background. It was taken just a short time after the tornado passed through. (Courtesy Scott Beckwith.)

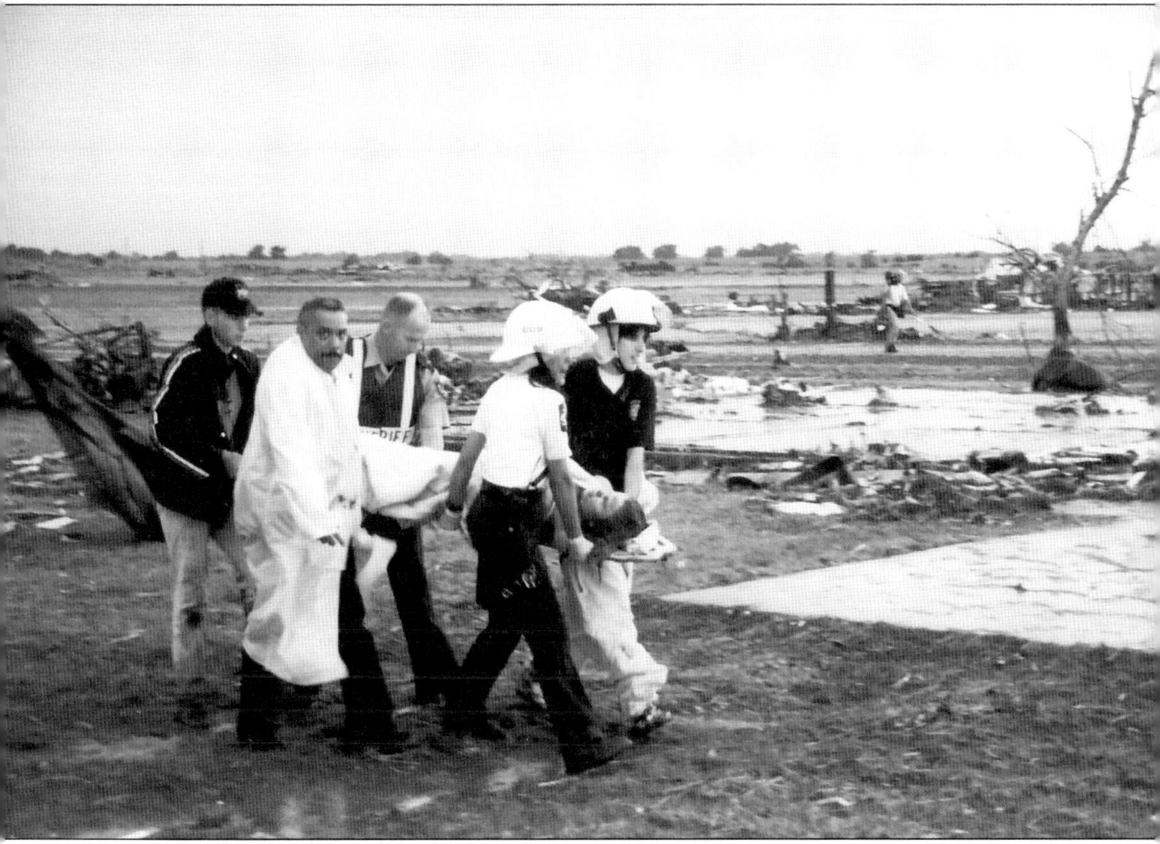

Emergency crews were on the scene trying to locate any possible survivors. They were few and far between. This picture shows the heroic effort on the part of local responders. Twenty-seven people lost their lives. Included were young people, children, and two entire families. Many others were injured. An impromptu morgue was set up in the Jarrell Volunteer Fire Department. Volunteers searched for survivors until they were completely exhausted. Identification of victims was difficult at best. Others began to organize to meet the needs of the survivors. A makeshift shelter was set up, food was donated and prepared, and once again, the community came together. Lives were completely interrupted and many lost everything. Also seen here is the central debris field left by the storm. There was not much need for heavy equipment; there was nothing left. (Courtesy Scott Beckwith.)

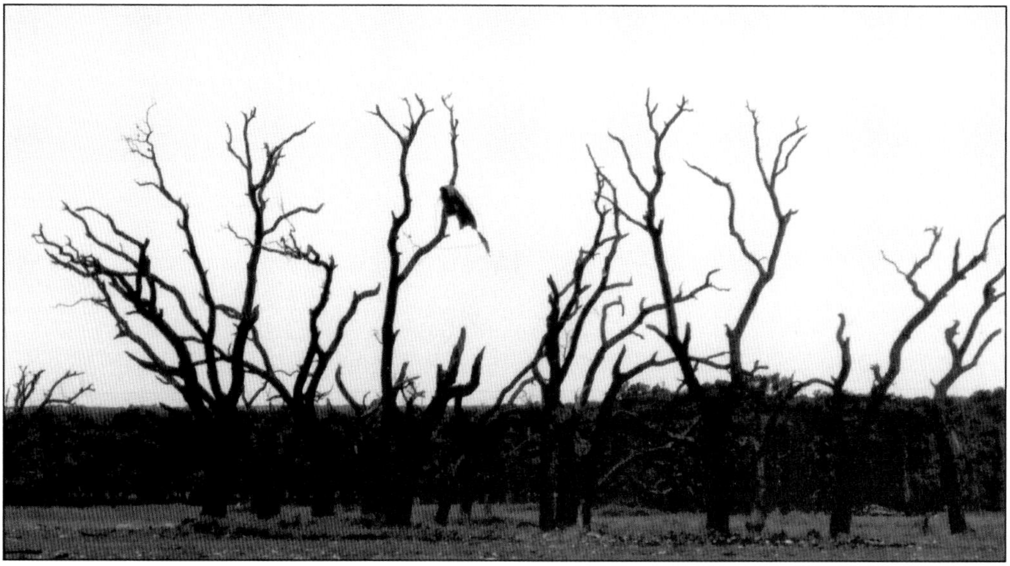

The tornado subsided in a densely wooded area just past Double Creek Estates. These photographs show what were once large oak trees, now barren silhouettes against the sky, ground down to half their original size. The appearance of the landscape after the storm was completely unreal and totally foreign. The oak tree has become a symbol of Jarrell and its people. Today these trees, though crippled and stunted, have leafed out and grown new branches. They have weathered and withstood extreme adversity, but they are still here, insisting on being a part of Jarrell's future. (Both courtesy Charlotte Vancil.)

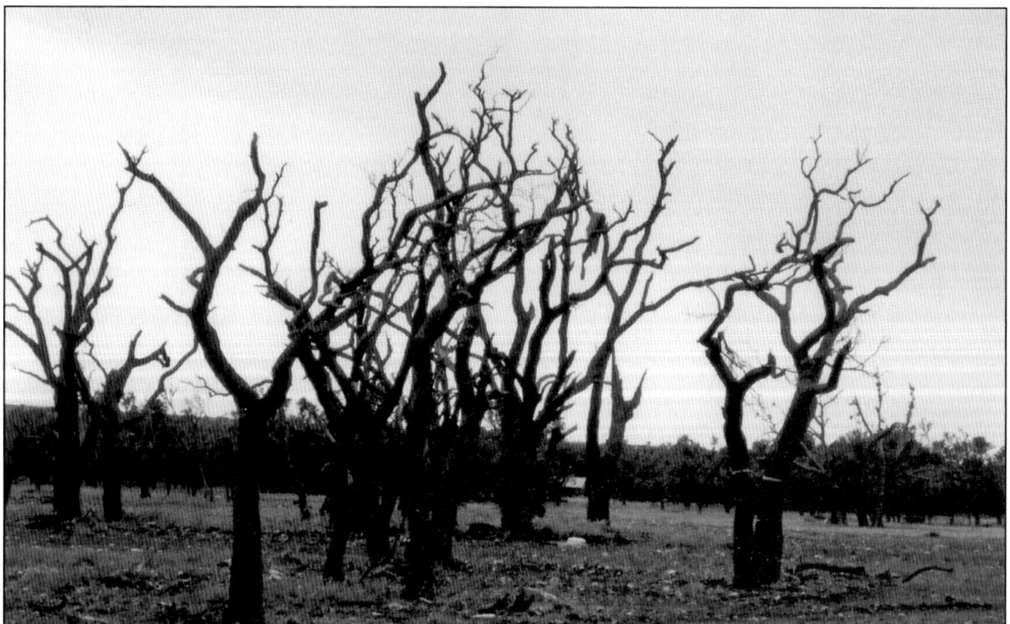

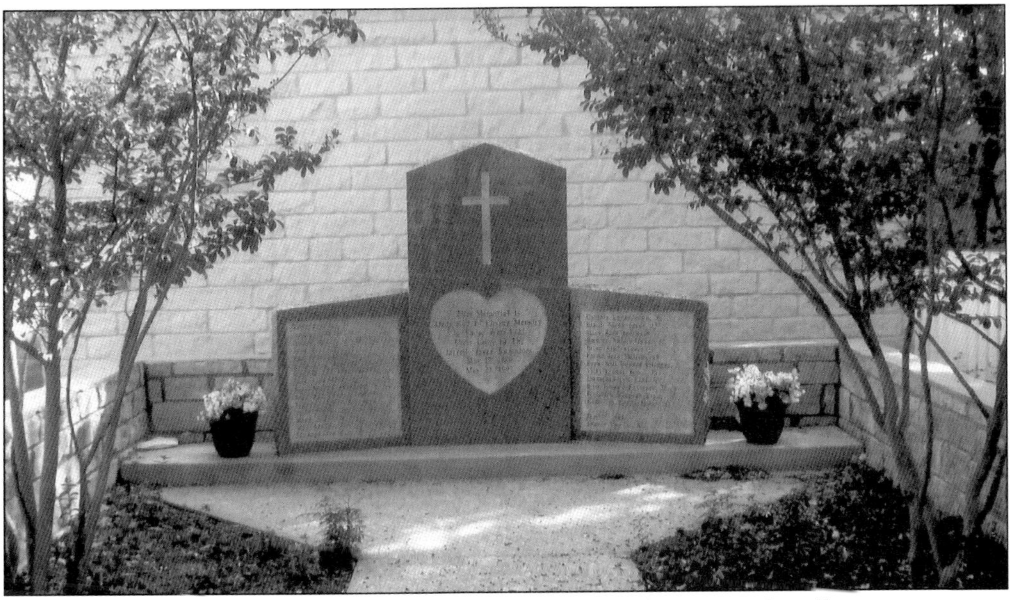

This beautiful granite memorial, placed in the middle of downtown Jarrell, is a permanent tribute to the victims of the Jarrell tornadoes. It is placed there in memory of the loss of life but also of the indomitable spirit of the Jarrell community. The true tribute is to the community that endured unprecedented loss but has managed to rebuild lives and even look forward to the future with optimism.

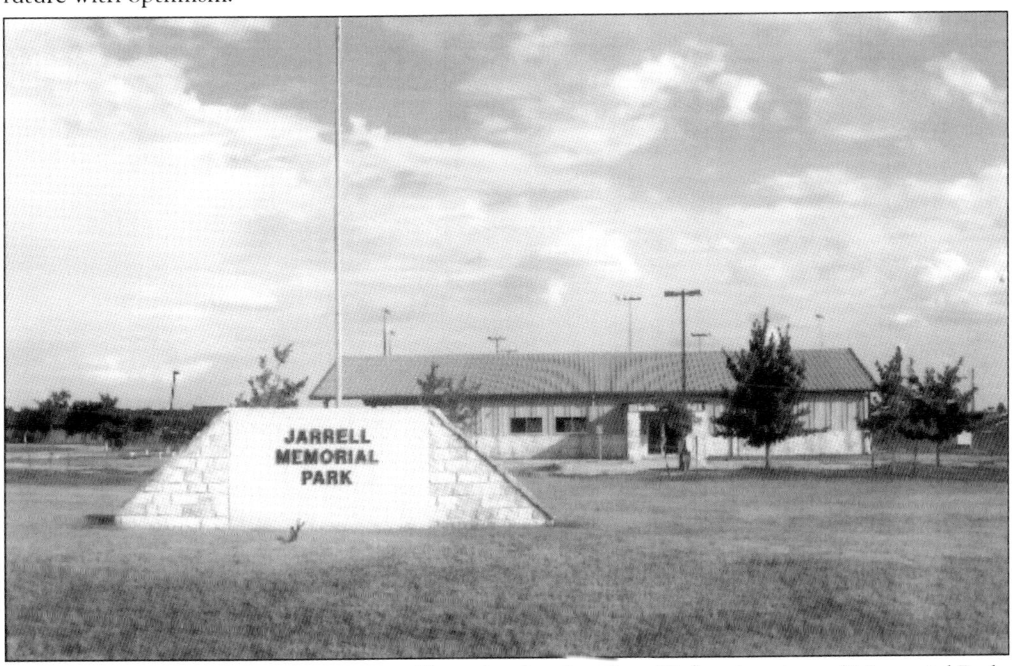

Built on land belonging to the Larry and Joan Igo family is Jarrell's family-oriented Memorial Park. All five members of the Igo family lost their lives in the storm that fateful day. This property, on which their home stood, was donated in their honor in order to build a community center, playground, and Little League ball fields, a fitting tribute to a civic-minded family that was an important part of Jarrell.

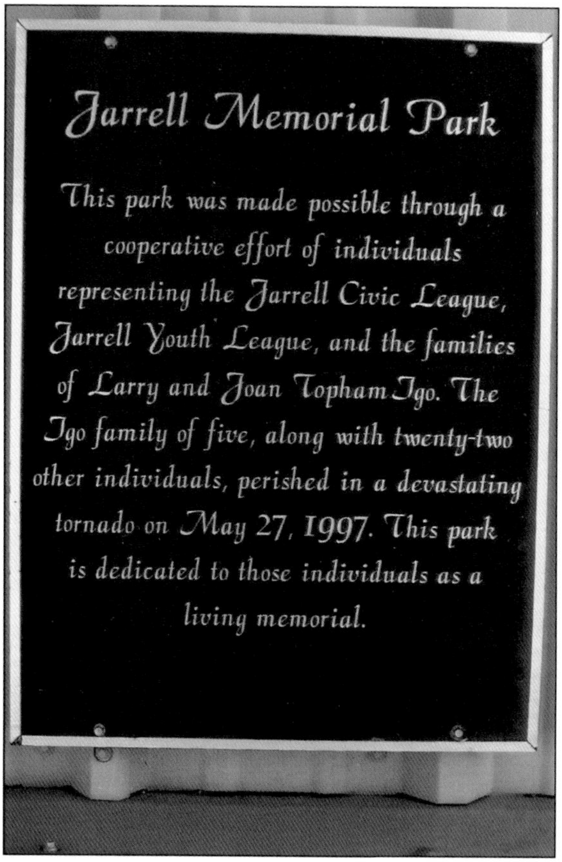

This plaque can be found at the entrance to the Jarrell Memorial Park Community Center. It tells the story of the Igo family and how the park came to be. This facility is used extensively by the community and has become a focal point for activities, both civic and social.

On the five-year anniversary of the 1997 tornado, a community service was held in the shadow of the memorial stone dedicated to the victims. It was a difficult day, a day when so many dark and dreadful memories tried unsuccessfully to choke out the bright sunshine. Here the local Boy Scout troop participates in the ceremony. (Courtesy the City of Jarrell.)

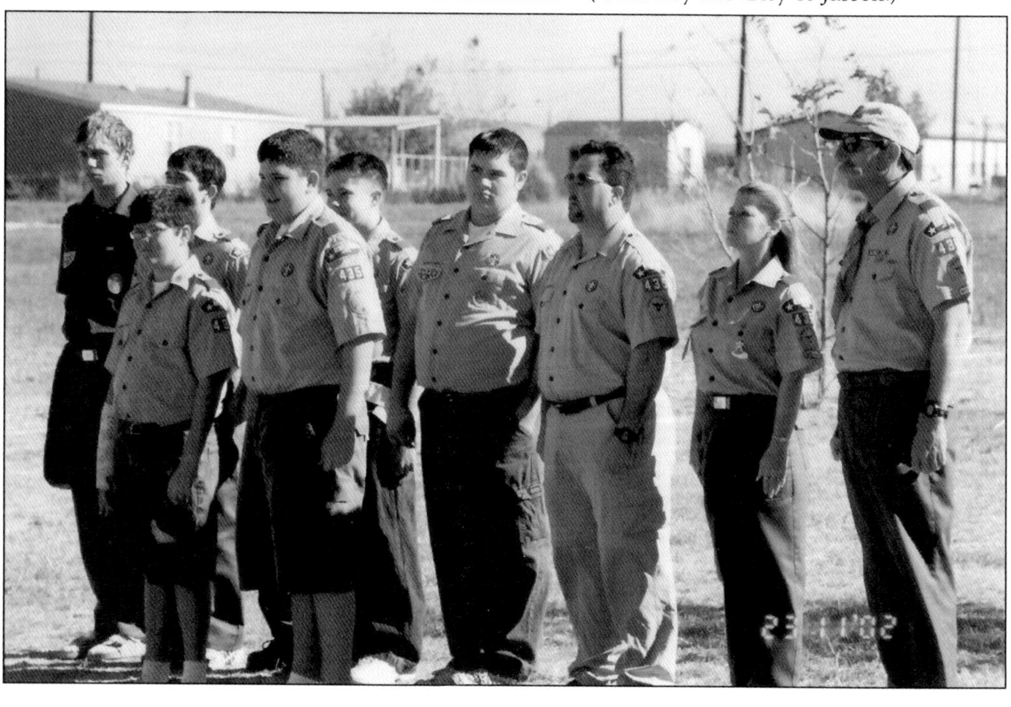

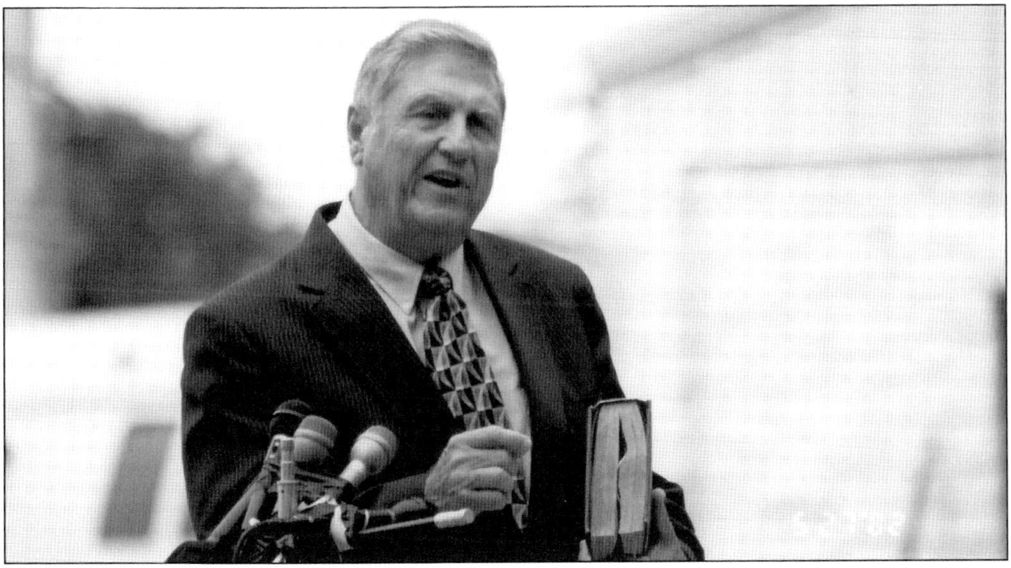

The townspeople gathered at the memorial that had been erected near the fire department on the main street in town. Shown here is Rev. Max Johnson, pastor of the Jarrell Baptist Church, giving words of encouragement. Reverend Johnson and his congregation deserve recognition for the large part they played in meeting the needs of the community during those difficult days. The crowd watches and listens—and they remember. They remember those they love and draw encouragement from the friends around them. (Courtesy the City of Jarrell.)

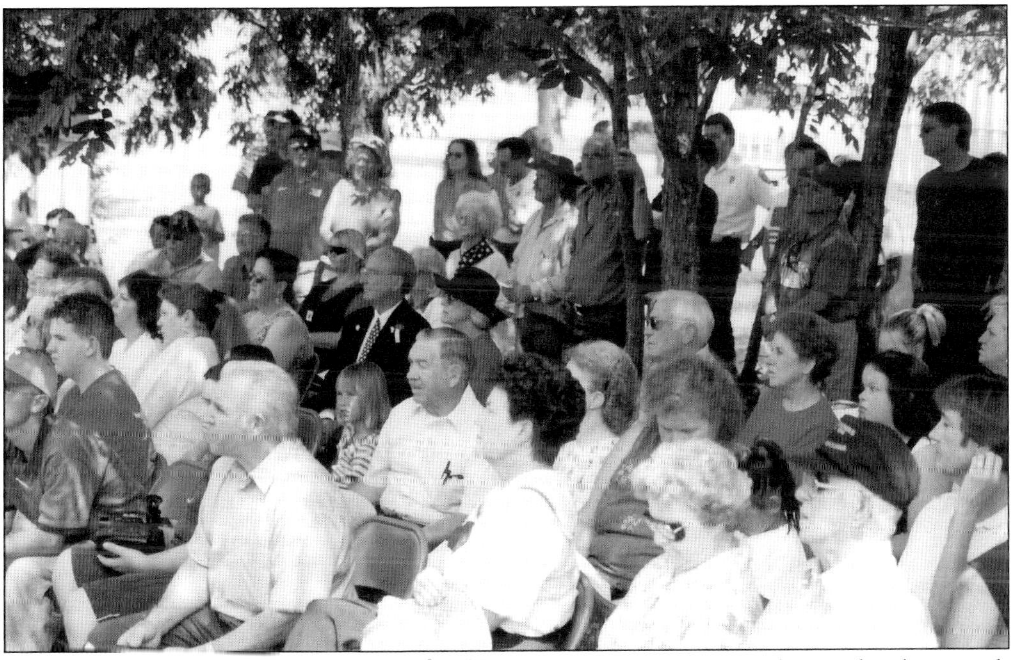

Looking out over the crowd, it is obviously a bittersweet occasion. Not evident in the photograph are the encouraging words and beautiful music shared that day. This memorial service reminded the residents of Jarrell that loss of life and property, although devastating, can bring a community closer together. It can also instill an innate sense of responsibility to help others in times of need. Especially since the tornadoes, Jarrell is known for its kindness in reaching out to others.

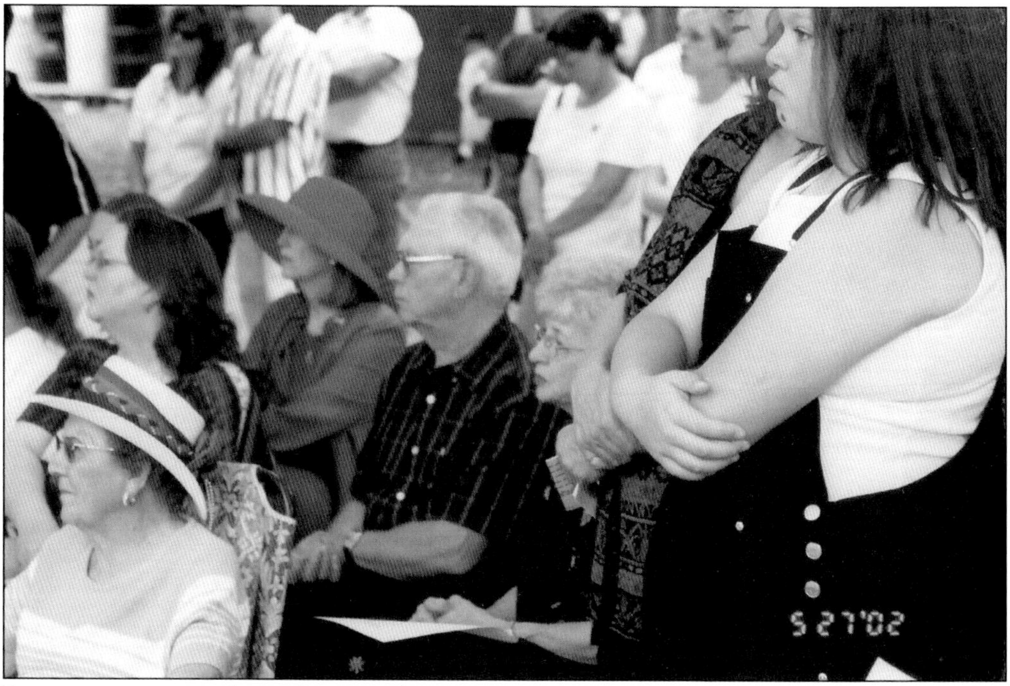

Five years is not very long when it is the anniversary of so many friends and family lost. When something as tragic as this occurs, everyone talks about what happened but few talk about their feelings. That comes with time. The picture above shows people attending the five-year anniversary of the tornado. The somber crowd looks on as words are spoken, songs are sung, and memories are relived. Shown below are Kermit and Juanitta Petersen and their granddaughter Bonitta, whose losses were significant. The looks on their faces say it all. (Both courtesy the City of Jarrell.)

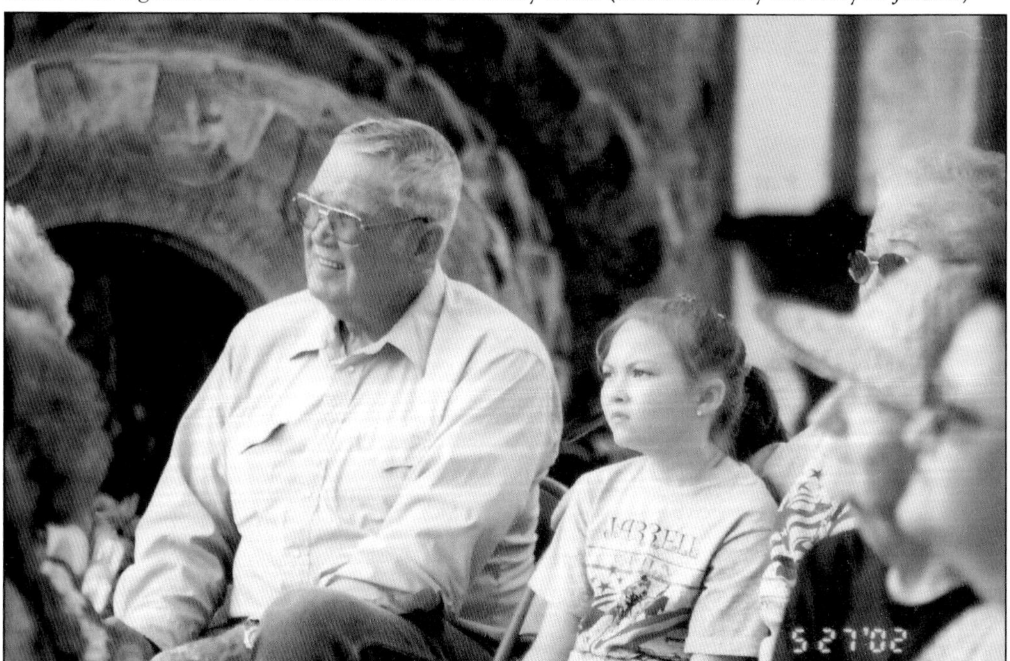

Eight

Past, Present, and Future

Small towns all over America have attempted to help their citizens improve and maintain quality of life. Although loosely structured, Jarrell had provided, in its own unique way, the things people needed. This chapter celebrates the beginnings of services to Jarrell residents in the early years. Water wells had been drilled, a volunteer fire department was in place, and law enforcement was provided by the Williamson County Sheriff's Department. With the tremendous growth in the Central Texas area, Jarrell faced one of the biggest challenges of its century-old history: incorporate and become an official city or be swallowed up by burgeoning communities nearby. Known for their independence, the citizens of Jarrell wanted to maintain the town's individual identity and have some control over its future. Residents voted to incorporate. Incorporation meant Jarrell was now a stand-alone city that needed a mayor and a city council, additional law enforcement, and increased fire protection. This chapter will introduce some new folks in the community, both leaders and neighbors. Finally, the reader will witness history repeating itself as a real estate developer once again recognizes the potential for growth and brings a whole new era to the small Texas town of Jarrell.

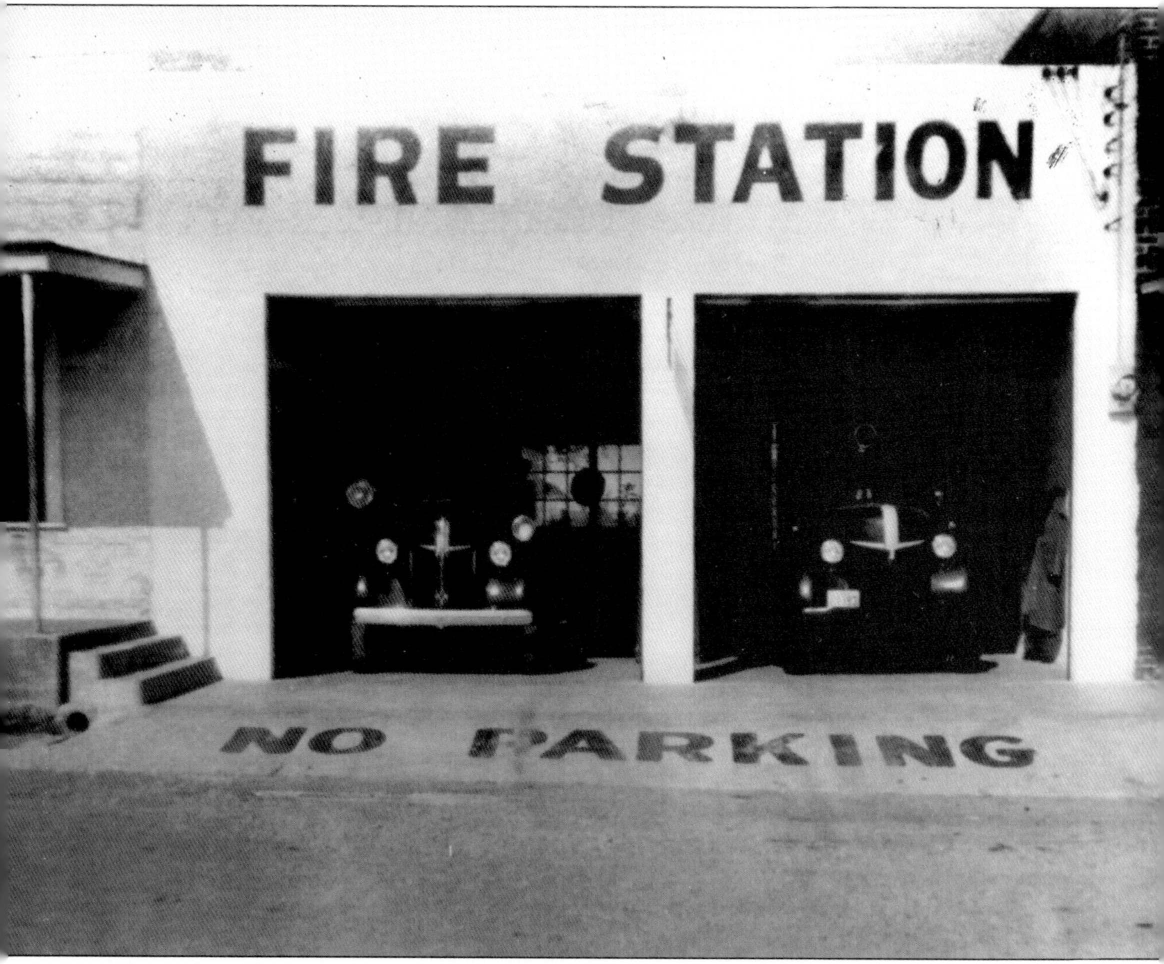

This is the old fire station that was in the Woodsman building south of the original downtown mercantile. In the two bays, the fire trucks are ready to respond. Darrell Conlee was instrumental in helping to establish the volunteer association. He even had a makeshift ambulance, which was a station wagon with the back seats taken out, a place for a stretcher, and a red emergency light on top. The firemen were all volunteers and worked at various jobs. When a call would come in, the fire whistle would start to sound and would continue to blow until someone got there to turn it off. It could be heard all over town. The first firemen to arrive at the station would board the trucks and respond to the emergency. Others would follow in their own vehicles, mostly pickup trucks. Over the years, the fire hall was the scene of lots of activity, even a wedding. Esther Tschoerner reports that she and her husband, Eddie, were married in the fire hall in 1955 by justice of the peace C. W. Whitlow. (Courtesy the Jarrell Volunteer Fire Department.)

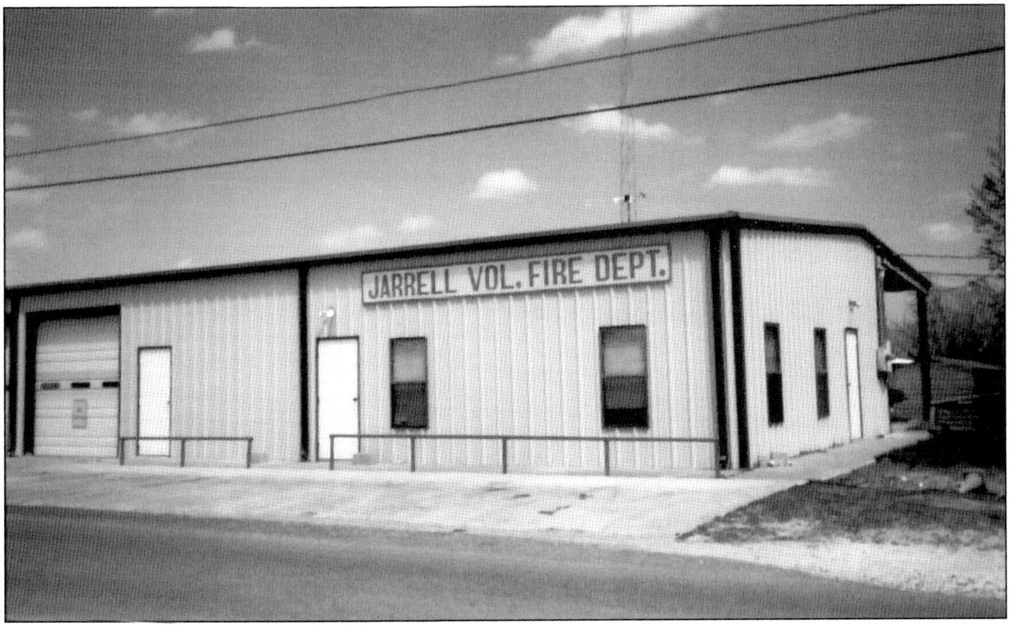

Above is the current fire station in Jarrell. Things are very different now. On duty are firefighters who are trained in modern firefighting techniques. The volunteers are still there, however, helping in any way they can. Each year, the Jarrell Volunteer Fire Department holds a fund-raiser. For many years, an annual barbeque and street dance were held to help provide needed equipment for the department. It is this community spirit that has helped the fire department stay alive. These were and continue to be dedicated men and women who give many hours of their time to provide protection to Jarrell and the surrounding rural area. Below is a picture of one of the older fire trucks participating in a local parade. Notice the Glass Hotel in the background. (Above, courtesy C. B. and Mary Hodge; below, the Jarrell Volunteer Fire Department.)

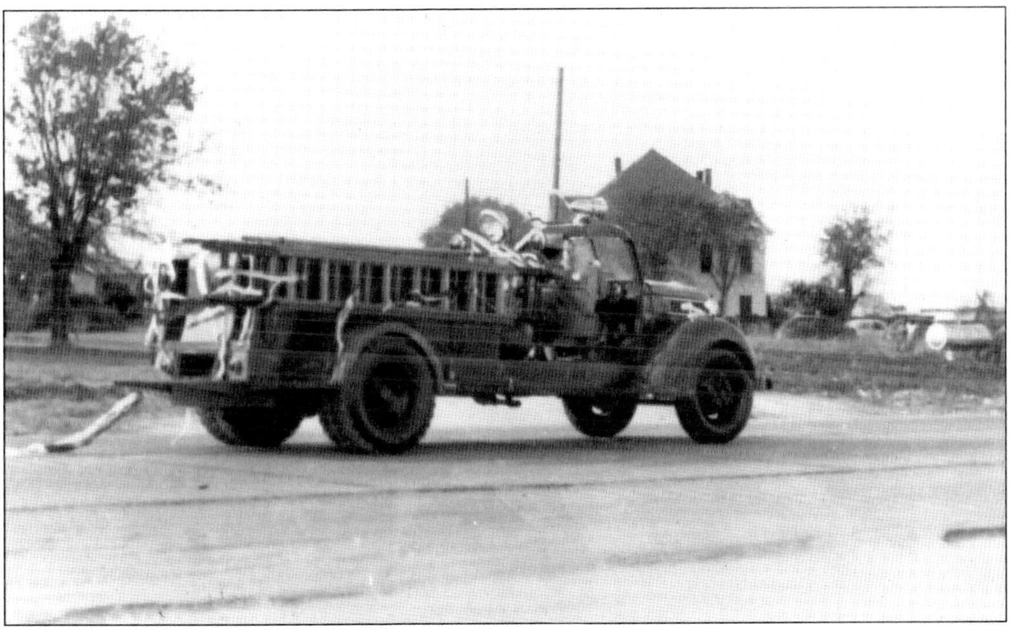

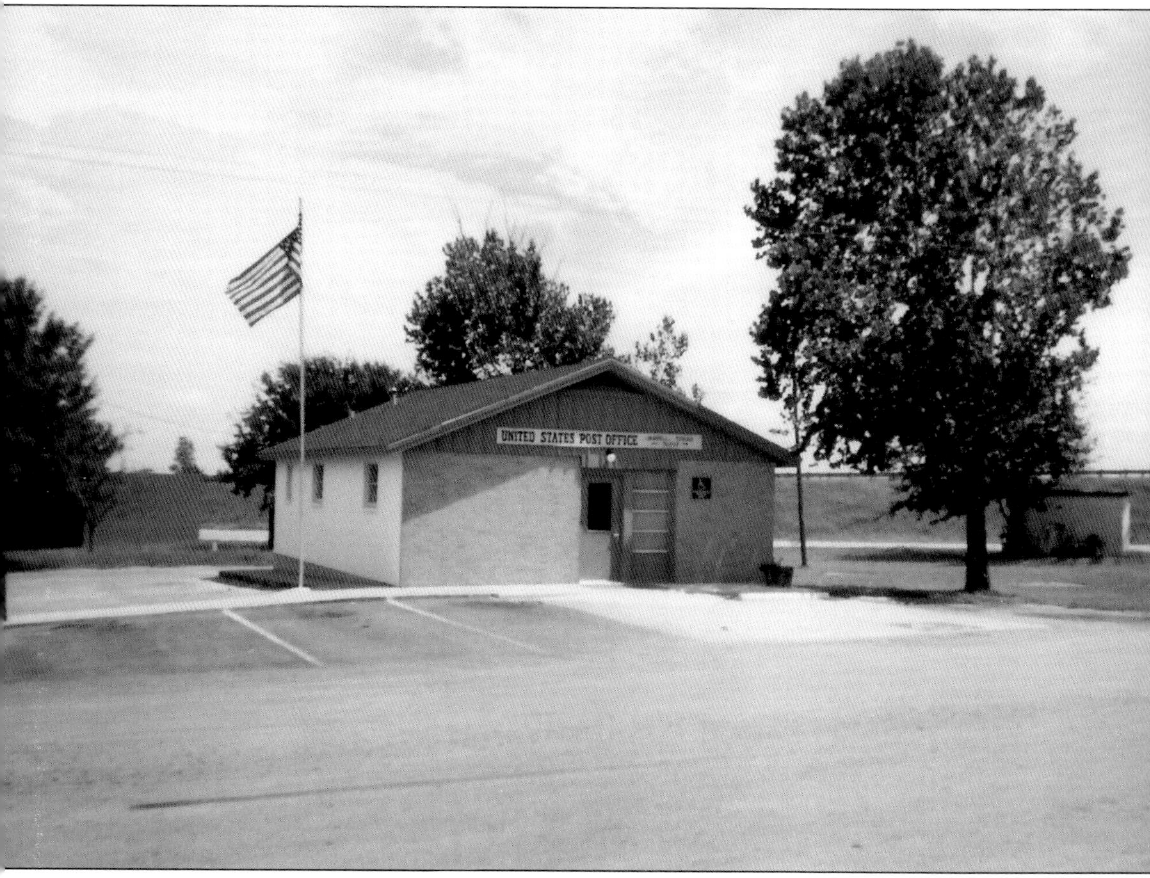

After moving from Corn Hill, the post office in Jarrell was located on old U.S. Highway 81 behind the hardware store. Ginger's Beauty Shop (shown on page 80) was the original post office building. At some point it was moved to its present location and continued to serve as the post office until 1969. It was then that the building shown in this photograph was constructed "just across the street." With its central downtown location it was a hub for town news and goings-on.

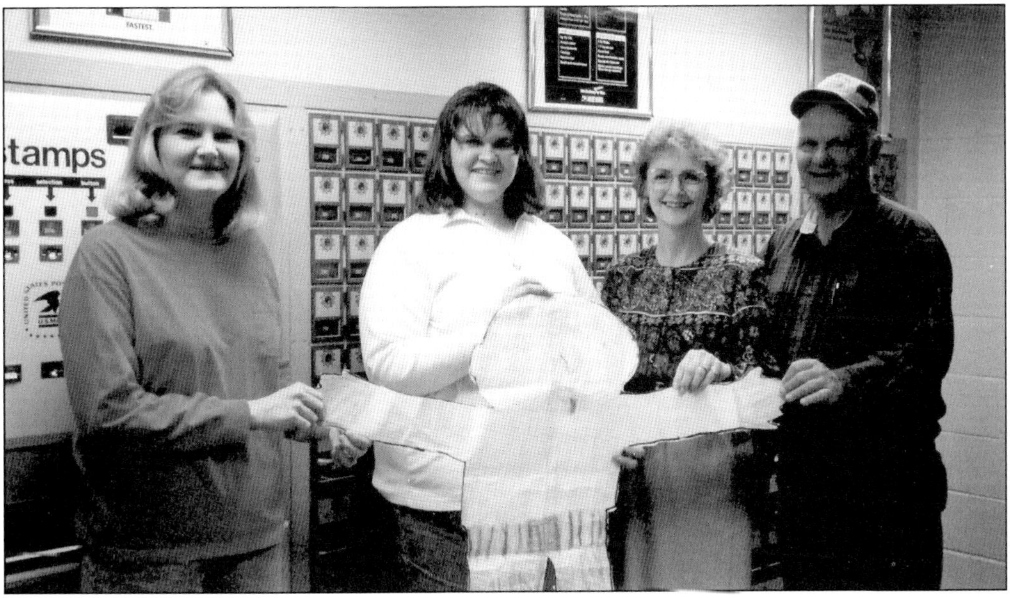

Most people in the Jarrell area got their mail on a rural route. Almost everyone's address was RFD 1, standing for Rural Free Delivery. The background of this photograph shows the post office boxes for those who preferred to get their mail at the post office. Pictured above from left to right are Theresa Schwertner, Terri Haley, then postmaster Boots Brizendine, and longtime mail carrier Frankie Vrabel. The photograph below is the working part of the post office hosting a third-grade field trip. Notice the boxes where the mail was distributed and the enthusiasm of the children learning more about the postal system. Two of the recognized faces of the children are Raina Fuller (back right) and Joseph Klepac (smiling, right of the desk). Their teacher that year was Charlotte Vancil. (Both courtesy Charlotte Vancil.)

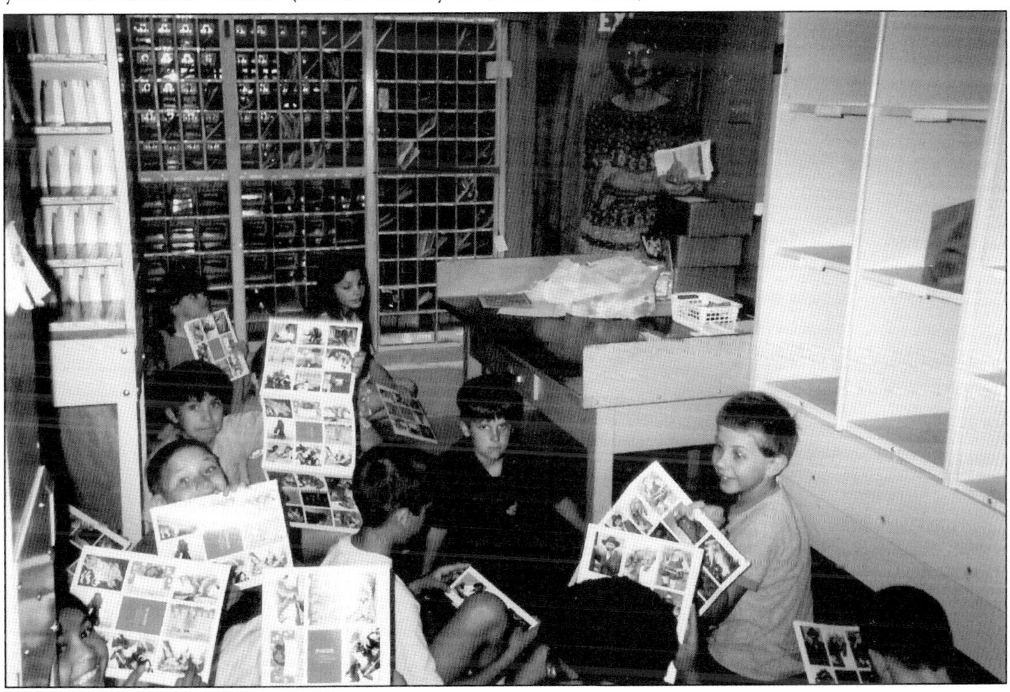

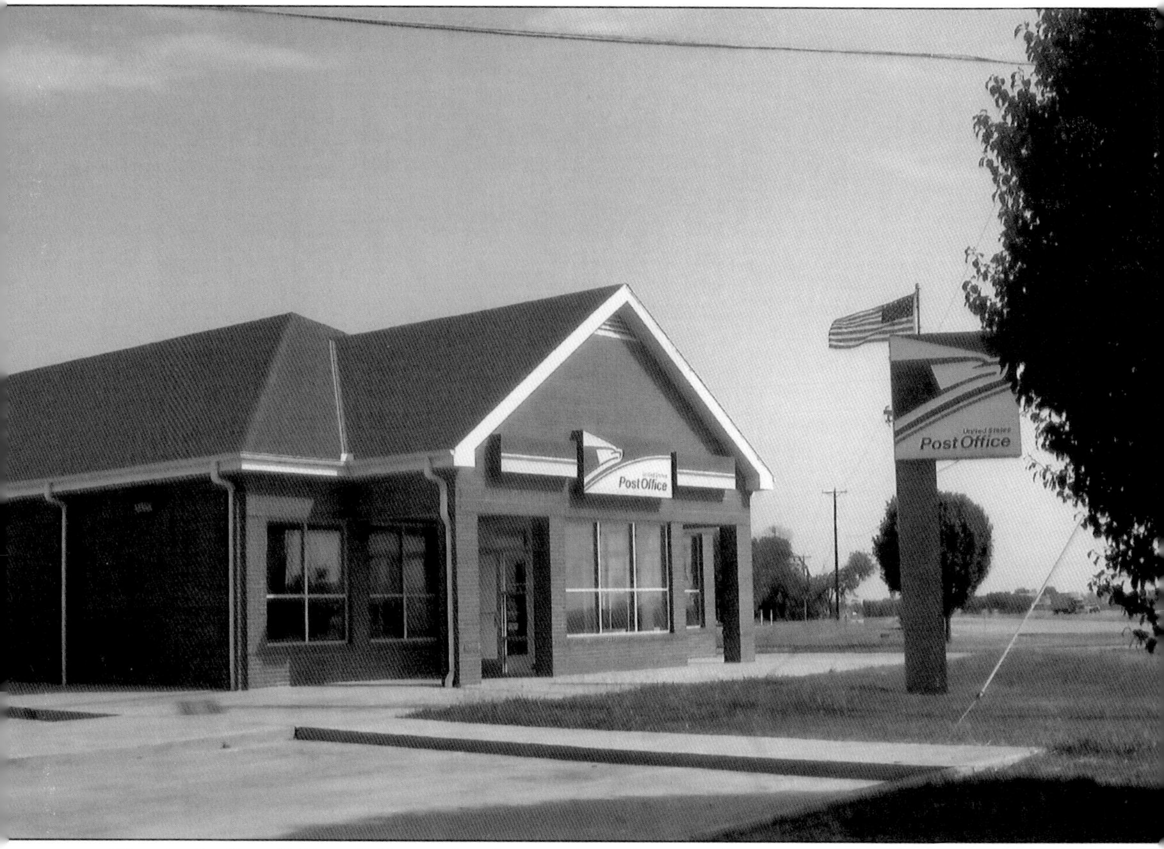

This is the Jarrell Post Office today. Located on the west frontage road of I-35, it still stands as a place where folks come daily and exchange greetings. Postmasters who served Corn Hill and their first year of service includes the following: John E. King (1855); Hiram Wood (1867); Tilman Lea (1871); Andres Pearce (1875); Otto Felthouse (1878); Montgomery Hair (1879); Roberta Hair (1882); George Weatherford (1886); William Shaver (1891); Columbus Jackson (1892); Thomas Dunn (1894); Rufus Brown (1902); William Foster (1903); James Smith (1904); and Thomas Thoma (1906). The Corn Hill Post Office closed in 1912. Postmasters who served Jarrell are the following: Thomas Thoma (1912); William Votaw (1914); Maynard Watkins (1950); James "Buck" Jones (1962); Walterine "Boots" Brizendine (1991); and George Balady (2002).

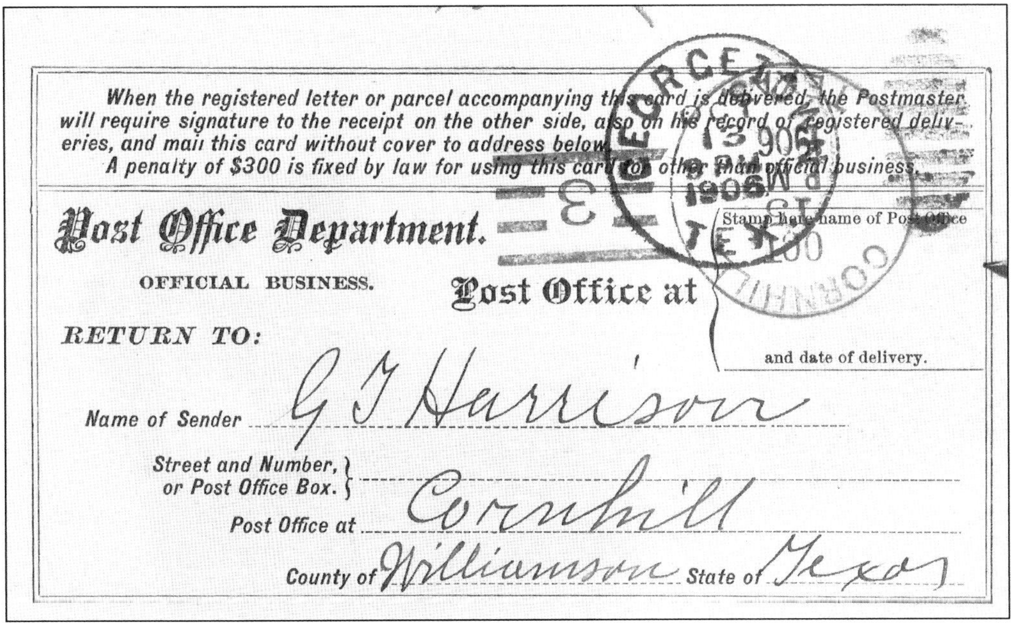

When the registered letter or parcel accompanying this card is delivered, the Postmaster will require signature to the receipt on the other side, also on his record of registered deliveries, and mail this card without cover to address below.
A penalty of $300 is fixed by law for using this card for other than official business.

Post Office Department.

OFFICIAL BUSINESS.

Post Office at

Stamp here name of Post Office and date of delivery.

GEORGETOWN OCT 13 1906 TEX. — CORNHILL

RETURN TO:

Name of Sender G T Harrison

Street and Number, or Post Office Box.

Post Office at Cornhill

County of Williamson State of Texas

This is a card mailed at the Corn Hill Post Office on October 3, 1906. It would have accompanied a letter or parcel. It was mailed by G. T. Harrison and sent to the First National Bank in Georgetown, Texas. The card shows both the Corn Hill and Georgetown postmarks. When the bank received the accompanying registered letter or parcel, a signature was placed on the card and returned to the sender, letting him know the letter had reached its destination. Postcards like this, from closed post offices, are rare and highly sought after by collectors.

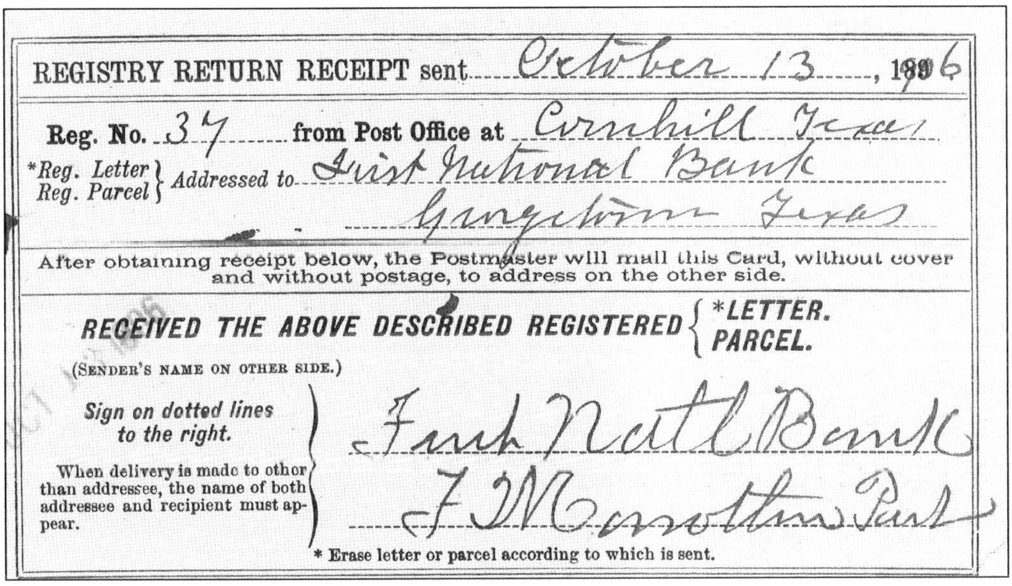

REGISTRY RETURN RECEIPT sent October 13, 1906

Reg. No. 37 from Post Office at Cornhill Texas

*Reg. Letter / Reg. Parcel } Addressed to First National Bank Georgetown Texas

After obtaining receipt below, the Postmaster will mail this Card, without cover and without postage, to address on the other side.

*RECEIVED THE ABOVE DESCRIBED REGISTERED { *LETTER. PARCEL.*

(SENDER'S NAME ON OTHER SIDE.)

Sign on dotted lines to the right.

When delivery is made to other than addressee, the name of both addressee and recipient must appear.

First Natl Bank
F M Morrothin Pact

* Erase letter or parcel according to which is sent.

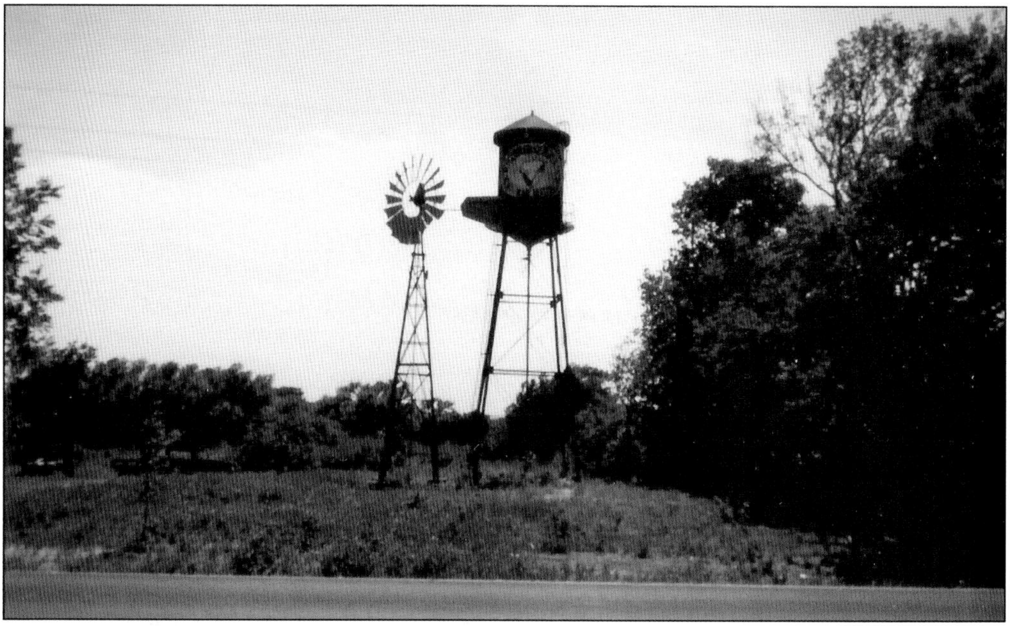

Unhappy with the prospect of having to dig personal wells or hauling water from another location, citizens organized the Jarrell Water Works and drilled a community well. Johnny Hall operated the well, and O. D. Jarrell was the president of the organization. The company was later sold to S. C. Bryce and then to K. W. Havins. Eventually it was sold to Frank Viktorin, who operated it until 1971. Pictured is the original water tower that supplied "running" water to the homes and businesses in Jarrell. Now owned by the Jarrell-Schwertner Corporation, water is supplied from a number of wells, including the one shown below. (Both courtesy Charlotte Vancil.)

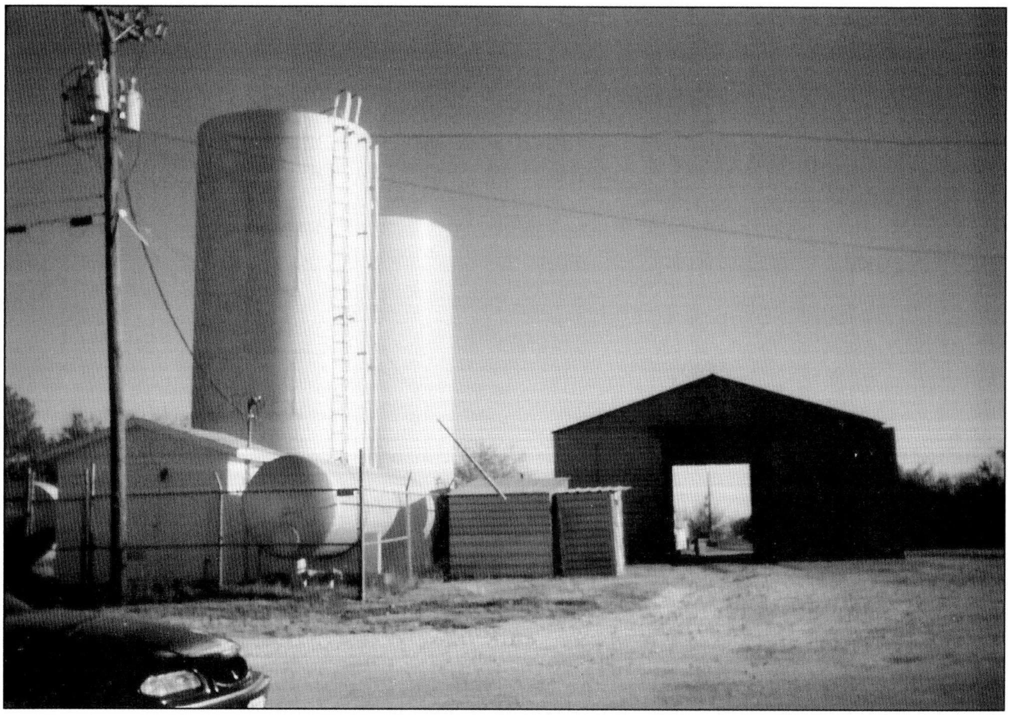

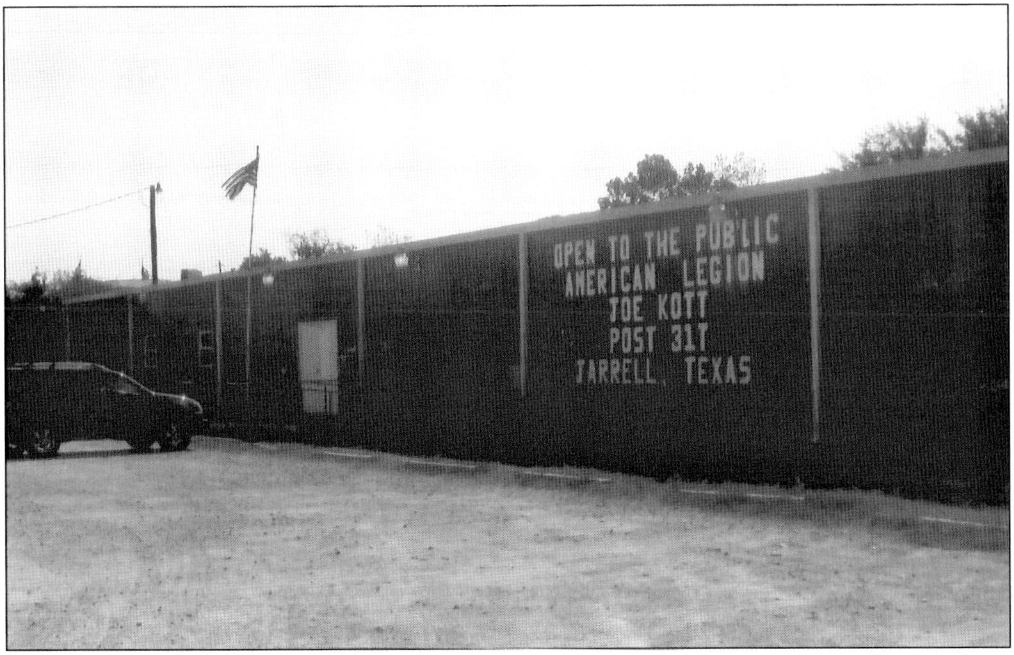

The American Legion is a national association with membership open to all war veterans. Chartered in Jarrell in 1938, Post 317 has served as an important part of the Jarrell landscape as a social gathering place, a civic-minded organization, and a community hall for special events. The original building, constructed in 1964, burned and the new one was built in the same location.

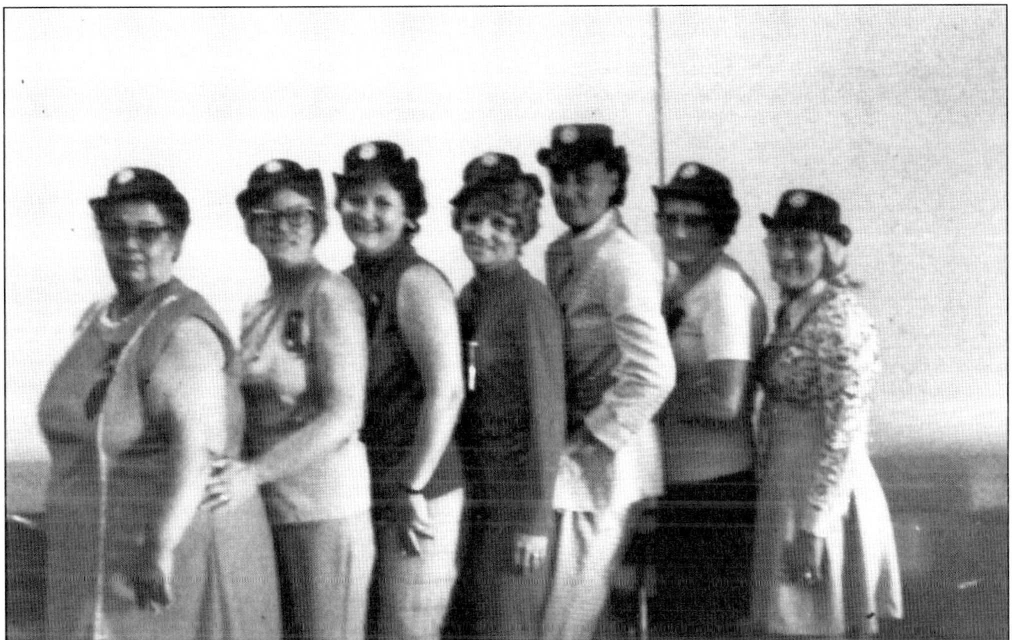

Taken in the 1960s, this is a photograph of officers of the American Legion Auxiliary. Pictured are, from left to right, Naomi Mersiovsky, Catherine Weir, Gertrude Brabandt, Charlotte Horton, Esther Tschoerner (president), Billie Kelly, and Pat Upthegrove. (Courtesy Esther Tschoerner.)

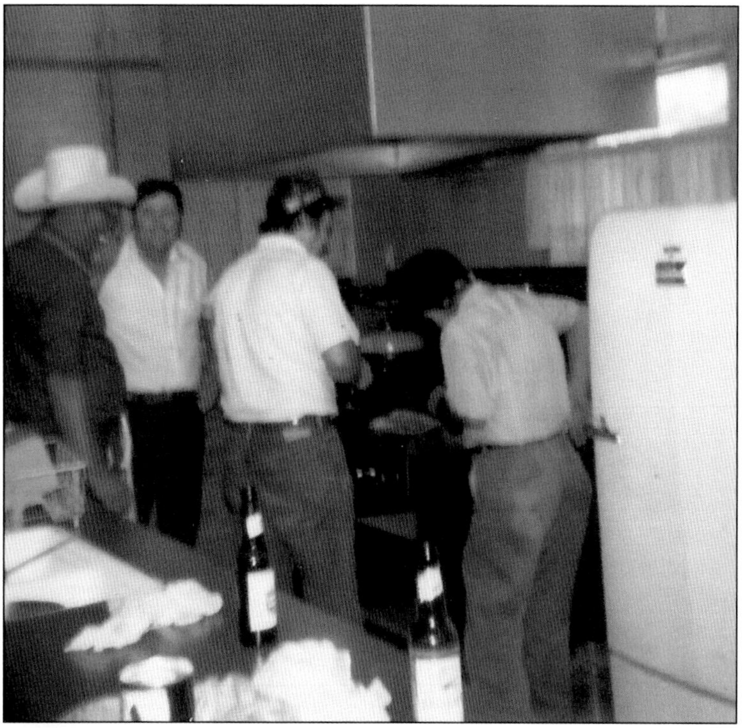

A big portion of the activities of the American Legion revolves around celebrations and food. Barbeque and chili cook-offs guarantee great food and great fun. In a picture taken in the 1970s in the Legion's kitchen are, from left to right, Clem Kubacek, Eddie Tschoerner, Jerry David, and Tim Tschoerner. (Courtesy Esther Tschoerner.)

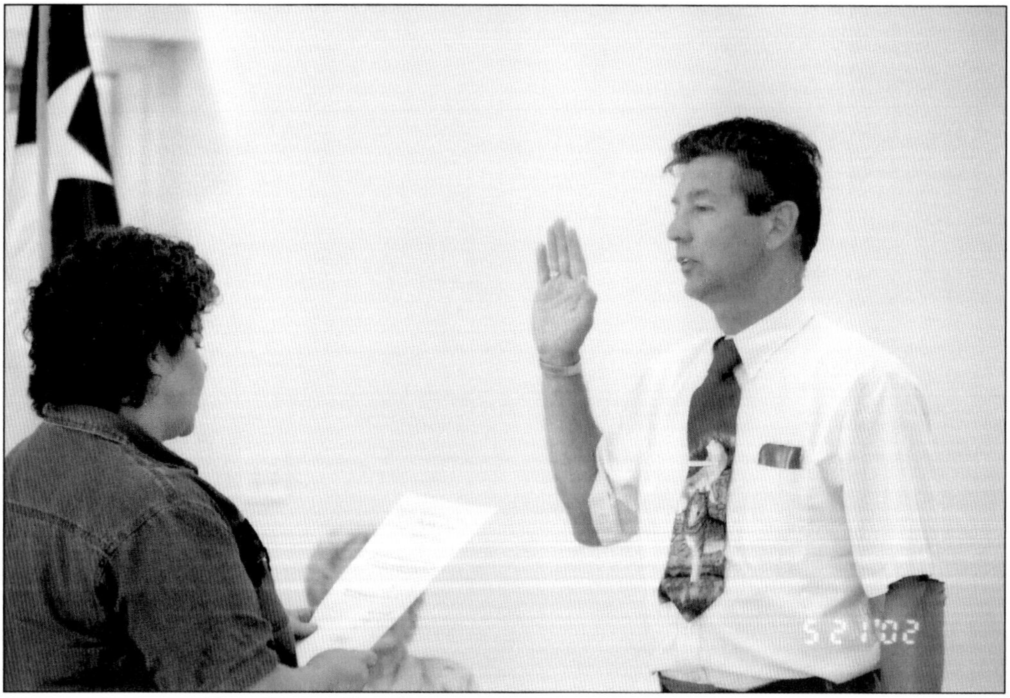

In 2001, the City of Jarrell was officially incorporated. Jarrell would now be able to maintain its own unique identity. With that came major changes, including the need for city government. Shown here is Wayne Cavalier, the first mayor of Jarrell, being sworn into office by city secretary Alana Hoffman Enriquez. (Courtesy the City of Jarrell.)

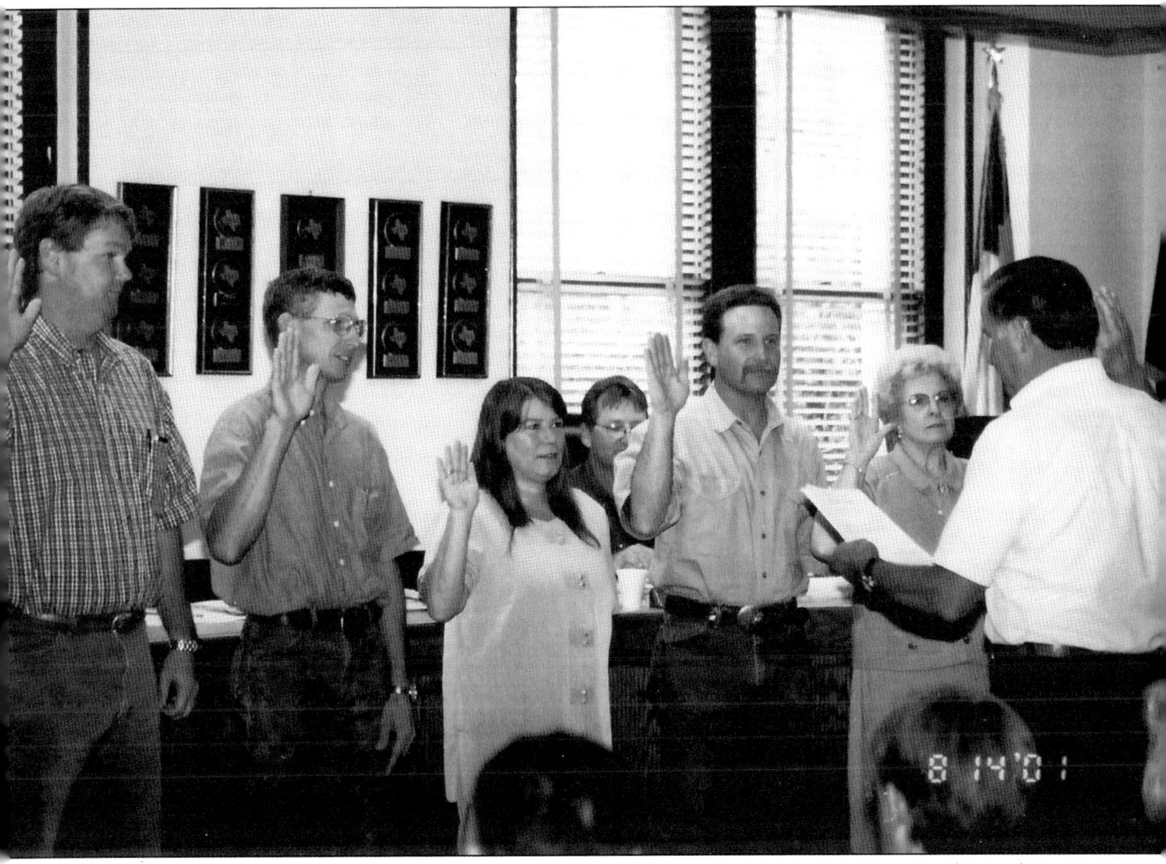

In August 2001, the first city council for the City of Jarrell was elected by its citizens. Shown here being sworn into office by county judge John Doerfler are, from left to right, Jeff Stockton, Greg Danek, Sharon Bell, Mack Parks, and Dorothy Jones. (Courtesy the City of Jarrell.)

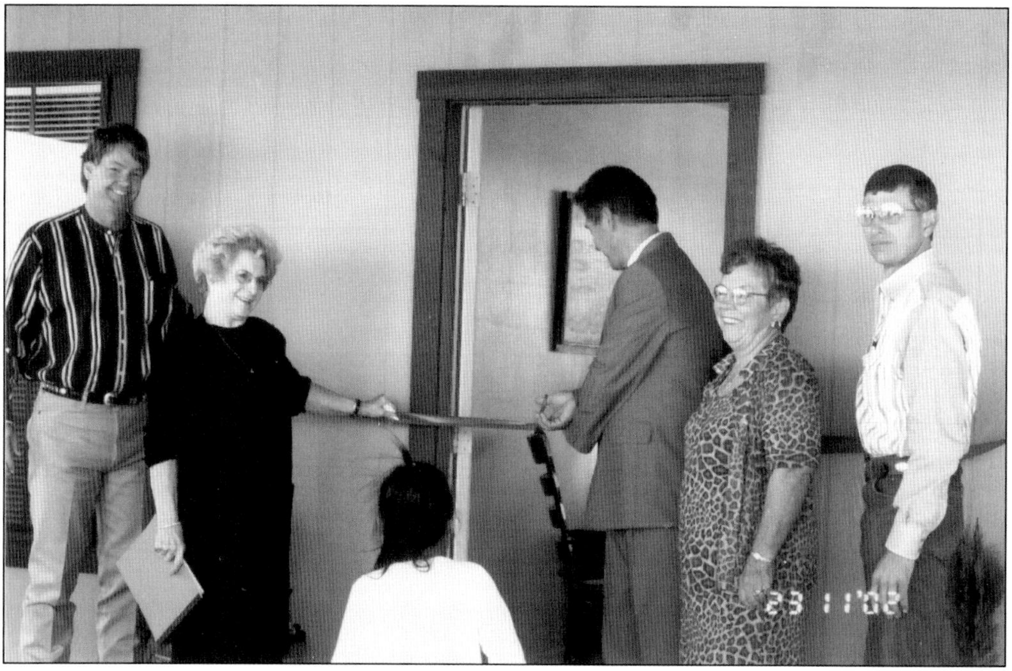

Pictured here is the ribbon-cutting ceremony for city hall. This building would now house the city administrative office and the mayor's office, along with space for city council meetings and for Jarrell's first municipal court. Shown here from left to right are Jeff Stockton, Dorothy Jones, Mayor Wayne Cavalier, Ruth Dotson, and Greg Danek. (Courtesy the City of Jarrell.)

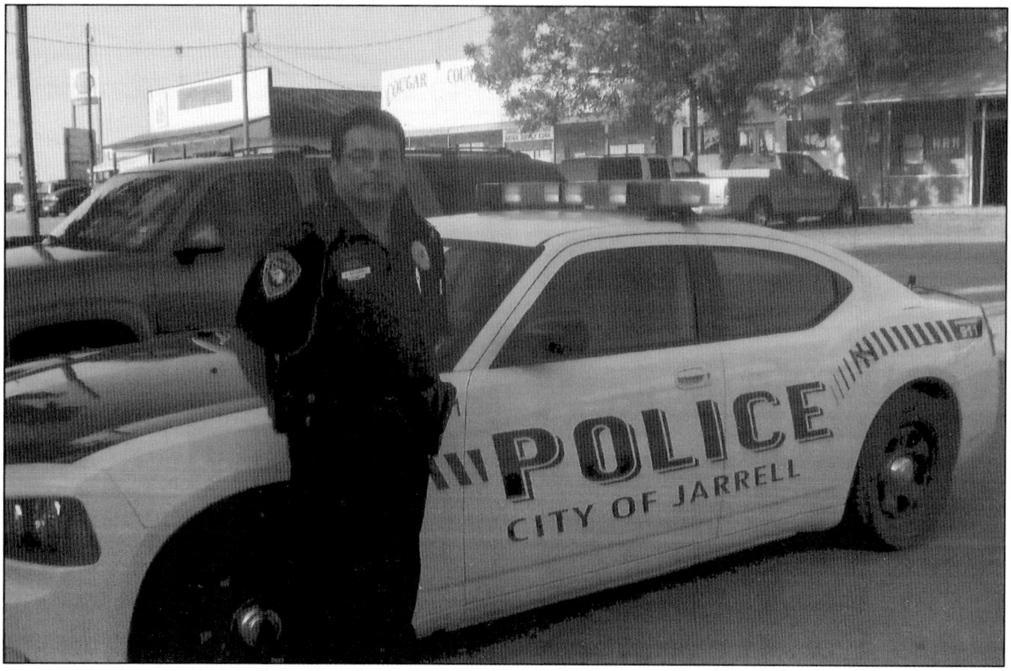

Pictured is Jarrell's first police chief, Andres Gutierrez. He is standing beside the first official police car for the City of Jarrell. Chief Gutierrez was hired in June 2006 to establish the Jarrell Police Department and to provide additional safety and protection for its citizens.

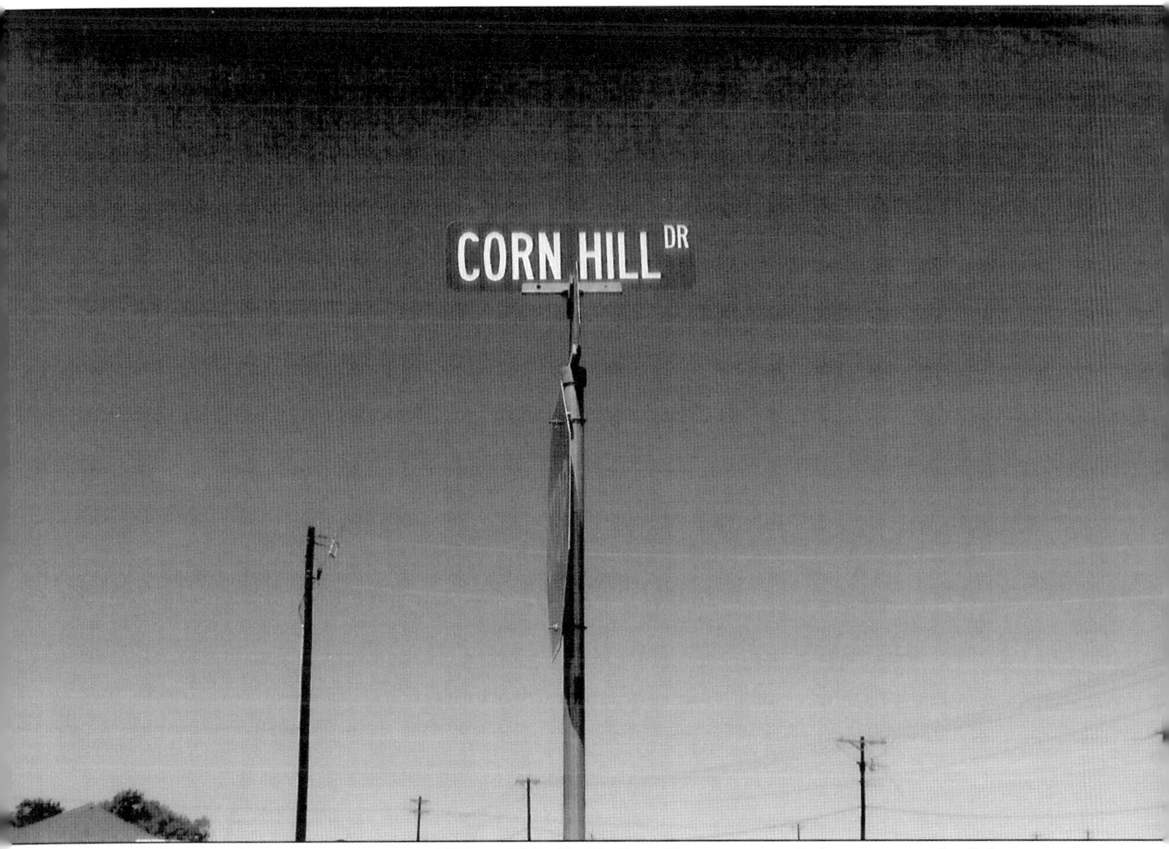

Everyone knows history repeats itself. In 1909, O. D. Jarrell recognized the potential of the area and developed the Jarrell Townsite. He promoted and sold lots, people built homes for their families, businesses grew and flourished, and the community of Jarrell began. Today a major subdivision called Sonterra, developed by Theron Vaughn, is becoming a significant part of Jarrell. It encompasses the land where Corn Hill once stood. Once again, the area has been recognized as having good potential, lots in the development have been sold, many homes have been built, and commercial enterprises are rapidly becoming a part of the scene. Does anything sound familiar? Pictured is Corn Hill Drive street sign in the Sonterra subdivision. It lies only a few yards from the site of the original main street of Corn Hill. Somehow it seems fitting that the last photograph in this book is evidence of Jarrell re-creating itself once again. The meaning of Sonterra is "celebrate the land." If the past is any indication, the residents of Jarrell, both old and new, can look forward to a bright and vibrant future underpinned with 100 years of strength, flexibility, and resilience

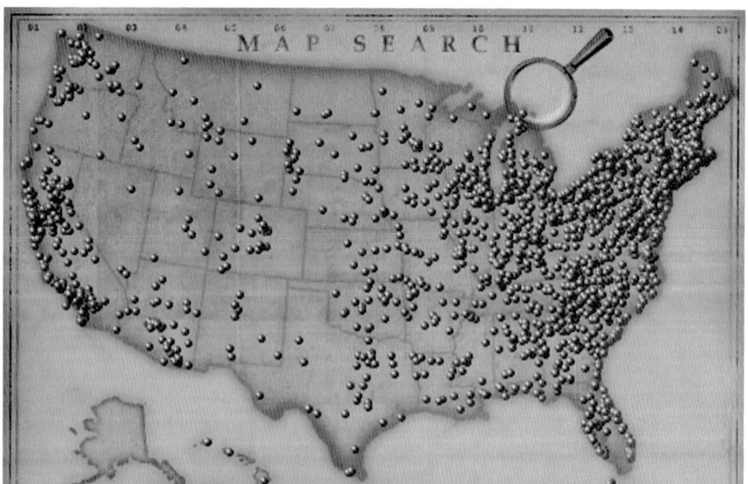
MAP SEARCH